Henry Edward Watts

The Christian Recovery of Spain

being the story of Spain from the Moorish conquest to the fall of Granada -

711-1492 a.d.

Henry Edward Watts

The Christian Recovery of Spain
being the story of Spain from the Moorish conquest to the fall of Granada - 711-1492 a.d.

ISBN/EAN: 9783337230814

Printed in Europe, USA, Canada, Australia, Japan

Cover: Foto ©ninafisch / pixelio.de

More available books at **www.hansebooks.com**

THE CHRISTIAN RECOVERY OF SPAIN

BEING THE STORY OF SPAIN FROM
THE MOORISH CONQUEST TO
THE FALL OF GRANADA
(711-1492 A.D.)

BY

HENRY EDWARD WATTS

NEW YORK
G. P. PUTNAM'S SONS
LONDON: T. FISHER UNWIN
1894

PREFACE.

IF only on the score of its novelty, seeing that I attempt what to my knowledge has never been done before, I may claim some indulgence for the present work. The object is to give the general student a sketch of the process by which the Spanish nation was formed. The story of early Spain, from its loss to Christendom to its recovery, is really the story of some four or five nations, which, though springing from the same root, followed each its separate law of development, blending finally into one nation rather through the accidents of war and policy than by deliberate choice or any natural process of concretion. Their unity, when finally achieved, was thus rather an agglutination than an association—which, indeed, remains true of the Spain, or Spains, of the present day. Leon has become merged in Castile—Catalonia in Aragon; but each of the great provinces composing the Spanish nationality has had its independent history, and each retains its individual character, formed by its own struggle for existence and developed by its peculiar natural conditions.

To follow the course of that struggle as a whole, and to weave into one connected story the tangled threads of that diverse and confused life, is a task which needs some hardihood to undertake, in which I do not know that I have any predecessor. The only history of Spain in English is the general one, embracing the whole Peninsula, from the earliest times to the close of the Eighteenth century, by Dr. Dunham, which was published sixty years ago, in five volumes of Lardner's Cabinet Cyclopædia. Of this learned and laborious historian I would desire to speak with all respect; but his work is certainly too much flattered by Buckle when he declares it to be " the best history in the English language of a foreign modern country." Writing without the light which recent Arabic scholars have turned upon the early annals of Spain, with no authority better than the frail one of Conde, and Conde only in the faithless French version of Marlès—Dunham is now entirely out of date. Nor was Dunham gifted with the instinct of history to guide him through the mists and mazes of the early Spanish chronicles. He is obstinate and credulous — over-fond of parading his authorities, which are like a stage army, formidable rather by repetition than by weight or multitude—strangely partial in some of his judgments, especially of the kings of the Bourbon dynasty—with prejudices and passions, which blind him to some of the ugliest features of the political condition—tedious and obscure in his narrative, feeble and platitudinous in his too frequent moralisations. The best part of Dunham— the part which doubtless captured the judgment of

Buckle—is his account of the civil and social institutions of the early Spaniards. The worst feature of Dunham is the unfortunate scheme of arrangement, according to which the history of one nation is taken separately for a chapter or two, and then left suspended for the history of another. With all his faults, however, it would be ungrateful in me not to acknowledge my indebtedness to Dr. Dunham for much of the knowledge which I have endeavoured to use in this simpler and more condensed narrative, where the growth of all the Christian kingdoms is told as one story.

The sources of Spanish history are twofold—Christian and Arabic. The bald, scanty chronicles of the early Christian writers, who were all ecclesiastics, are supplemented by the fuller and more ornate narratives of the Moorish historians, of which latter by far the most valuable are those in the collection translated and published by Don Pascual de Gayangos in his "Mahommedan Dynasties," which may be said to be the beginning of all our real knowledge of early Spanish history from the Moorish side. The work of comparing the two and gleaning the truth from the rival utterances has never been thoroughly done. The late Professor Dozy of Leyden, in his "Récherches sur l'histoire et la littérature de l'Espagne" and other works, displayed an excellent acumen and a true historical sense. Dozy is discursive and pugnacious, who will stop in the middle of an important research to fight with some rival Arabist, and in the ardour of battle is apt to forget his reader. But for what the Leyden professor has done in interpreting the old monkish legends by the light of learning and common sense he is entitled to the gratitude of all students of Spanish history.

The authorities from the Christian side are the monkish chroniclers, who wrote in Latin, of whom Isidorus Pacensis, wrongly termed Bishop of Beja, who dates from 754, is the first. Next to him, who does not seem to have been acquainted with his predecessor's work, was Sebastian, a monk of Salamanca, who composed his chronicles in the reign of Alfonso III. (866-910). The Monks of Silos and Albelda wrote about 881-3. The works of these, with other fragments of contemporary and later chroniclers, are preserved in some of the many volumes of Florez, his "España Sagrada"—a monumental work, entitling the learned author to be called the Muratori and the Montfaucon of Spain, in which is enshrined all that remains of old Spanish history. The "España Sagrada" has been brought down from 1754 to 1850 by successive continuations, and now extends to forty-seven volumes, containing a mine of history which has hardly yet been thoroughly explored. For the dark period of the Tenth and Eleventh centuries the record is imperfect, the chief light being furnished by the Arabic historians, Ibn Haiyân, who wrote in the Eleventh, and Ibn Khaldoun in the Thirteenth, centuries. For the special history of the Cid the documents, from the Christian side, are, first, a fragment of a Latin Chronicle written in 1141, together with the contract of the hero's marriage with Ximena, originally published in 1601; secondly, some brief notices in the Latin annals of Toledo and Compostella of the

Thirteenth century; thirdly, the "Gesta Roderici Campidocti," discovered by Risco in the convent of S. Isidore at Leon, bearing internal evidence of having been written before 1238; fourthly, the "Poema del Cid," which is as much history as poetry, to which Dozy assigns the date of 1207; fifthly, the "Chrónica Rimada," a fragment in rude verse, in which certain of the deeds of the Campeador are recited, obviously from living tradition and popular song; lastly, the so-called "Chrónica del Cid," to which an exaggerated historical value has been attributed by Southey and others, which is clearly proved to be only the fourth chapter of the General Chronicle of Alfonso X., retouched and with the Christian character of the hero revised and corrected by some ignorant monk of the Fourteenth century. To all these authorities, insufficient up to the time of Dr. Dunham to prove to all men the real existence of the Cid, there has now been added, by a happy discovery made by Professor Dozy in the archives of Gotha, a very curious and valuable document which settles for ever the question of the Cid's identity. This is a letter written by a contemporary and eye-witness, a Moor of rank who was the Cid's prisoner at the taking of Valencia, giving a detailed account of the calamities which had overtaken the city by that accursed "dog of Galicia," with a brief account of his career. This letter is preserved in a volume of Arabic manuscripts, being the third of a treatise on the men of letters who flourished in Spain during the fifth century of the Hegira, and is dated 505—corresponding to A.D. 1109, or ten years after the Cid's death.

The leading Christian chronicler of the Thirteenth century is Archbishop Rodrigo of Toledo, that same fiery prelate who bore his red cross before him at the battle of Las Navas de Tolosa. Archbishop Rodrigo, who has incorporated in his work the labours of all his predecessors, supplementing and enlarging them out of the resources of his own fruitful and daring imagination, is as intrepid in history as he was in battle, and cannot be trusted to tell the truth when it bears against the Faith and his nation—a characteristic which he shares with nearly all the chroniclers of his race.

The first to gather up all the traditions and stories of Christian Spain into one history was the learned King Alfonso X., who caused to be compiled, and partly wrote, the "Chrónica General." This, which is the earliest book of any importance written in the Romance or Castilian tongue, has a value as literature far transcending its historical worth. It is one of the monuments of the Spanish language, to which, seeing that it has not been reprinted since 1604, and was never properly edited, scarcely sufficient justice has been done by the modern scholars of the two Royal Academies who have charge of Letters and of History in Spain. Alfonso, who is said to have been assisted in his labours by learned men of the Moorish nation, begins his history with the creation of the world, and ends it with the death of King Fernando, his father, in 1252. It is divided into four parts, of which the third and fourth only treat of the affairs of Spain. The value of the General Chronicle as history may be said to be mainly of a subjective character.

It is as a series of pictures of national life and manners, rather than as a storehouse of facts, that his book is most precious. History in the Thirteenth century, in Spain as elsewhere, was an art rather than a science. To tell the story as the people had it, this was the chronicler's function. To sift the truth of the accepted belief was no part of his duty. We may be grateful to King Alfonso for that, in spite of his learning, he was not in this respect superior to his age. He has included in his Chronicle everything that his people believed and sung, about the things that had happened in the world. For this service, at least, let his memory be respected. An enormous number of ballads—the earliest of all historical documents—of popular legends, of familiar traditions, of vulgar stories and sayings of the common people are here preserved, which but for this book would have perished—of an intrinsic value far transcending any facts, or theories about facts, which Alfonso was likely to have possessed. Whether the material from which Alfonso and his scribes worked was mainly the ballads of the country, or whether, as others have maintained, it was the ballads which were made out of the rich imaginative stuff here contained, is one of those questions which scholars will never cease to debate. Probably the truth lies midway between the two theories. Doubtless many of the ancient ballads are to be found embedded almost whole in the narrative, often with rhyme and metre intact. Certainly, also, the narrative itself has furnished the ballad. Out of the rich mine of ore, almost pure metal in its bed, it was not difficult in that easy melodious Castilian, with its double resource of consonant and assonant rhyme, to carve out verses almost ready made; and thus, doubtless, sprung most of the profuse ballading of the Fifteenth and Sixteenth centuries.

The example of Alfonso X. in compiling the annals of his country was followed by his successors. From that time forward every monarch had his chronicler, and it is to these individual chronicles, unequal as they are in merit, that the historian of Spain is chiefly indebted for his knowledge of the later reigns, down to that of Isabel and Ferdinand, who crowned the edifice of Spanish nationality, and were the first, as they were the last, of the pure Spanish sovereigns. Henceforth we are on firmer ground and work with solid material. Some of these individual chronicles of the kings, beginning with that of the chivalrous Alfonso XI., were reprinted during the last century under the care of the Spanish Academy; but the series is by no means complete. In this, as in other points of the especial duty pertaining to it, as in the neglect of the grand old chronicle of Alfonso X., which is extant only in the two rare and corrupt editions of Zamora (1541), and Valladolid (1604), the Spanish Academy of History has done little to earn its name.

Emerging from the region of contemporary chronicle and tradition the student of early Spanish life receives but small aid from the recognised professors of history. The national historian is Mariana, the Jesuit, who wrote his great history, first in Latin, then in Spanish, in the first decade of the Seventeenth century. Mariana, a true soldier of the order he professed, first brought himself into notice as the author of a work in which the lawfulness of regicide, in the cause of the Faith, was maintained and justified. His history of Spain has become a classic for its style, which is of the purest and most elevated Castilian— simple, dignified, rich, and picturesque. He is the Spanish Livy; equal to his model in liveliness of narrative and in imagination. He is one of the first of the historians who cultivated the art of telling a story, who offered the charm of style as a substitute for truth. Unlike some later professors of the art rhetorical, Mariana made no pretence at truth telling. He is perfectly frank about his scheme of writing. "I never undertook," he says, "to make a history of Spain in which I should verify every particular fact; for if I had I should never have finished. I undertook only to arrange in a becoming style what others had collected as materials for the fabric I desired to raise." In this more modest design Mariana has been completely successful. Except that he is not to be trusted for any single fact or date, Mariana is one of the best of historians. His style is admirable, though in parts careless and diffuse. He has caught the trick of narrative. His speeches—who cares whether they were delivered by the very persons in whose mouths they are put?—are full of eloquence. He has the art of story-telling in perfection, with all the prolixity and impressive dwelling on details which belong to the highest professors of the fiction which would be accepted for truth. He will continue to be read, for his style, among the masters of the Castilian tongue. As to the rest, which to him was the smaller part, the retailing of facts, he is not to be trusted. It is not that he distorts the truth, but that he has no idea that it is his duty to separate the true from the false. Enough for him that the story is to be found in some old writer; that it is picturesque, and tending to the honour of his Church and his nation—the Church being always preferred to the king or to the people. He records, with admirable gravity and precision, the most fantastic stories; and believes everything he records—miracles, apparitions, heavenly interpositions in battle, improbable feats of war, and the strangest tales of slaughter. For all that Mariana is a delightful writer, who is justly reckoned an honour to his country.

Of his rivals and contemporaries, nay, of most of those who came after him, it cannot be said that they were any better in truthfulness, while they were vastly inferior in art. Morales is even more credulous, thoroughly dull, and intolerably tedious. His contemporary, Zurita the Aragonese, who wrote the Annals of his country in 1562, must be placed higher than any of them in all that constitutes the true and sober historian. He is the first of those who wrote of events in Spain who cared to trouble himself about the truth, and though he leans to the side of his country throughout, he is commendably free from the usual vices of the Spanish annalist, and can be trusted to speak honestly even of the king and of the Faith.

The modern native historians who deal with the early life of Spain are numerous, but not distinguished for critical insight or philosophical impartiality. Their prevailing faults are tediousness and an incurable propensity to give to the ancient story a practical and political application. In credulity and in defect of the sense of proportion and perspective they are not much better than the older writers, while they are far less picturesque and lively. One of the most recent, who is also the most ambitious, of the modern Spanish historians, who claims to deal with the past from the superior point of modern enlightenment, is Lafuente, whose twenty-ninth volume comes down to Isabella the Second. It is a work more conspicuous for largeness of margin than for greatness of soul, and is on a scale too grand for its spirit of candour. While ashamed of the absurdities to be found in the old chronicles, Lafuente is too timid or too patriotic to correct them all, himself repeating many of the mediæval legends, with a fond relish, as pertaining to the glory of Spain. Of Lafuente's quality of enlightenment we may judge by the fact that, while mildly condemning the decree for the expulsion of the Moriscoes, he claims the result as conducive to the integrity and greatness of the country.

This is the besetting sin of all the Spanish historians, who, more, I think, than those of any other nation, are prone to believe it to be a point of patriotism to make out such a story as shall best redound to the honour and glory of Spain.

A vast mass of material for the history of Spain, which still needs sifting and sorting, lies buried in the multitude of volumes published by the Royal

Academy of History under the title of "Coleccion de Documentos Ineditos para la Historia de España"—a publication which has passed its ninetieth volume, and is still proceeding.

CONTENTS.

PAGE

INTRODUCTION 1-15

I.

THE RALLY IN THE ASTURIAS, AND THE FOUNDATION OF THE CHRISTIAN KINGDOM. 711-866 16-41

The landing of Tarik—The Berbers and the Goths—The Battle of Guadalete—Advance of the Moors—The Christians under Theodomir—The Retreat to the Asturias—Pelayo chosen Leader—Covadonga—The rally in Asturias—The Christians take heart—Recovery of lost territory—The romantic Episode of Charlemagne—Charlemagne's invasion—The dolorous Rout of Roncesvalles—The Spanish side of the Story—The Version in the Spanish Ballads—Bernardo del Carpio—A doubtful Hero —The reign of Alfonso II.—Apocryphal Victory of Clavijo —Saints in Battle—Ordoño I.

II.

THE KINGDOM OF LEON—RISE OF CASTILE—THEIR TEMPORARY UNION. 866-1109 . . . 42-70

The second Founder of the State—The policy of disruption—Leon made Capital—Period of confusion—Rise of the Counts of Castile—Leon and Castile—Rise of Almanzor—Legendary

Battle of Calatañazor—Partition of his States—Siege of Zamora—The Cid and the King—Rise of the Almoravides—Almoravides usurp Moorish Dominions.

III.

THE STORY OF CID. 1026–1099 71–91

The ideal hero—His character—Alfonso's Standard-bearer—The Cid's marriage with Ximena—The Cid starts on his adventure—The Cid in battle—At war with Raymond Berenger—A dinner with the Cid—The Cid in death—Death of the Cid.

IV.

THE PERIOD OF DISSEVERANCE—RISE OF THE SMALLER STATES—CASTILE AND LEON DIVIDED AND UNITED 92–120

Anarchy in Mahommedan Spain—Growth of Navarre—Battle of Alcoraz—Early Counts of Barcelona—War between Castile and Aragon—Discord under Queen Urraca—Alfonso the Battler—Separation of Aragon and Navarre—Rise of the Almohades—Another separation—Great defeat of the Christians—Las Navas de Tolosa—A crowning Victory—Queen Berengaria.

V.

UNITED CASTILE AND LEON—RISE OF ARAGON. 1217–1254 121–144

Campaign in Andalusia—Defeat of Pedro of Aragon—Jayme meditates conquest of Valencia—Mahommed-ibn-Alhamar—Aragon aids Castile—Character of King Jayme—Conquest of Seville—Death of San Fernando—Alfonso the Sage—Character of Alfonso.

VI.

LAWS AND GOVERNMENT OF CASTILE AND ARAGON
—THE CORTES AND THE FUEROS—PROGRESS
OF ARTS AND LETTERS 145–171

The *Fuero Juzgo*—The *Siete Partidas*—The Cortes—Laws of Aragon—Aragonese Barons—The Mozarabic Ritual—Religion influences National Character—The Ballad—Poetry and Science—Handicraft—Romanesque Churches—Architecture.

VII.

THE REIGNS OF SANCHO IV., FERNANDO IV., AND ALFONSO XI. IN CASTILE—VICTORIES OVER THE MOORS—AFFAIRS OF ARAGON. 1284–1387 173–194

Alonso the Good—Troubles of the realm—Civil War—War between Castile and Granada—Battle of Salado—Siege of Algeciras—Death of Alfonso—Aragon's entry into Italian affairs—War in Sicily—Pedro IV. of Aragon.

VIII.

REIGN OF PEDRO THE CRUEL—THE GREAT CIVIL WAR—ENGLAND AND FRANCE IN SPAIN. 1350–1369 195–215

Queen Blanche of Bourbon—Butcheries of the King—Character of Pedro—Pedro's wanton murders—Murder of Queen Blanche—The Black Prince to the rescue—Battle of Najera—An Episode of Chivalry—Pedro falls into a trap—The end of the tyrant.

IX.

THE DYNASTY OF TRASTAMARA—ENRIQUE II.—JUAN I.—ENRIQUE III.—AFFAIRS OF ARAGON. 1369-1412 216-231

John of Gaunt a claimant to the throne—Portugal sides with the English—The Portuguese defeat the Castilians—John of Gaunt marries his daughters—The adventure of Alcántara—Issue of the religious raid—Aragon in Sardinia—A Prince of Castile reigns in Aragon.

X.

THE REIGN OF JUAN II.—THE AGE OF CHIVALRY. 1407-1454 232-255

The beginning of Art and Letters—The King's favourite—The Constable in his glory—The Constable meets the King—Dignities and revenues of Don Alvaro—The Pact of Tordesillas—Execution of Don Alvaro—The Spanish Raleigh—Growth of Chivalry—Jousts and Tournaments—An Honourable Passage of Arms.

XI.

REIGN OF ENRIQUE IV.—CIVIL WAR AND DISORDER—MARRIAGE OF FERNANDO AND ISABEL—UNION OF CASTILE AND ARAGON. 1454-1474 257-276

A burlesque Crusade—Revolt of the Nobles—Two Kings of Castile—Death of Prince Alfonso—Isabel's wooers—Isabel betrothed to Fernando—Demoralisation of the country—The King of Aragon in Naples—Aragon mistress of South Italy.

XII.

REIGN OF ISABEL AND FERNANDO—UNION OF CASTILE AND ARAGON—PEACE AND ORDER IN SPAIN—THE INQUISITION—WAR WITH THE MOORS AND CAPTURE OF GRANADA—THE END. 1474-1492 277-301

Queen Isabel as Bride—Early troubles of the Queen—Union of the Two Crowns—The Holy Brotherhood—Civil Reforms—The Holy Inquisition—The relations with Granada—Capture and Defence of Alhama—The two Abdallahs—The Siege of Baeza—The Siege of Granada begun—The final Victory.

APPENDIX 303

INDEX 311

LIST OF ILLUSTRATIONS.

	PAGE
PORTRAIT OF QUEEN ISABEL THE CATHOLIC, FROM THE PICTURE IN THE MUSEO AT MADRID . *Frontispiece*	
MAP OF THE SPANISH PENINSULA TO ILLUSTRATE THE POLITICAL DIVISIONS . *Facing*	1
CROSS OF PELAYO	24
TOMB OF ORDOÑO II. IN LEON CATHEDRAL	46
BURGOS CATHEDRAL . . .	48
CATHEDRAL OF ZAMORA, ELEVENTH CENTURY .	55
BAS-RELIEF FROM MONASTERY OF S. DOMINGO AT BURGOS . . .	57
PORTICO OF ZAMORA CATHEDRAL	60
VIEW OF TOLEDO . .	65
PORTRAIT OF THE CID RODRIGO DE BIVER	72
CHURCH OF S. PEDRO AT CARDEÑA	90
CRYPT OF MONASTERY OF S. SALVADOR DE LEIRE, NAVARRE . . .	94
EFFIGY OF QUEEN URRACA IN THE CHURCH OF S. VICENTE AT AVILA	102
TOMB OF ALFONSO EL BATALLADOR AT MONTE ARAGON	104

LIST OF ILLUSTRATIONS.

	PAGE
ELEANOR OF ENGLAND	110
EFFIGY OF QUEEN BERENGARIA IN TOLEDO CATHEDRAL	118
EFFIGY OF S. FERNANDO FROM THE CLOISTER OF BURGOS CATHEDRAL	122
HELMET AND STIRRUPS OF KING JAYME EL CONQUISTADOR	132
COSTUMES OF THE THIRTEENTH CENTURY, KINGS AND NOBLES	135
MAP OF THE POLITICAL DIVISIONS OF SPAIN AT THE DEATH OF S. FERNANDO III., 1252	138
ARCH IN CHURCH OF S. MIGUEL DE LINO	146
COSTUMES OF THE THIRTEENTH CENTURY, COMMON PEOPLE	151
ROMANESQUE CAPITALS	168
PORCH OF CATHEDRAL AT LERIDA, THIRTEENTH CENTURY	170
INTERIOR OF S. ISIDORO AT LEON, WITH TOMBS OF THE ANCIENT KINGS	172
RUINS OF MONASTERY OF S. JUAN DE DUERO AT SORIA	178
TOMBS OF THE KINGS OF ARAGON IN THE MONASTERY OF POBLET	188
A KNIGHT ON HORSEBACK, GALA ATTIRE	233
EFFIGY OF DON ALVARO DE LUNA FROM HIS TOMB IN TOLEDO CATHEDRAL	248
TOMB OF JUAN II. AND HIS QUEEN IN THE CARTUJA DE MIRAFLORES	250

LIST OF ILLUSTRATIONS.

	PAGE
ARMOUR OF FIFTEENTH CENTURY	252
ARMOUR AND HELMETS FIFTEENTH CENTURY	254
ARMOUR OF ISABEL THE CATHOLIC	256
ALCAZAR OF SEGOVIA, REBUILT BY ENRIQUE IV.	264
CROWN OF ISABEL THE CATHOLIC	278
PORTRAIT OF KING FERNANDO THE CATHOLIC	280

[*The illustrations of architecture and old buildings are taken from "España, sus Monumentos y Artes," the most recent work on Spanish topography, published at Barcelona during* 1886-90. *The ancient arms and armour are from the Royal Armoury at Madrid, as figured in Jubinal's "Armeria Real." The portraits and effigies are reproduced from Carderera y Solano, their "Iconografía Española." The costumes are copied from "Los Estudios de Indumentaria Española," Barcelona,* 1890. *The head of the Cid (probably a work of imagination) is that which is prefixed to Father Risco's "La Castilla y El Mas Famoso Castellaño,"* 1792.]

THE RECOVERY OF SPAIN.

INTRODUCTION.

ONE day, after a battle seven days' long, saw the ruin of Spain—that fatal day in July, A.D. 711, when Roderick, the last of the Goths, lost his army, his kingdom, and his life, on the banks of the Guadalete. Nearly eight hundred years were spent by the Christians in undoing that day's work and in winning back their country from the Moslem. The story of the conquest has been told, from the Moorish side, in a former volume of this series.[1] It remains for me to tell of the fortunes of the conquered—of the long and slow process by which Spain was recovered to Christendom, and of the rise of the nation into its full stature under Ferdinand and Isabella.

The fall of Granada, in A.D. 1492, which brought the long controversy between Christian and Moor to an end, seems a fitting conclusion to this story of the Recovery of Spain. By that date the union of the crowns of Castile and Aragon had been happily accomplished. The tide of African invasion had been stemmed; and the Peninsula was once more Christian,

[1] "The Moors in Spain." By Stanley Lane Poole. 1886.

from Gibraltar to Biscay, from Lisbon to Valencia. The whole country called Spain, with some trifling exceptions on the northern border, had become an independent nation, co-extensive with the territory so named, under one government and one dominion. For the first time in history, the people, though various in origin, and divided by old jealousies and rivalries, differing in laws and institutions, and not yet welded into harmony, were united in a common polity, and were able to take their place as one Power in the system of Christendom. The redeeming of the soil from the Moslem; the re-conquest of the land, step by step, by the Christians from the Moorish invaders; the long and slow process, often suspended, but never wholly lost sight of, by which the Spaniards recovered their hold of the country, and formed themselves into one nation—this is the story which I propose to tell.

Never in the annals of the world was a victory more complete than that of Tarik, on the banks of the Guadalete. The result of the seven days' fighting was not only to leave the lieutenant of Musa in possession of the field of battle, but to establish the dominion of the Khalif (then seated at Damascus) over the whole of the Peninsula. No second blow was needed to rend this important limb from Christendom, to secure what till then was the most valuable prize won by the newly-risen Crescent. The Gothic dominion was broken for ever. The ruin of the Christians was so thorough as to justify the pious chroniclers of the nation in ascribing the event to the direct intervention of Heaven. Nothing less than a stroke of Divine vengeance, provoked by the manifold and crying sins of the Gothic kings and the impious neglect of the Church by the people, could account, it was supposed, for a catastrophe so sudden, so complete and unheard of, as the defeat of Roderick and his splendid host by the scanty force which Tarik had brought over from Africa. After the battle, the Goths seem to have abandoned all hope of resistance. The victorious army of Islam poured over the country like a deluge. City after city yielded without a blow. Within two years the army of Musa, though still in number inconsiderable, had advanced to the Douro, and even to the foot of the Pyrenees. A year or two more, under Musa's son Abdelaziz, saw the whole Peninsula, from sea to sea, subject to the Moors. The tide of conquest even burst the bounds of the Pyrenees, and flowed into Southern France. It was not until Charles Martel met and stemmed the onward wave at Tours, in A.D. 734, that Western Christendom felt itself safe from the terrible soldiers of the False Prophet, though it was not until the close of the Eighth century that the soil of France was finally cleared of Moors.

The rapidity and the thoroughness with which the Ruin of Spain (*La Perdida de España*) was accomplished have greatly exercised the ingenuity of the patriotic historians. The wickedness of King Witiza (a graceless monarch, who even went so far as to ask the clergy to marry, and compelled them to do so), the incontinence of King Roderick, the vindictiveness of Count Julian, the treachery of the Jews (since heavily atoned for), the disunion among the nobles, and the general corruption of morals and decay of faith, are the favourite excuses made by the native writers to account for a calamity so little creditable to Spanish manhood and to orthodoxy. Even if we accept the highest estimate of the numbers of the conquerors, the companions of Tarik and Musa could not have come over in any great multitude. Among them the Arabs, the countrymen of the Prophet, who might be supposed to possess in the highest degree the genius and the fervour of triumphant Islam, must have been always in an insignificant minority. The greater part of Tarik's army, with Tarik himself, were Berbers, newly converted to the Mahommedan faith. They were probably not the least hardy among the warriors of Mahommed, being, indeed, of blood akin to the Goths; who, as descendants of the Vandals, were but returning to the land once occupied by their race. As to the assistance derived from treason within the Gothic camp, this may account for the initial victory of the Moors, but hardly for the ease and rapidity with which its fruits were reaped, and for the success of the Moslem domination. The Jews —who formed then, and for some centuries afterwards, a body considerable in number, and still more important by their wealth and intelligence, in the chief cities of Spain—are accused, probably not without reason, of helping the Mahommedans to their conquests. The Jews had much cause to complain of the Christian rule, under which they had been grievously oppressed and plundered. They not unnaturally regarded with favour an invasion headed by Semitic warriors of their own kindred, which promised to avenge them on their oppressors and to increase their influence.

But chief of all the causes which led to the fall of the Gothic kingdom and the triumph of the Moors was doubtless the demoralisation of the people. The gross corruptions of the Court, and the debasement into which the once proud and manly race of the Visigoths was sunk, through long disuse of the "honourable exercise" of war, and indulgences in the vices of peace; the lack of all sympathy between the nobles, who were exclusively Gothic, and the mass of the nation; the utter absence, in short, from the Christian Spain of that day, of all the elements of a healthy and living nationality, were sufficient to ensure the easy triumph of the fierce warriors of the Prophet, fresh from their conquests in Asia and Africa. The Visigoths, though they had borrowed the language and assumed the habits of the Romans, had never really mastered the secret of Roman dominion. The old Roman civilisation, which the Celtiberians had been so quick to adopt, sat awkwardly on these newer barbarians. It was a heritage to which they had not succeeded of nature, and a burden too great for them to support. The Romans had made one nation and one people of Spain. The Visigoths were not much more than an encampment. Unlike their brethren of the North and East, they could not assimilate what they won. They were a race apart from the body of the people. There was no fusion of conquerors and conquered. The king and the nobles—and all Goths were *nobiles*, while all others were *viliores*—were a caste, with which the Spaniards proper were not suffered to mix. It was not until the reign of Recceswinth, who died in A.D. 672, that the law prohibiting a Goth from marrying a native was repealed. The mass of the Spanish nation, at the date of the Moorish conquest, were slaves in name and in fact. They could have but small motive to resist a foreign dominion, even though subjection involved the subversion of their national faith. Their masters, the Goths, had only become orthodox Christians, in passing from Arianism to Catholicism, during the last hundred and fifty years. The condition of the Church was an open scandal. The mass of the Latinised Iberians were probably in their hearts almost as much pagan as their ancestors. How should they be expected to resist the influx of a power which showed them a way to freedom, and set them an example of faith; of which the goodness and truth seemed to be affirmed by the miracle of victory? The decrepit edifice needed but the touch of the vigorous hand of nascent Islam to crumble to pieces. In fine, Gothic Spain fell because it deserved to fall. King, Church, and people were equally debased; nor was the gain of Mahommedanism wholly a loss for Christendom.

The easy progress of the Moors and the rapid subjugation of the country were doubtless, not wholly due to the martial superiority of the conquerors. The path of the invaders had been made plainer through the policy of King Witiza, who, at the end of the sixth century, had levelled all the fortresses for the better promotion of peace. There was but little fighting anywhere after Guadalete had been won. The great cities yielded without a blow—only Cordova making a show of resistance. Toledo, the Gothic capital, which, being one of the few cities exempted from Witiza's fatal decree, might have been expected to offer an obstacle to the invaders, opened her gates, and yielded a vast amount of spoil, the accumulated treasure of the Gothic kings, with their crowns and emblems of sovereignty. The Jews are said to have betrayed the city to the Moors. The flying Goths had only time to carry off a chest containing sacred relics — precious bones of saints and martyrs, with a tooth of Santiago, an arm of Eugenius, and a sandal of Peter.

Within the space of two or three years the Moors had reached the Pyrenees, and, indeed, had crossed that barrier into France. From east to west the whole Peninsula was theirs—Musa himself following up the conquest, in jealous emulation of his lieutenant. Only in the mountains of Asturias did the Goths make any stand. The greater part of the interior table-land, where the climate and soil offered but few attractions to the conquerors, was overrun and ravaged rather than occupied. The Moors, indeed, were established in the north and in Castile only as a military camp. They never settled there as in their beloved *Andaloos* and in Valencia.

That the process of regaining possession of their own country should have occupied the Christian Spaniards a period of nearly eight hundred years, is not wholly flattering to the national character. But the marvel of the Moorish occupation, which must always have been the rule of a minority, becomes less when we examine into the circumstances of the two peoples. The Moors, although at first a mere handful of warriors, cut off from the centre of their power, opposed to a whole nation with all the European chivalry at its back, and the resources of Christendom to draw upon, were not so unequally matched as it might at first sight appear. On their side they had all Northern Africa, and all Islam, for a reserve and a base of operations. As soon as it became apparent that the original conquerors and their descendants, the Arabs and the Berbers, were unequal to the task of maintaining themselves against the Spaniards when united, and that Andalusia and Valencia, at least, were worth holding as homes for the Faithful, vast hordes of Africans, including Egyptians, Nubians, and negroes from the Soudan, were poured into the South of Spain. After the fall of the Cordovan Khalifate, in fact, the contest resolved itself into one between Castile and its allies on the one hand, and the powerful Empire of Morocco, including Barbary and the Mahommedan countries in the Mediterranean, on the other. The forces were not unequal, for though the Christians fought on their own ground, they had to encounter not only the native-born Mahommedans, who in Andalusia and the favoured provinces of the south had greatly multiplied; but the contingents of hardy and warlike barbarians also flocked to the assistance of their co-religionists from Africa. There were at least two great waves of invasion, after the first one—under the Almoravides in the Eleventh, and under the Almohades in the Twelfth century. Indeed, so long as the supremacy in the narrow seas lay with the Moors, as it did almost up to the fall of Granada, the straits of Gibraltar were but a bridge between Morocco and its dependencies in Spain. Every young Moor of ambition, every aspirant for a paradise, either in this world or the next—every candidate for martial glory—every founder of a new sect in Islam—every purifier of the Faith—when seized with the spirit of adventure, or an access of devotion, or inspired by greed of land, or in quest of social distinction, sought his career and his field in Christian Spain.

But more than all, what delayed the Recovery of Spain and prolonged the period when the cities of the South, including the richest and the fairest portion of the Peninsula, were under the sway of the unbeliever, was the incessant quarrelling among the Christian princes, out of which came

> Red ruin, and the breaking up of laws.

For nearly eight hundred years the duty of rescuing Spain from the infidel, supposing such a duty to have been included among those incumbent on a Christian Spanish prince, was habitually postponed to the task of self-aggrandisement and the work of mutual destruction. Even before the heroic age was past, when as yet it was thought shame by Christians that Paynim feet should press the soil of Spain, king fought against king, Castile with Aragon, Aragon with Navarre, Portugal with either or both—whenever the internal state made the kingdom secure, and there was no intestinal war for the kingship, or strife of nobles with nobles—rather than seek honour or increment by battle against the Moors, singly or in union. The Moors, indeed, had their divisions and distractions as well, which would have made it all the easier for the Christians to compass their expulsion. But the Spaniards seem to have had no great heart for the work until quite a late period of the national history. As for the people, it may be doubted whether, in spite of the exhortations of the priests, they ever had that wholesome hatred of Moorish dominion which was necessary for the redemption of the soil. Those who were directly subject to the Moors had, from the first, no great reason to wish for a change of masters. The Mahommedans, here as elsewhere, showed an example of tolerance such as never found imitators among those who claimed to be of the purer Faith. After the conquest those who preferred to remain in the country occupied by the Moors were guaranteed the undisturbed enjoyment of their property and their religion. They were permitted to have their own district governors and judges, who administered their own laws. They retained most of their churches, and were allowed the exercise of all their religious functions. In Cordova seven churches, in Toledo six, were throughout the Moorish occupation open to Christians, with a full service of clergy, who were even permitted to celebrate in public the rites of the Romish Communion. The taxes were light, and, with the exception of the poll-tax, which secured immunity from military service, were such as were paid by all citizens, by Moors and Jews as well as Christians. Indeed there is no reason to doubt that the position of the Christian artisan and husbandman was better under the Moors than under the Spanish kings of Castile or Aragon.

That a great number, including even men of noble race, became converts to the Moslem faith, preferring to share their life with the conquerors, with its freedom and gaiety and opportunities of adventure, to remaining in subjugation as an inferior race, deprived of all incentives to ambition and all hope of rising, is certain; although the fact is passed over delicately by the native historians. As renegades they became highly distinguished among the champions of Islam, and the fiercest assertors of the new religion. Some of the stoutest warriors and most successful chiefs under the Crescent were those who had put off the Cross—making their presence known in the pages of history by the quaint Arabicized forms of their baptismal names. There is much evidence, in fact, to show that the distinction between Moor and Christian was but lightly regarded in the early days. They intermarried not infrequently, even Christian kings giving their daughters to Mahommedan Emirs. Thus Theresa, the daughter of Bermudo II., King of Leon, was married to Almanzor, the famous Mahommedan hero and conqueror, in A.D. 993. In Aragon we are told of an ancient family of Visigoths who embraced Mahommedanism, and became the Beni Casî—rising to be independent Emirs of a province. One of these, under the name of Mousâ I., had for a spouse a daughter of Iñigo, the first King of Navarre, in A.D. 788.

The intercourse between Moor and Christian—in

the intervals when they were not fighting—must have been at least as familiar as between Castilian and Aragonese, or Aragonese and Navarrese, when these were not fighting. The career of the great Cid himself—*Mio Cid*—the legendary hero of Spain, and supposed champion of the Faith, is full of instances illustrative of the easy passage from Moor to Christian, even in the heroic age. The Cid himself fought sometimes under the Moorish flag, as when in the service of the Beni-Hud, the Emirs of Saragossa. In his expeditions for plunder he was quite impartial, pillaging the Christian churches as freely as the Moorish mosques. He had a large number of Moorish mercenaries in his pay, and was not over-nice how he used them, whether against Moor or against Christian—nay, leading them upon occasion even against his liege lord, the king. In matters of chivalry, involving gentleness, honour, and truth, the cavaliers of Granada were admitted to be equal with the Christian knights; and they fought together, whether in battle or in tourney, with perfect good humour and all courtesy. There were passages between them in which it was not always the Moor who was deficient in good manners. The Christian king was sometimes helped in his trouble by his Mahommedan neighbour. The communications between the rival courts, even in time of war, were conducted with all civility. The few instances where the honourable rules of chivalry were broken are, unhappily, to be found on the side of the Christians. On the whole, except among the professional fanatics on both sides, who sought to please God by maiming and slaying His creatures, there was much good-will between the two nations, and an extent of mutual toleration and good-neighbourliness, when kings and priests did not set them by the ears, which could hardly have been possible had there been that opposition of race to race or religion to religion such as is required by the theory that the Christians were constantly engaged in the pious attempt to turn the Moors out of the country.

The long duel with the Moor and the constant struggle for political supremacy in the name of religion were the chief factors in the development of the Spanish nation, and in the formation of its character. But to suppose that the two races were in perpetual conflict is to misread the record. They agreed fairly well, and fought no more bitterly—at least during the first four or five hundred years—than the Christians did with Christians while the question of supremacy among them was still undecided. At a later period, it is true, there was imported into the conflict with the followers of Mahommed a hotter spirit, as the religious feelings deepened with the growing influence of the Church; but at no time, while Moordom was still a living power in the Peninsula, was there so much bad blood between the two races as under the government of Philip II., when all question of national rivalry was at an end, and only the religious feud was alive. Now and then the spirit which led the knights of Western Europe to engage in the enterprise for the redemption of the Holy Sepulchre would break out even in the Peninsula; but the crusade in Spain was shorn of a good deal of its lustre from the very proximity of the enemy. The Paynim being always to be found at home, and his home but on the other side of the river, the adventure was reduced to a simple reckoning of nicely-balanced profit and loss. In vain did the popes and sometimes the local archbishops urge the Christian monarchs to unite against the unbeliever instead of tearing each other's throats. When Castile or Aragon had no other enemy handy, he would sometimes be induced to attempt to take a few cities from the Moor; but the campaigns against the people of the opposite faith were rarely more than forays, undertaken as much for plunder as for piety. No Christian king, in fact, could afford to be long away from his own territory, for fear that, while he was engaged in subduing the infidel, the faithful among his brother kings or his own subjects might be tempted to spoil him at home. On the rare occasions when two or more kings joined their forces against the Moors, the chief anxiety of each seems to have been lest his ally should anticipate him in profiting by the expedition. Even after the crowning victory of Las Navas de Tolosa in A.D. 1212, which drove the Moors from off the central tableland and brought the Castilians to the crest of the Sierra Morena, Alfonso VIII. did not attempt to pursue his advantage into the plains below, the true home of the Moors and the centre of their power. It was not until the union of the crowns under Ferdinand and Isabella that a systematic crusade was made against the unbelievers with the object of expelling them from the soil, or at least of extirpating the religion of Mahommed from Spain.

For the greater part of eight hundred years Spain was divided as much by political and racial differences as by the strife of religion with religion—the contests of race and of state being as much among the Moors as among the Christians. This is the leading fact in the early history of Spain, which, unless we understand, we cannot read aright the story of the nation and of its making. The accession of Ferdinand and Isabella, which put an end to the political differences among the Christians, enabled Spain, for the first time, to attempt the extinction of the religious trouble. By the capture of Granada, the last rallying point and refuge of the Moors, the citadel and stronghold of the Mahommedan power, Spain got back all that she had lost, and took her place for the first time among the Powers of Europe. With the year 1492, memorable on another account in connection with the rise of the national greatness and the extension of the national dominion by the discovery of America, this story of the Recovery of Spain may fitly end.

I.

THE RALLY IN THE ASTURIAS, AND THE FOUNDATION OF THE CHRISTIAN KINGDOM.

(711–866.)

On the 30th of April, A.D. 711, Tarik, the lieutenant of Musa, the Khalif's general in Africa, landed at Algeciras, with an army of seven thousand, which was destined to overthrow the power of the Goths and to establish the Mahommedan power in Spain. There is no reason to doubt the opinion of the best authorities, Spanish and Moorish, that the expedition had for its immediate object the ravaging of the Christian lands, the report of whose wealth and fertility had excited the cupidity of the Moors. That the extension of the domain of Islam was the ulterior purpose of the Mahommedan leaders we may reasonably believe, but Tarik was first sent to plunder and spy the land rather than to conquer and occupy it. Traitors in the Gothic camp, among whom were the two sons of Witiza, who had been dethroned and put to death by Roderick, had reported the weakness of the Christians. Even Count Julian, however, with his brother apostate, the Bishop Oppas, whose names are coupled as the two foremost of those who, by their treachery, brought about the ruin of Spain, are not charged with having designed a consummation so thorough as the subversion of the Christians.

The story of Florinda (*La Cava*), the Helen who wrought this woe on Spain, which fills so prominent a place in Spanish romance, is now rejected by all sober historians, and is believed only by the all-believing Mariana. That there was a Count Julian, who had wrongs to avenge on King Roderick, and that he took an active part in bringing about the invasion, is likely enough to be true, whether it was his daughter or some other woman who "seduced him to that foul revolt." The Arab general, Musa, who commanded in Africa for the Khalif, proceeded with caution in the enterprise. Tarik was first sent to make a reconnaissance on Spanish ground with one thousand five hundred horsemen. Landing near Gibraltar, which has since borne his name, Tarik ravaged the country round about and returned with much spoil in treasure and captives. He must have reported favourably of the chances of a larger enterprise, for he was sent over again with a considerably increased force to make a foray over a wider field.

The Moslem army consisted almost entirely of Berbers, a fierce and warlike race, but lately converted to the new faith, whose appetite for war and conquest in Spain was whetted by the prospect of revenge. The Berbers were the descendants of the Vandals, who had been driven out of Spain by the Goths some three hundred years before. Tarik, their chief, was himself a Berber, and therefore of blood akin to those who had conquered Spain from the Romans. No doubt some of the leaders of the enterprise, and some who were most conspicuous thereafter in guiding it to results beneficial to mankind and to civilisation, were Arabs; but it has not been sufficiently noted that the conquest of Spain was no exception, as at first sight it would appear to be, to the general law which rules the history of European nations, by which the conquerers come from the North. The invading Berbers, under Tarik, were but a reflex wave of the great Scandinavian stream. The Goths were to be replaced by a more vigorous shoot from the same stock.

King Roderick, warned by Duke Theodomir, the governor of Andalusia, of the landing of the invaders, hastily gathered an army and advanced towards the enemy. The forces of the Christians mustered ninety thousand strong, while Tarik, who had received a reinforcement of five thousand men, did not have more than twelve thousand under his command. This disproportion was probably more nominal than real. The Goths had grown effeminate by long disuse of arms and indulgence in luxury. The canker of a long peace had entered into their hearts and sapped their ancient martial virtue. The spirit of their Scandinavian sires was almost extinct in the nation. Shut up in their peninsula, they had abandoned themselves to the indulgences of social life, careless of the enemy which their isolated position seemed to exclude. The mass of the footmen in Roderick's host were probably of the nation whom the Visigothic laws branded as slaves, who cannot be supposed to have had much stomach for battle. On the other hand, the Berbers were trained to arms and accustomed to fighting.

They were inspired by the flaming zeal of new converts—conscious of being the soldiers of a faith who had overcame the proudest empires—who had humbled the Emperor of the East, and conquered Syria, Persia, Egypt, and Barbary. They had Paradise before them and behind ; for the living, Andaloos ; for the dead, eternal bliss. Tarik was specially strong in cavalry, in which arm Roderick was weak. On the 19th of July the two armies met on the plains of Xeres, within a mile of the sea, on the banks of the Chrysos—a river since known as the Guadalete, a corruption of *Wad-el-leded*, the river of delight. For seven long days—according to the chronicles—the battle raged from dawn till sundown. Roderick, the king, bore himself valorously like a Christian knight. The Moors fought desperately, as knowing that for them there was no retreat. At last their disparity in numbers began to be felt, and they were gradually giving way when Tarik rushed in front and invoking the name of Allah, plunged singly into the Gothic ranks. The Moors were aroused to new ardour. Then, at the crisis of the day, according to the Christian chronicler, treachery began to do its work. The sons of Witiza and Oppas deserted their posts, and either joined the enemy or fled from the field. Roderick himself fell, slain by the hand of Tarik ; or, if we believe the legend preserved in the Spanish ballads, was permitted to retire and expiate his sins in a neighbouring monastery. The fate of the last Gothic king was never clearly ascertained, though, according to the Arabic writers, his body was found in the field and his head sent to Musa, to be forwarded to the Khalif at Damascus.

Thus ended the Gothic dominion in Spain, which had endured for three hundred years, dating from Atawulf, the first who invaded the country. The victory of the Moors was complete, nay, the success of Tarik was so signal, and the prospects opened to the conqueror so dazzling, as to fill Musa with envy. He sent orders to Tarik to remain inactive, on the plea that he needed reinforcements. Meanwhile the Arab commander-in-chief prepared to pass over with his whole army to Spain, writing to the Khalif to claim for himself all the merit of victory, and extolling the value of the new conquest. Tarik, relying upon his popularity with his men, paid no heed to his superior's orders, but struck out boldly for the heart of Spain, reaching Toledo and taking possession of the royal city of the Goths without a blow; while two of his lieutenants occupied Cordova and Malaga.

Henceforth our story requires us to follow the fortunes of the conquered, who, the Gothic dominion being at an end, may from this time be spoken of as Spaniards. From the fatal field of Guadalete the survivors seem to have fled in two main streams—one of which was directed by the prudent Theodomir, the Duke of Andalusia—one of the few who foresaw the calamities of his country. Theodomir, who claimed to be the rightful successor to Roderick, took his way with his followers towards the hills of Murcia. The other portion of the beaten Goths, including, as from the sequel we may suppose, the most patriotic and independent of the Christians, fled northward to the mountains of Asturias. Under Theodomir, a skilful

and crafty leader, some attempt was made to arrest
the progress of the conquerors. His followers, however, before they could form, were overtaken and cut to
pieces by the Moslems—Theodomir himself escaping
with his life. Afterwards, when in most desperate
straits, he succeeded by dint of ingenuity and daring
in making terms with the unbelievers. The letter of the
convention is still extant in a contract made between
him and Abdelaziz, son of Musa, dated 713, by which
Theodomir was permitted to remain in undisturbed
possession of his states, on promising fidelity to the
Khalif and paying him tribute—the Christians to
preserve their religion and their churches, and their
wives and daughters to be respected. These states
of Theodomir, which included Murcia and parts of
Valencia and Granada, were henceforth called by the
Arabs the country of Tadmir, and bore that name
for four hundred years. Theodomir and Athanagild,
his son, enjoyed their qualified independence, under
the terms above recited, for some thirty-five years,
when their territory was absorbed into a neighbouring Mahommedan kingdom. Some confusion has
been made between Theodomir and his contemporary
and rival, Pelayo (of whom we have presently to
speak) by the Christian writers. While some omit
all mention of Theodomir, others place him above
Pelayo, whom they reduce to insignificance or pass
over without a word. There is a third party, which,
out of pure mischievousness as it would seem, is
supported by Voltaire in his "Essai sur les Mœurs"
which make one and the same individual of Theodomir and Pelayo. For ourselves, we may drop

Theodomir altogether out of the story, as he was at best but a passing episode—a Spaniard, who made terms with the Moor, surviving only for himself, and contributing nothing to the re-making of Spain.

The remnant of the Gothic host, together with all who were, as we may suppose, true and patriotic Spaniards, who scorned to submit to the infidel invaders and yet were unable to make head against them in the open country, fled from the field of battle towards the mountains of Asturias. There, entrenched within the rocky fastnesses which had been the immemorial refuge of Spanish patriotism—which had defied Carthaginian, Roman, and Goth—in the midst of a race who had never bowed the neck to any conqueror, the hardy Asturians, of the Cantabrian stock—the same whom the Roman poet declared to be "indomitable by cold, by heat, or by famine"—a people to whom "life was insupportable without battle"—the survivors of the Gothic army were secure. Thither were brought away from Toledo, by a happy provision of the ministers of religion who remained true to their faith, the holy relics of the saints, together with the books of the law, and the most precious of the ecclesiastical apparatus and furniture—a salvage held almost to compensate for the disgrace of surrender, which doubtless had a certain efficacy in keeping alive the sacred flame of patriotism, with which henceforth was inseparably combined faith in the one Catholic Church. Out of this small germ grew by slow degrees the tree of Spanish nationality. The remnant who survived to reach their Asturian retreat was but small—nay, according to the ridiculous legend preserved in the chronicles, only thirty obeyed the call of their chief. Thus reduced and humbled the Goths had time to reflect on the sins which had brought them to ruin. Compelled by defeat to resign their pretensions to exclusive nobility, they were brought into touch with the native Spaniards whom they had despised and neglected. There was not room in the narrow Asturian valleys for more than one people. The claims of wealth and high descent had to be abandoned where all were from and on the same level. In Asturias was laid the foundation of the Spanish nation, and hence sprang that new nobility which knew no differences of race. Goth and Iberian thenceforth existed no more, being merged into one people, to be called Spaniards. The nobles were they who fought most stoutly. The king was the select man of the nobles. Henceforward it was from Asturias that all that was best in Spain descended—Asturias, which was the cradle of the nation, where every mountaineer was an *hidalgo*.

The refugees chose for their leader Pelayo, or Pelagius, not so much perhaps because he was a descendant of Chindaswind, of the Gothic blood royal, as because he was the most capable man for that burdensome honour and painful trust. The process of election was according to the old Visigothic custom, by the general voice of the people. It may be presumed that the electors in such a case were not inconveniently numerous. Pelayo established the seat of his authority at Canga de Onis—now an insignificant mining village in a picturesque Swiss-

CROSS OF PELAYO.

like region, with a dominion, scarcely yet to be called a kingdom—extending east and west as far as the Christians were yet unsubdued, bounded on the north by the sea and on the south by the mountains. Of Pelayo very little is known, except that he fought for the life of his infant state, and won the famous battle of Covadonga in 718. Covadonga, which is a name as sacred to Spaniards as Marathon was to the ancient Greeks, is memorable as the first victory gained by the Christians over the Moors—a victory which gave assurance to the world of the life which still resided in the Christian body and hope of resurrection. The Moors, who had hitherto neglected this mountain region as being not worth conquering, hearing of the stand made by "one Belay" sent a force under Alxaman to crush the nascent insurrection. Alxaman was accompanied and guided by the renegade Bishop Oppas to the retreat of Pelayo, which was a cavern, *La Cueva de Anseva*, up the small river called the *Rio Bueno*. We may presume that the cavern did not hold all the array of the Christian leader, for it is incapable of harbouring more than three hundred men. The Moorish army crossed the mountains, and descending on the other side came to where Pelayo's small force was entrenched. They were met in a narrow pass by a shower of rocks and stones from the neighbouring heights, which threw the unbelievers, unaccustomed to such a mode of warfare, into confusion. Following up his artillery Pelayo and his band rushed from their hiding-places and made havoc of the Moors—slaying their leader with a hundred and twenty-four thousand of his men.

Sixty-three thousand more were drowned in the river. The remainder took refuge in France, where three hundred and seventy-five thousand were put away. So gravely assert Sebastian, Bishop of Salamanca, who composed his chronicle in 866–910, and Paul the Deacon who wrote after him.[1] Seeing that the nucleus of Pelayo's force is said to have been but thirty men, it must be confessed that this was a very handsome return for the heroism expended. At this rate the Moors should have been wiped off the Peninsula much earlier; and it is all the more credit to Pelayo that he did this execution on the miscreant children of Mahommed, seeing that he had no assistance from any of the fighting saints, such as afterwards was so freely rendered to the Christians.

But the glory of Pelayo's exploit happily does not rest upon this terrible slaughter. The monkish chroniclers, writing in an age when there were few to read and none to contradict them, were most murderous in the treatment of the enemy, and not over-careful in their authorities. Seeing that in this case no miracle was pretended, later Spanish writers admit the number of the slain to be excessive. Not one-tenth part of those generally alleged to have fallen under the edge of Pelayo's sword and the rocks and stones of his mountaineers could have found standing room, much less sustenance, in that narrow valley. What is certain, however, is that a decisive blow was dealt at the Moorish power. The advancing tide of conquest was stemmed. The Spaniards gathered heart and hope in their darkest hour; and the dream

---

[1] *Como canta el Abad responde el Sacristan !*

of Moslem invincibility was broken. Covadonga remains a word for ever linked with the holiest memories as the cradle of Spanish independence. The work done on that day by the sturdy mountaineers of Asturias was the making of the new Spain. The Moors made no further attempt to disturb Pelayo in his rocky nest, affecting to despise him as an enemy unworthy of serious notice. So they left him alone in peace, and never again attempted to break through the mountains. Asturias remained free, and thither, doubtless on the strength of that immunity, came all who were dissatisfied with the Moorish dominion, all who clung to the hope of a Christian revival, all who detested Mahommed, or who had cause to quarrel with the new order of things, including, as we may suppose, the best and stoutest among the old Gothic nobles. They began, we are told, to extend their bounds, to build new houses, to repair those that had been destroyed, and to cultivate the land. Of Pelayo, the hero of Covadonga, nothing more is known, though one chronicler, Archbishop Rodrigo of Toledo (writing five centuries afterwards) speaks of other battles won from the Moors. The first of the Christian leaders (it does not appear that he ever called himself king) died in 737, and was buried in the small church of S. Eulalia, at Cangas de Onis, near the scene of his great victory. To him succeeded his son Favila, who, after a brief reign of two years, was killed by a bear while hunting—a fact which is enshrined in " Don Quixote " (chapter xxxiv. of the second part), and commemorated, as is still to be seen, in the doorway of the church of Villanueva, built by his successor. Alfonso, the first of that popular name (which is the same as Alonso and Ildefonso, in Latin Alphonsus, Ildephonsus), surnamed the Catholic from the zeal which he displayed in the restoration of the churches, who came after Favila, was the son-in-law of Pelayo, who was chosen not because he was the direct heir to the throne, but because he was the best able of the family to support the weight of sovereignty. The law of hereditary succession was unknown to the old Visigoths, whose practice—invoked and imitated at a later age as we shall see—was to elect to the throne the eldest or the strongest of the royal race. Thus, the uncle was preferred to the nephew, the second or other son to a grandson, the eldest of a collateral branch to the younger of the main stock. Mariana, the historian, tells us indeed that Alfonso inherited under Pelayo's will ; but Mariana was a zealous advocate of the kingly right divine, and there is here, as always, great reason for not believing him. It is doubtful whether any of the royal Gothic family could write, and even if Pelayo had possessed this rare accomplishment, more than doubtful that he should nominate his next but one successor. Alfonso, who in the old days had been commander of the Gothic militia, proved his right to the throne by the vigour he displayed in its defence. He made large additions to his state, which under his management grew to proportions which might fairly entitle it to the name of kingdom. He annexed nearly all Galicia, a province which the Moors had never fairly occupied, including what is now Portugal as far as the Douro. He retook Leon, Salamanca, Zamora, Astorga, and Ledesma—extending his boundaries even to Castile, by the reduction of Avila, Segovia, and other important places. Eastward his dominion embraced Biscay and Navarre. These conquests, which included nearly a fourth of all Spain, are a testimony to the vigour and ability with which Alfonso took up the task of recovering the country from the Moors, and entitle him to the distinction which he enjoys in history as the greatest of the new race of kings. It is true that these conquests were made at a period when the Mahommedans were engaged in an intricate series of civil wars, before the establishment of the Cordovan monarchy; but the rapidity with which Alfonso extended his dominion seems to prove that in the northern provinces the Moorish hold was a slack one, and that their so-called colonies were really only military camps. Most of the places we have enumerated fell again into the hands of the Moors, to be taken and retaken many times in the course of the next two or three hundred years. In fact, in these early days, the measure of the Christian dominion was the character of the reigning monarch. The able and warlike king had a large territory; the feeble and the incompetent was reduced to a narrow kingdom. The true home of the Christians, during the early years, was in the mountainous country; just as the true home of the Moors was in Andalusia and the South. All between was debateable land, perpetually fought for, won, and lost, but not valuable as a possession, being by reason of chronic disturbance and frequent changes of owners, desolate and uncultivated.

Alfonso I. died in 757, and his son Fruela reigned in his stead. Fruela, who governed but for six years, is not known for any good. He was a cruel and sanguinary tyrant, who is said by the early Christian chroniclers to have won a great battle over the Moors. But he is claimed by the Moorish chroniclers as a tributary to their great king, the first Abderahman. It is certain only that Fruela lost some of the ground his father had gained, and was done to death by his own people in 768. Aurelio, his successor, was a nephew of Alfonso I., who lived in peace with his Moorish neighbours; which makes credible the report that he was really a tributary and vassal of Abderahman. Of Silo, his brother, who succeeded him in 774, and reigned for nine years, even less is known. In his reign the seat of the court was moved to Pravia, on the western border of Asturias. Of Mauregato, the bastard son of Alfonso I., who came next, the name is held in evil memory; for it was he who, according to Rodrigo de Toledo and the ballads, agreed to pay Abderahman a yearly tribute of one hundred beautiful maidens, in return for Moorish help to secure him on his ill-gotten throne. Of this shameful bargain nothing however is said by the Mahommedan writers, who would scarcely pass over such a matter in silence. Against the weight of tradition and the authority of the Archbishop of Toledo is to be set the improbability of Abderahman, who was a man of taste, exacting, or of Mauregato being able to furnish, the hundred beautiful maidens from out of his scanty dominions. The maidens of Asturias, though dowered with every excellent virtue, are not beautiful. It may be, as has been suggested, that the agreement with the Moors only went to the extent of the two kings encouraging marriages between their respective subjects, which would be a policy quite in accordance with Abderahman's enlightened and liberal character, though naturally odious to the severer Christians. On the death of Mauregato in 788, Bermudo I., a nephew of Alfonso the Catholic, was elected to the throne— Alfonso, the son of Fruela, being passed over by the nobles lest he might be tempted to revenge on them the death of his father. Bermudo had taken holy orders, but he was compelled, much against his will, to accept the royal office, which included a wife. The double burden, however, was found too much for him, and after a short reign of three years he put off his wife, and retired in favour of his cousin.

But before we proceed with the story of the kings it is necessary that we should speak of an episode in the history of Spain, which, though it had no direct bearing on the destinies of the country, is still of importance as throwing light on the character of the age, and on the relations of Christians and Moors. This is the famous expedition of the Emperor Charlemagne into Spain, which, with all that rose out of it—a very rich and rampant growth—fills the early romantic literature of the three Latin races. Out of the dense mist which tradition and romance, aided by a lying chronicle and a forged record, have thrown over the story—a story which has furnished more matter to the poets and balladists than any subject ever selected by man on which to exercise his imagination—a few leading facts are to be discerned. To Charlemagne, the Emperor, at Paderborn, there arrived in 777 an embassy from the Sheikh Suleiman-el-Arabi (the Alarabi of the Spanish chronicles), praying for aid against Abderahman, the Emir of Cordova, who had, to the scandal of the orthodox Mahommedan world, usurped the title of Khalif, together with the independent sovereignty of Spain. Charlemagne, as is well known, was an ally of Haroun-er-Rashid, the Khalif of Bagdad, in support of whose superior claims to the headship of Islam a large number of the Spanish Mahommedans, including the turbulent Berbers, were in arms. Alarabi himself, with his followers, had seized Saragossa, and was holding it against Abderahman's governor, Abd-el-Melic. For objects, doubtless, of his own policy, which we may fairly suppose had little to do with religion, seeing that he was asked to intervene in support of one Mahommedan against another, Charlemagne agreed to furnish the aid required, and marched into Spain with a large army in 778. His first conquest, to the disgust of all good Spaniards, was the Christian city of Pampeluna, in which there were no Mahommedans. Thence he passed into Aragon, where he received the submission of Saragossa, then in the occupation of the rebel Berbers, though he was refused admission into some other towns—a characteristic incident of Spanish alliances, which is curious as showing that even thus early some Moors had become good Spaniards. It does not appear that Charlemagne fought with any Moors, or that he did anything whatever to justify the character he enjoys in the French *chansons de geste* of being a Christian champion. As for

Marsilio, his great antagonist, the arch-Paynim of the Italian and French romances, he is entirely a figment, unless we take him to be founded on Abd-el-Melic, the rightful Wali of Saragossa. But Abd-el-Melic is not known to have come across Charlemagne's path, nor his master Abderahman to have interfered in any way with the expedition of the Frankish Emperor. Doubtless Abderahman had learned to know that the enterprise of Charlemagne was not directed against him or his religion.

Leaving Alarabi established in Aragon, and setting governors of his faith (the Mahommedan faith) over principal cities, Charlemagne made a somewhat hurried retreat from the country—compelled to return, it is said, by news of a revolt among the Saxons. While passing through the defiles of the Pyrenees, the rear-guard of the Frankish army, under the famous Roland, the Emperor's nephew, which was encumbered with a vast load of spoil, taken either from Christians or friendly Moors, was set upon by a mixed body of Navarrese, Basques, Gascons, Spaniards, and even Moors, and cut to pieces to a man. *Usque ad unum omnes interficiunt,* says Eginhard, the Emperor's secretary.

Upon this slender basis of fact, not very honourable to Charlemagne or to Christendom, has been reared that huge pile of fiction, the legend of Roland at Roncesvalles, which to France has given an epic, to Italy two great romantic poems, and to Spain innumerable ballads. How the legend which describes the fight as one between the Christians and the heathen, with Roland or Orlando as the Achilles of the host on one side, and Marsilio the king of the Saracens or misbelievers as the Paynim Agamemnon on the other, with armies drawn from Egypt, Persia, and Tartary—with the treachery of Ganelon, which brought about the disaster at Roncesvalles, and the moving incident of the dying Roland with his ivory horn, whose echoes reached eight miles away—how this fiction, the fruitful mother of many fictions, arose, and of the many winding ways into which it wandered, it is no part of my duty to tell, however tempting is the digression. What is pertinent to our subject is to inquire into the part played by the Spaniards, whether Christian or Moor, in these transactions. And first, it is to be noted that the story of Charlemagne's expedition, even from the poetical side, is told quite differently in Spain from that of Theroulde, or Thorold, whoever he may be — the French *jongleur* who in the Thirteenth century composed the *Chanson de Roland.* According to the Spanish ballads — some of which relating to this matter are at least as old as the *Chanson de Roland*, while they must be credited with an authority even greater, seeing that they speak of events which happened on Spanish soil and reflect Spanish opinion —Alfonso the Chaste, being old and having no heirs, assigned his kingdom to Charlemagne on the condition that the Frankish Emperor would help him against the Moors. It is to claim the performance of this compact that Charlemagne crosses the Pyrenees. But Bernardo del Carpio, who is the son of Alfonso's sister, Ximena, hearing of the shameful bargain by which he would be disinherited, defies the king—vowing that rather than submit to the Franks he will summon all the youth of Asturias and Leon to arms to repel the invader :—

> Y ese rey de Zaragoza
> Me prestará su compaña,
> Para salir contra Francia
> Y darle cruda batalla.
>
> (And that king of Saragossa
> Shall lend to me his company,
> To march against the Frenchman
> And give him bitter battle.)

Elsewhere the Moors of Aragon are claimed as allies of the Asturians, Bernardo even going to Granada to invoke the assistance of certain Moorish heroes against the Frankish invaders.

Here, then, is quite another story, in its essence more consistent, as I believe, with the truth of history, however the details may have been distorted or exaggerated. It is Charlemagne who is the national enemy, who is driven back from an unholy purpose. Roncesvalles is a glorious victory, achieved by native valour against a barbarous horde of foreign invaders. In this war Moors or Paynims do not appear except as allies of the patriot heroes who drive the French away. Roland himself cuts but a poor figure in the legend under his Spanish name of Roldan, for there is a better than he, even Bernardo del Carpio. He it is who leads the combined host, Christians and Moors, against the French, who, after performing prodigies of valour, ends by catching Roldan in his arms and squeezing him to death, as Hercules did the giant Antæus. The French may sing of Roland, the Italians of Orlando; but it is Bernardo who is the

Spanish ballad-monger's joy, the hero of innumerable romances, admitted by the excellent Don Agustin Duran, acutest of Spanish critics, to be a true type and representative of pure Spanish *caballerismo* or knighthood.

With the hero of romance we are not here concerned, but with the hero of history. Who then was Bernardo del Carpio, the famous champion of united Spain against the French invaders in the Eighth century? If he is historical, his actions shed much light upon the character of the age. But unfortunately there is much reason to doubt whether there lived any such person. The first mention of Bernardo del Carpio is in the General Chronicle of Alfonso X., compiled in the Thirteenth century, assuredly out of the popular legends and romances. He is not known to any of the contemporary chroniclers, as he certainly would have been had he lived and performed the actions attributed to him. Again, the leading circumstances of his life and the dates of his performances do not correspond with the historical record. He is said to have been the son of Alfonso II.'s sister, by a secret marriage with the Count Saldaña. He is represented as opposing the king in his scheme of surrendering his dominions to Charlemagne, and as heading a revolt of the Asturians and Leonese successfully against this project, for which offence, and for the crime of being his nephew, the king punishes him by imprisoning his father, the Count of Saldaña. But none of these circumstances of the fable will square with history. Alfonso II., surnamed on account of a virtue uncommon among kings, the Chaste, is not known to have had a sister. There was no Count of Saldaña. The events which form the main burden of the romances, the defeat of the Franks and their slaughter at Roncesvalles, occurred not later than 780. But at that date Silo was king of Asturias. Alfonso II. did not begin to reign till 791, when he must have been a young man, seeing that he lived to 842. He could hardly, in 780, have had a nephew old enough to be the recognised champion of his kingdom. Again, Alfonso is represented in the ballads as having reigned more than thirty years, and white-haired, when the invasion of Charlemagne occurs. All this makes it difficult to reconcile the story of Bernardo del Carpio with the strict letter of history, although the main facts of that story may be true, as they indisputably are picturesque, and valuable as illustrating the national character.

But as myths do not grow out of nothing, there may be in this legend of Bernardo del Carpio (apart from what we know to be historical), a germ of truth, that is, as regards the hero himself. Even in the monstrous fable of Roland which has thrown its shadow over all Western romance, there is a grain of fact. We know from two lines of Eginhard that there was a Roland, that he was "prefect of the marches of Brittany," and that he died at Roncesvalles. So his rival may have had a real existence in some popular leader of those who fell upon Charlemagne's rear-guard, around whose name there clustered, in the process of ages, the wonderful deeds which were done in that adventure. What there is of interest to us in the history is the light which is thrown upon the national character which, even at this early date, we find to be imbued with one leading Spanish feature, which is jealousy of the foreigner, Leonese and Asturians joining with Moors to resist an interference with their internal affairs, and hatred of the French overriding all differences of race and religion.

Alfonso II. reigned for over fifty years, a fact which alone justifies his being regarded as the best and most popular of the early kings. This long reign was not, however, unmarked by some of the incidents which hereafter will occur so frequently in the history of the Spanish kings. He was taken prisoner by a body of rebels and confined in a monastery. But he was rescued and brought in triumph to Oviedo, which henceforth he made his capital and where he established his court, enlarging and beautifying the city. He built a church and founded a bishop's see, which were endowed with special rights and privileges. Here Alfonso II. lies buried, in the beautiful cathedral erected in place of the original edifice in 1388, together with many of the early kings. During his reign, which lasted to 842, we hear of no wars with the Moors or accretions of territory. His successor was Ramiro I., son of Bermudo I., called the Deacon—the ex-monk who had preceded Alfonso. He had to dispute the throne, as usual, with some members of his family, but succeeded in disposing of them in the milder form, by putting out their eyes and shutting them up in monasteries. He won more renown by encountering and defeating the Norman freebooters, who for the first time appeared on the Spanish coast to ravage the land and seek for a settlement, landing at Corunna, where they were defeated and lost seventy ships. A grander achievement, which Archbishop Rodrigo of Toledo in the thirteenth century and Mariana in the seventeenth century have invested with extraordinary lustre, namely, the victory of Clavijo where seventy thousand of the misbelievers fell, and Santiago appeared in person "on a white horse, bearing aloft a white standard on which was depicted in red the form of a cross," to direct the fight and increase the slaughter, is now proved to be an impudent invention. No such battle was ever fought, no such victory was gained. No writer before the Thirteenth century, either Christian or Mahommedan, mentions such an event. Nor had any of the early monkish chroniclers a motive for the invention, seeing that the shrine of Santiago at Compostella was not established until A.D. 1120, so that there was no necessity for working up the miracle and calling for gifts and offerings to the saint. The very words of Mariana in relating the story, which Morales declares " none but a heretic could disbelieve," betray the object and purpose of the invention. "This battle was fought," he says, "in the year 846, being the second of King Ramiro. The victorious army, in gratitude to God for the divine aid, vowed to Santiago, under whose leadership the victory had been obtained, that all Spain should thenceforth be tributary to the church of Compostella; and that every acre of ploughed and vine land should pay each year a bushel of corn or wine to that church."

This is the first of the many childish legends intended to confirm and refresh the faithful, palpably invented in the interests of the shrine, which we shall find frequently in the annals of Spain, such as even her modern historians are not ashamed to repeat. Neither the patriotism nor the valour of the Spaniards need any such extraneous aid; and it is surprising that the native historians do not perceive how much they damage the reputation of their countrymen by attributing their successes in battle to supernatural agency. The schoolboy who reads of the meddling of the Homeric gods with the battles of the heroes, if of a healthy and manly turn of mind, is disgusted with the story, and certainly thinks no better either of the divinities or those they befriend. When Æneas is whisked away in a cloud by his mother, or Diomed is saved a beating by Juno, we are aware of an outrage on fair-play as well as on art. The story becomes insipid when we know beforehand that one of the combatants is secure of victory, having divine help—while another, though braver, fights in vain, being destined to defeat. The tendency of these legends, designed to glorify the national faith at the expense of the national valour, is to increase our sympathy with the Moors, who had no such preternatural allies, but fought against odds, with carnal weapons, and with only their stout hearts and arms to help them.

The next to succeed after Ramiro was Ordoño, his son, whose principal work, during the sixteen years of his reign, was to fortify his frontiers and to re-people the outlying districts which had been laid waste by the Moors. As we hear of Leon and

Astorga among the towns so restored, we must presume that these places, which had been won by Alfonso I. a century before, had since been either deserted or had fallen back into Moorish dominion. Ordoño was victorious over the unbelievers without magic or miracle, winning a signal victory at Albelda over Musa, one of the rebel Moorish kinglings, and compelling his son, who had seized Toledo from the rightful Emir, to become his vassal. These successes were brought about as much by craft as by valour, Ordoño taking advantage of the dissensions between Mahommed I., the incapable son of Abderahman II., and his rebellious Emirs, and allying himself with Moors on terms of mutual help, whenever it suited him to do so. Before the close of his reign in in 866, Ordoño had greatly extended his patrimony, the Christian state now reaching as far south as Salamanca.

II.

THE KINGDOM OF LEON—RISE OF CASTILE—THEIR TEMPORARY UNION.

(866–1109.)

THE reign of Alfonso III., the son of Ordoño, marks the beginning of a new epoch for Christian Spain. The native Spaniards had now regained a large portion of their lost territory. Within the space of a century and a half they had thrown back the Moorish dominion at least to the Douro, and even, in one direction, to the Guadiana. They were undisputed masters of all the mountain region to the sea. The whole of Asturias, Biscay, Galicia, and Northern Portugal, with a great portion of Navarre, was theirs. In Castile, still but a waste land studded with castles (whence the name is supposed, by a dubious etymology, to be derived), they were supreme as long as they could command the field. For this happier condition of things, which lasted for a hundred years, the Christians were indebted to the valour and firmness of Alfonso III., who is fairly entitled to be regarded as the second founder of the state. Some of the ground he won by the sword was lost indeed by the fatal policy which he was the first to introduce, of providing for the division of his estates after death —a policy which led to unnumbered evils in the hands of his successors, and was a principal cause of the retardment of Spain; but Alfonso, as great in war as he was in peace, must be reckoned one of the ablest of the early monarchs. His long reign of forty-four years, ending in 910, was disturbed at the outset by the usual troubles from two of his turbulent nobles; but the *Cortes* of Oviedo helped him to get rid of one of his rivals by assassination, and he himself put down the other by war. To secure a barrier in Navarre against the French, Alfonso set over that unruly province, which constantly abused its privilege of being neither wholly French nor purely Spanish, one Sancho Iñigo, a local nobleman of great influence. This was the beginning of much trouble to the public peace, Navarre being from that time forth an abiding thorn in the side of Spain, and by its double character and divided allegiance, sometimes French, sometimes Spanish, a perpetual source of quarrel between the two countries. In his wars with the Moors, which continued almost without intermission during his reign, Alfonso was more successful, beating them in several great battles, gaining victories over both the Khalif and the independent Emirs, raising the character of the Christians in arms to a higher point than it had ever reached, and establishing the kingdom on a solid basis. But what the unbelievers could not do was effected by domestic treason. A palace intrigue was got up against Alfonso in which his wife, his son

Garcia, and his son's father-in-law, Nuño Fernandez, the Count of Castile (a title which figures for the first time in the story) took leading parts—the object of which was to deprive the old king of his throne and set the young prince thereon. At first the king was successful in putting down the revolt, but the populace being moved to rise in behalf of Garcia, Alfonso was forced to abdicate in favour of his eldest son; to Ordoño, the second son, being granted the government of Galicia, and to Fruela, another son, that of Oviedo. Thus an example was set of that fatal policy of partition, by which the natural accretion of Christian Spain was arrested, and the work of recovery undone. This policy, which more than once set the clock backwards—the good done by one able monarch in his life being spoilt at his death—was doubtless in accordance with the humour of the age, which was one impatient of unity and jealous of the kingly power. The nobles and the great fief-holders would rather be separated than united. The king was but the chief of the nobles, not always the richest or strongest of them. The idea of a state, in the modern sense, had not arisen, nor was there any deliberate or concerted design, as the frequency with which these partitions occurred seems to prove, of turning the Moors out of the country. When there was nothing particular doing at home in the way of internal battle and slaughter, the Count would take a hand in helping to ravage the Moors. Very often the crusade was got up, as other crusades have been, to keep the nobles out of mischief; while the prospect of their being thinned off in the war was probably not without its attractions both to king and people.

On the death of Alfonso III., after a last foray into the land of the Moors, Garcia moved the capital from Oviedo to Leon. Thenceforth the kingdom, which hitherto had been regarded as too loose in its borders and too unfixed in its foundations to have any particular designation, was called and known as the kingdom of Leon. The change of the seat of government was significant of the larger security and increased importance which the state had acquired. The Christians had now fairly emerged from their mountain shelter, and had arrayed themselves face to face against the usurpers of their soil. Oviedo was in the middle of a region which had scarcely known the presence of the Moor. Leon, half-way between the sea and the Douro, lay in the open plain in the full front of the enemy. The choice of such a spot for the centre of their strength seems to show that the Christians deemed themselves now on an equality with the Moslems, and had fairly entered into the struggle for ascendency in the Peninsula.

The short reigns of Garcia and his brother, Ordoño II., are marked by perpetual war with the Moors, of which the result was, after various alternations of fortune, to strengthen the new frontiers and even to extend the power of the Leonese. Between the conflicting accounts of the chroniclers of the rival faiths it is difficult to make out the truth respecting the various stubborn battles fought about this period between the Christians and Moors, but it is certain that, after defeating the Moorish army under the

TOMB OF ORDOÑO II. IN LEON CATHEDRAL.

general of Abderahman III., Ordoño himself encountered a signal reverse at Val de Junquera in 921, where two of his fighting bishops were made prisoners. The succeeding period is one of the most confused in the Spanish annals, king resembling king in all the general features of his reign, so that Fruela II., who followed Ordoño II., and Alfonso IV., who succeeded Fruela II., are scarcely to be discriminated. Ramiro II. came to the throne in 930, after putting out the eyes of all the nearest of his relations, and won what is admitted to be a decisive victory over the Moors at Simancas. In his reign which lasted for twenty years, Castile first rises into historical prominence, under its famous Count Fernan Gonsalez—that is, Fernan (Ferdinand) son of Gonzalo.[1] Castile, hitherto a dependency of Leon, now began to lift its head as the land, once a march of the Christian kingdom and but a chain of scattered fortresses, came to be settled and repeopled. Fernan Gonsalez was the first of its counts who aspired to independence. Revolting against Ramiro II., he was beaten and confined in a castle. Afterwards on paying homage and making submission, he was restored to liberty, his daughter Urraca (not to be confounded with a more celebrated princess of the same name who comes hereafter) being married to the king's eldest son, Ordoño. This, which might appear to be an auspicious event for the two countries, was but the beginning of more troubles between Leon and

---

[1] The final *ez* in Spanish marks a patronymic. Thus Perez is the son of Pedro, Sanchez the son of Sancho, &c.

BURGOS CATHEDRAL.

Castile, which in the next hundred years distracted the realm, throwing back the work of reconquest and giving the unbelievers (who, indeed, rarely lacked of such good fortune) much increase and encouragement. Ordoño III. had scarcely mounted the throne in 950, before he was confronted with rebellion in his own household, fomented by his own father-in-law, the turbulent and ambitious Count of Castile. Fernan Gonsalez, on whom many ballads were made (mostly Castilian), behaved with less magnanimity than might have been expected from a hero of romance. He sided with Sancho the king's brother and Count Garcia of Navarre against his daughter's husband; but after invading Leon at the head of a body of Castilians and Navarrese, unheroically retired, without battle, on finding the king well prepared. Ordoño III. punished him by putting away Urraca and marrying another lady—to the scandal of the Church, but by a license not uncommonly assumed by the early kings of Spain. Sancho, the first of that name, surnamed the *Fat*, had not long to wait for the throne, succeeding his brother in 955. He was himself to experience the vicissitudes of kingship, suffering at the hands of the unprincipled Count of Castile precisely the same fate which he had designed for Ordoño. Fernan Gonsalez found another Ordoño, son of Alfonso IV., who had been put away and blinded several reigns earlier, to whom he married his daughter, the divorced Urraca. The new Ordoño was set up as king against Sancho, who retired into exile—owing his ruin it appears, as much to the disfigurement of his person by excessive obesity as to any other cause. Sancho was more fat than king beseemed — cursed with a corpulence revolting to Christian opinion. In this affliction poor Sancho turned for relief to a quarter which we should scarcely have suspected as being open to a dethroned and helpless Christian prince, the descendant of kings who had laid their chief glory in the harrying and slaying of the Moslems. Despairing of the Christian leeches Sancho wrote to Abderahman III., the Khalif of Cordova, to beg that he might be allowed to consult some of the famous *Hakims* of the Moorish capital upon his case. Abderahman sent a courteous reply. Sancho was hospitably received and splendidly entertained, and by cunning simples—the juice of certain herbs, we are told—his superfluous fat was removed, and his shape restored to its original grace and a slenderness consistent with princely dignity. But Sancho (who had probably that result in his eye when he went to Cordova) found relief for more than his bodily afflictions. He is said to have made himself so agreeable to Abderahman and the Moslem court that they gave him help in men and money to enable him to recover his kingdom. At the head of an army of Moors Sancho returned to Leon, driving the usurper out amidst the acclamations of his subjects. Ordoño, in his turn, was abandoned by the shifty and unscrupulous Fernan Gonsalez, deprived of his wife and children, and driven to take refuge with the Moors. The whole episode is of interest as confirming the views we have expressed as to the close communion of Moors and Christians in those early times, in spite of their frequent wars and desperate battles. At this time, indeed, as both before and after, Cordova was the chief seat of European civilisation, and under the enlightened rule of the Omeyyad Khalifs, distinguished throughout the world for her eminence in learning and science, no less than as the centre of courtesy and the school of good manners.

The reign of Ramiro III., the son of Sancho, began with a long minority, and was marked throughout by disturbance and rebellion. The Normans, who were now in their flush of victory and height of power, made a determined attempt at the conquest of Galicia, penetrating to Compostella, and occupying the province for two years, until at last the people arose and expelled them. Afterwards a desperate civil war, fomented as usual by the Count of Castile, who had raised up Bermudo, grandson of Fruela II., as a competitor for the throne, rent the Christian realm in two. The calamities of the kingdom were aggravated by the disasters caused by the inroads of the Moors, who, under their celebrated leader, Almanzor, entered upon a career of victory such as recalled to the affrighted Christians the age of their first humiliation, and spread terror throughout Christendom. A humble letter-writer at the gate of the palace, Almanzor, who is ranked among the greatest heroes of the Arab race, rose, by one of those turns of fate so common in the East, and only possible under a system like that of Mahommed, where talent irrespective of birth had a free field and ample opportunity, to be the most powerful man in the Peninsula—the mightiest of the soldiers of the Crescent since Tarik and Musa. Raising a large army, and proclaiming a *jihad*, or war of faith, Almanzor marched into the Christian kingdom, driving all before him, and scattering Castilians and Leonese as the Goths had been scattered three hundred years before. Town after town fell into the hands of the conquerors. In ten years Almanzor had nearly recovered all the territory which had been lost by the Moors. In 996 Leon itself fell, with all its treasures—the entire population being put to the sword. The sacred shrine of Santiago at Compostella felt the fury of the conquerors, who must have had a special grudge against this fighting saint. The newly-built cathedral was razed to the ground, and the idols of "the polytheists," as the Moslem writers irreverently call them, overthrown and mutilated. The tomb of the tutelar saint himself was only saved from desecration by "a divine splendour," which, according to Mariana, appeared from within, and dazzled the eyes of the audacious invaders. The bells of Compostella were sent as trophies to Cordova to be melted into lamps for the service of the great mosque. The terrified people seemed to have offered but little resistance, and we are told of counts and nobles who met the conqueror at Zamora and begged to be allowed to share his spoil. The ruin of the Christian state would have been complete but for the death of Almanzor, when his whole work, as usual with Oriental conquests, which have no other assurance than the life of the conqueror, fell to pieces.

Bermudo II., the son of Ramiro, who came to the

throne in those evil days, was little able to stem the torrent of ill-fortune, his nobles either openly joining the Moorish invaders, or stirring up dissension among the people. His son, Alfonso V., was only five years of age when he succeeded to his broken estate in 999. Two years afterwards, however, the great Almanzor himself died—out of chagrin, the Christians declare, at the loss of the battle of Calatañazor, where for the first time the three Christian states of Leon, Castile, and Navarre united their forces against the Moors. Over Calatañazor itself, the victory, there has raged a fight quite as hot, not only between Christian and Moor, but between Christian and Christian, as to whether such a battle ever took place, and whether it was not the Mahommedans who won and not the Christians. The latest authority on this subject, Dozy, pronounces the whole story to be a pious fiction. No Arab chronicler speaks of the battle; no Christian writer previous to the Thirteenth century has a word about it. The monk of Silos, a contemporary, draws a gloomy picture of the calamities which the terrible Almanzor had inflicted upon Christian Spain, but consoles himself by saying: "At the end God took pity on our great misery." But the relief he speaks of came by the death of Almanzor, whom "a demon" carried off—not by his defeat. For their consolation the Christians said, in this black hour of their adversity, what was said of Roderick and the "dolorous rout" of Guadalete—that Bermudo and his people, for their many sins, had deserved this chastisement. The Moors, for their acts of sacrilege, were punished by a dysentery which carried off their entire army, so that not a man of Almanzor's impious band returned to Cordova alive. The honour of Santiago and of the nation, however, demanded that Almanzor should be beaten in the field; and beaten he was accordingly at Calatañazor—by the Christian historians.

The death of Almanzor in 1002, which was followed by the rapid dissolution of the domains he had raised by his valour and genius, was the turning-point in the fortunes of Islam. With this great chief—the last who led the united Moors against the Spaniards—fell the Khalifate; for though the Omeyyad dynasty lingered for a few years longer, the power of the house was broken and the empire of Cordova dissolved for ever. Thereafter, the struggle of the Christians is with the petty Moorish kings, who were divided among themselves even as the Christians were. That at this period, even with the horrors endured by the faithful at the hands of the demon-inspired Almanzor fresh in their recollection, the king, Alfonso V., should not hesitate to give his sister in marriage to Mahommed, the King of Toledo, proves that there was much comity of feeling between Christian and Moor. We must conclude, either that Alfonso could not help himself, which implies his subjection to the infidel king, or that he could, which argues him to be careless of the national faith. In this reign Leon was rebuilt and re-occupied, and the mischief done by Almanzor repaired. To get rid of the eternal jealousy with Castile, a bargain was struck by which, while the states were dissevered, the reigning families were united. The king's son,

CATHEDRAL OF ZAMORA, ELEVENTH CENTURY.

Bermudo, was married to Ximena, the daughter of the Count of Castile, while the Count's son, Garcia, was wedded to the King's daughter, Sancha. On the Count of Castile was conferred the title of king, and he was made independent of Leon. This compact brought present peace but a crop of future troubles to the two countries, whose rivalry was henceforth continued for two hundred years longer.

Alfonso V. dying in battle against the Moors in Portugal, the tranquillity of the realm under Bermudo III., his son, was disturbed by the ambition of Sancho, called the Great, King of Navarre—who had risen by force of character and the fortune of marriage to be the most powerful of the princes of Christian Spain. Besides Navarre and the lordship of Sobrarbe, he was master of Aragon (at least of that small part of it which was independent of the Moorish kingdom of Saragossa); and in 1026 succeeded, in right of his wife Elvira (daughter of Garcia the last count), to the newly-created kingdom of Castile. This was a dominion exceeding that of Leon in importance and wealth, if not in extent. Had he waited, Sancho would have acquired for his family the kingdom of Leon also, for Fernando, his son, was married to a daughter of Alfonso V., and Alfonso's son, Bermudo, was childless. But the lust of dominion, or the greed of land, was too strong to be resisted. Sancho twice invaded the kingdom of Leon, on the last occasion making himself virtual master of the country as far as Galicia. The fair prospect, however, of a united kingdom for Christian Spain was once more dispelled, and in the usual manner. On

BAS-RELIEF FROM MONASTERY OF S. DOMINGO AT BURGOS.

the death of Sancho the Great, in 1035, his states were divided between his three sons, who at once fell to war with each other. The King of Leon, taking advantage of the inter-fraternal strife, made an attempt to recover some of his own lost territory. In a battle with Fernando, the King of Castile, on the banks of the Carrion, Bermudo III. was slain, and with him ended the male line of the kings of Leon, of the blood of Pelayo.

Here opens a new chapter in the history of Christian Spain. Fernando, the first of that name, became by the death of Bermudo II., and in the right of his wife, King of Leon as well as of Castile, and for a life-time the two crowns were united and there was peace in the country. Fernando was an able, wise, and energetic ruler, who contrived to win the favour of the jealous Leonese, while retaining the allegiance of his own people of Castile. After overcoming his brother Garcia, the King of Navarre, who had invaded Castile in 1054 at the head of an army of mixed Navarrese and Mahommedans, Fernando devoted himself to the extension of his borders in the south and west. He recovered a large part of Portugal from the Moors. He advanced the frontiers of Castile from the Douro even to the Tagus. He would have taken the city of Toledo had not the Moorish king made submission and promised tribute. He carried his arms even into Andalusia, and went so far as to lay siege to the city of Valencia. He compelled the Emir of Seville to give up to him the remains of Saint Isidore, to cover which the present cathedral of Leon was erected by his son Alfonso in 1063. He would have done even more for the faith and for Spain, but that he fell ill of a sickness and had to return to Leon. He died in 1065 in what is called the odour of sanctity—doubtless one of the best of the Christian kings, whose love of justice and zeal for the welfare of his people were as distinguished as his piety and his liberality to the Church.

Fernando, by his will, left his kingdom divided among his sons; thus once more throwing back that Christian union through which alone the recovery of Spain was possible, and relieving the Moors, then in their darkest hour, of the dread of extermination. To Alfonso, his favourite son, were left Leon and Asturias; to Sancho, his eldest, Castile; to Garcia, Galicia with Portugal as far as the Douro. To Urraca, his eldest daughter, he gave Zamora, and to Elvira, Toro. The brothers of Leon and Castile reigned for two years in peace, when, in 1068, the inevitable fratricidal war broke out. After a series of indecisive engagements it was settled by the two brothers that a battle should decide their rival claims, the conqueror to be recognised, as in a duel, to have the better right and to acquire the double kingdom. On these conditions the battle was fought on the frontiers of the two kingdoms. For some time the issue was doubtful; but at last the Leonese were victorious. Their king, Alfonso, however, would not permit his soldiers to pursue their victory, as by the terms of the compact he was already master of Castile. In the Castilian camp, however, was one Rodrigo Diez, the king's standard-bearer—famous since to all ages as *The Cid*—by whose counsel the Castilians fell upon the vic-

PORTICO OF ZAMORA CATHEDRAL.

torious Leonese as the latter lay reposing in their tents at night, and dispersed them with great slaughter. Thus by a trick, of which no one in that age seems to have been ashamed (it was before the age of chivalry), Sancho got the better of Alfonso. The latter had to fly for sanctuary to the church of Carrion. He was dragged out thence and clapped into prison, but at the intercession of his sister, Urraca, permitted to retire into a monastery, whence he fled shortly after to take refuge with the Moorish king at Toledo. Sancho then turned his attention to the other members of his family, attacking his brother Garcia and stripping him of his estates, then assailing his two sisters. Elvira abandoned to him her town of Toro; but Urraca was obstinate, and defended herself stoutly in her fortress of Zamora. The siege of that place by Sancho endured so long as to have passed into a national proverb, *No se tomó Zamora en una hora* (Zamora was not taken in one hour). Foremost in the camp of the besiegers was the Cid Rodrigo, who witnessed with his own eyes, though he was unable to avenge, the death of his master, King Sancho, at the hands of Bellido Dolfus (Adolphus)—the murderer to be known throughout the realm of Spanish romance and fiction as the typical traitor, whose name is linked with the names of Judas, of Julian, and of Ganelon.

The death of Sancho left the Castilians no choice but to make Alfonso, the ex-king of Leon, their king. They did so most unwillingly, for they feared that Alfonso would make Castile subject to Leon, and punish all those who had helped to keep him out of his inheritance, and especially those who had defrauded him of the fruits of his victory of Golpejara. Chief among these, pre-eminent among the Castilian lords not so much by birth as by his skill in war and influence among the people, was Rodrigo Diez, the Campeador. The news of his brother's death came to Alfonso while staying at Toledo with the Moorish king, his father's tributary. Flying secretly from the city, where he had reason to believe that his host desired to detain him, Alfonso repaired to Zamora, whither the Leonese and the Castilians hastened to recognise him as their king. Being now in possession of the double throne, he next made himself master of Galicia, a province which had been left to his brother Garcia. Thus about the year 1073 the estates of Fernando were united and held under one authority, to the dismay of the Moors. Torn by their own civil wars and family quarrels the infidels appeared to be in the last stage of dissolution; and there is no doubt that, had the Christians remained in union, they had now a good chance of recovering their ancient dominion.

Alfonso VI., however, though master of Leon and Castile, had much to disturb him in the enjoyment of his power. His long reign was one perpetual conflict with adverse fortune; the contrary forces, tending to disorder and disunion, being recruited from quarters the most unexpected. In the first place, Alfonso had an enemy in the great Campeador, who had tried to cheat him out of his prize in the battle with Sancho (as we have related); who had done his best to oppose his election to the throne; and who, when he could no longer refuse to accept the Leonese for his king, tendered his allegiance in the manner most insulting to his sovereign. It was the Cid who was charged by the Castilian nobles to require Alfonso, as the condition of his being recognised as king, to make a solemn oath before twelve select nobles of Castile, that he had no part in his brother Sancho's death. Thus roughly did the Cid, according to one of the oldest of the ballads, perform that duty. I quote from the admirable English version of Mr. J. G. Gibson :—

> " Alfonso, and ye Leonese,
>   I charge ye here to swear,
> That in Don Sancho's death ye had
>   By word or deed no share.
>
> Alfonso, if thou tell not truth,
>   Be thine a death of shame ;
> May villain peasants strike thee down,
>   Not gentlemen of name.
>
> Not nobles of Castilian blood,
>   But, to thy foul disgrace,
> Asturian men of Oviedo,
>   That fierce and cruel race ! "
>
> " Amen, amen ! " Alfonso cried,
>   " I scorn so foul a thing ! "
> " Amen, Amen ! " the twelve replied,
>   " We answer for the King ! "
>
> Three times the Cid has given the oath,
>   Three times the King hath sworn ;
> With every oath his anger burned,
>   And thus he cried with scorn :
>
> " Thou swearest me, where doubt is none,
>   Rodrigo, to thy sorrow ;
> The hand that takes the oath to-day
>   Thou hast to kiss to-morrow ! "

The Cid's answer is very much to the point, and bears early witness to the business-like and practical character of that hero:—

> " Agreed, Señor ! " replied the Cid,
>   " If thou wilt give me pay ;
> As other kings in other lands
>   Do give their knights this day ;
>
> Whose vassal I consent to be
>   Must pay me like the rest ;
> If thou agree to do so now,
>   I yield to thy request ! "
>
> The King grew pale to hear his words,
>   And turned him from the Cid ;
> And from that hour for many a day
>   His wrath could not be hid.

After this the relations between the king and his great vassal must have been somewhat strained. Reserving for a separate chapter the recital of all the woes unnumbered that came out of this quarrel, with the story of the Cid Rodrigo Diez, and of his extraordinary adventures, we will follow the main current of Spanish history under Alfonso VI., of Leon and Castile. Though neither a great man nor a good king, Alfonso contributed materially to the development of his country. He has been somewhat unkindly treated by the tongue of contemporary report, being so unfortunate as to have the balladists against him—the balladists, who in Spain have made history. He has been so overshadowed by the towering figure of the great Campeador, and so dwarfed and obscured as that some of his own deeds, which were neither unimportant or inglorious, are forgotten or neglected. But it was

TOLEDO.

under the reign of Alfonso that Toledo, the old capital of the Goths, was recovered from the Moors. This event, which occurred in 1085, made a great noise throughout Christendom. Loud was the lamentations among the Mahommedans for the loss of that " pearl set in the middle of the necklace," that highest tower of strength in their empire. But the easy acquisition of Toledo, after a three years' siege, rather demonstrates the growing feebleness of the Mahommedan hold over Central Spain, than redounds to the credit of Alfonso or the Christian chivalry.

Toledo was given up, not won by force of arms, as part of a bargain between Yahia the Arab ruler, and the Castilians—a bargain doubly dishonourable to Alfonso, for it was made at the expense of an old ally, who had befriended and sheltered him when in adversity—and it was not carried out fairly. The bargain was that in return for the cession of Toledo Yahia should be put in possession of Valencia, Alfonso engaging to furnish him with men and funds to recover that rebellious city. But there was a lion in the path, as we shall see, who had marked Valencia for his own prey. Alfonso did nothing to help the unfortunate Yahia, having probably quite enough to do at this time to maintain his authority against his own turbulent vassals, not to speak of a new and very formidable danger which he had now to face, namely, the invasion of the Almoravides.

The Almoravides, or *Mourabitins*,[1] who derive their name from Arabic words signifying those who are

[1] From which is derived the modern word *marabout*, a Mahommedan fanatic.

consecrated to the service of God, were a sect who, by one of those revolutions which are so common in Mahommedan history, had acquired political supremacy in Morocco. Under the vigorous guidance of Yussuf, the son of Tashfin, who claimed to be of ancient Arab descent, they had overrun all Northern Africa, displacing the old worn-out dynasties in the name of the purer faith. To the Almoravides the Moors of Spain, in this their dark hour, turned for help. In a great conference of the principal Mahommedan chiefs and their representatives held at Seville, it was agreed to implore the assistance of the King of Morocco to resist the growing power of the Christians, and to preserve the Mahommedan realm from extinction. Yussuf at first pretended to be indifferent to the prayers of his co-religionists. But at last, on condition of the port of Algeciras being made over to him as a foothold and a place of retreat, he promised his assistance. Landing in Spain with a powerful armament, composed of much the same material as that of the conqueror Tarik, that is, of Berbers and Moors, with leaders of Arabian descent, Yussuf lost no time in joining battle with the Christians. Alfonso, who was then engaged in the siege of Saragossa, was invited in an arrogant letter, written in the strain of the early Moslem conquerors, either to embrace the faith of the Prophet or prepare for destruction. Alfonso collected all the forces he could muster, and with King Sancho of Navarre made haste to accept the challenge. The two armies met in the plain of Zallaca, on the banks of the Guadiana, between Badajoz and Merida. The battle which ensued was one of the most bloody ever fought between Christian and Moor. The softer Andalusians gave way before the shock of the Spanish horsemen, but Yussuf, with his body-guard of Africans, retrieved the fortune of the day, defeating Alfonso with great slaughter, so that the King of Castile himself, severely wounded, had to fly with but five hundred horsemen. This first encounter between the Christians and their new enemy was indecisive in its results, the Moors being too much weakened to follow up their victory. Yussuf returned to Africa, but came again the next year with a large body of Africans and proclaimed a *jihad*, or holy war, calling upon all the Mahommedan princes of Andalusia to join his standard. But whether by reason of their own dissensions, or from an apprehension which proved to be well founded, that they had as much to fear from the greed and ambition of their own ally as from the Christian enemy, the Mahommedans of Andalusia, who by this time had discovered the Africans to be rude barbarians, without culture or refinement, and had probably had reason to be offended by their excess of religious zeal, responded but languidly to the appeal. Again, a third time, Yussuf returned to Spain, but now he threw off the mask, and openly signified that his ambition was less to recover the dominion of Spain for the Spanish Mahommedans than to acquire what was left of the Mahommedan kingdoms for himself. At the head of a hundred thousand Africans devoted to his cause, Yussuf had an easy work in subjugating the kings of Seville and of Granada, then the two most considerable of the Mahommedan rulers. In vain did Alfonso send an army of twenty thousand men to aid the King of Seville. Valencia fell into the power of the conqueror in 1102. By the beginning of the Twelfth century the dynasty of the Almoravides was firmly established over all Southern Spain, with Cordova as their capital. Thus was new vigour imported into the effeminate and feeble race of Andalusians, and the date postponed of their final perdition. Henceforth Mahommedan Spain was but an appanage and a dependency of the African empire of Morocco, a change fatal to the Arab civilisation, and involving the work of the Christian re-conquest in new dangers and difficulties.

To strengthen himself against the formidable Africans Alfonso, whose talents were ever more conspicuous in diplomacy than in war, sought alliance with French princes. He was himself already connected with France, through his wife Constance, the daughter of Philip I.[1] To the Count of Besançon he gave his daughter Theresa, with a dowry which included all the territory he had won in Portugal from the Moors—a fatal gift, out of which rose all the subsequent mischief between Portugal and Castile. Andrea, daughter of Alfonso, was given to the Count of Burgundy with Galicia, while a third daughter was bestowed on the Count of Thoulouse. Thus did Alfonso VI., in imitation of his ancestors, repeat the error of dissipating at his death the estate he had

---

[1] Alfonso VI. was six times married—one of his wives being a Moorish princess, Zayda, the daughter of Aben Abet, King of Seville, with whom he got Cuenca as a portion.

accumulated during his life, thereby cancelling his good deeds and falsifying the character he had earned of one of the shrewdest and ablest of the Castilian kings. At his death in 1109—his only son Sancho having fallen in battle with the Almoravides—the united kingdoms of Castile and Leon fell to his eldest daughter Urraca who had married, for her second husband, Alfonso I. of Aragon.

But before pursuing the history of Castile and Leon, in which Aragon now for the first time finds a place, it is necessary that we should follow the story of the Cid, which is so large a part of Spanish life and so closely connected with the process of the national deliverance.

III.

THE STORY OF THE CID.

(1026-1099.)

THE history of mediæval Spain without the Cid would be something more barren than the Iliad without Achilles. He is the hero of the piece; the protagonist in the drama; the central figure in the picture. He is the epitome of all that is most characteristic of his age; an image in which is reflected the spirit of that heated and bustling period, the Eleventh century, which in Spain was the turning-point in her fortune. To omit his story from this narrative, though it has been told many times before, were to rob my readers of much entertainment and deprive the history of Spain of its most delightful and fascinating chapter. All that is most heroic and splendid and magnanimous of Spanish achievement is centred in the Cid. He is the glory of Spain and the envy of the surrounding nations, the darling of his race and people, in whom are embodied all the virtues Castilian in their purest form and most potent efficacy. His enchanting personality has taken captive the Spanish imagina-

THE CID, RODRIGO DIEZ.

tion, and dominates all Spanish literature. No hero of romance or history — no Arthur, Roland, or Rustum — has so deep a hold of the national heart in any age or country. He is the incarnation of all the highest aspirations of the people; the realisation of all that a Spaniard would wish to be. He is the perfect warrior, the ideal man-at-arms, the shining model of that kind of fighter in that kind of fighting in which Spaniards are always most excellent, the *guerillero*, of the type of Sertorius, *El Empecinado*, and Zumalacarreguy.

There are some, it is true, of an incredulity incredible, bold enough to assert that there never was a Cid — that his whole story is a fabrication. There have been found, even in Spain, historians of a scrupulousness so nice and so rare as to reject the Campeador altogether as a fabulous monster. The Jesuit Masdeu (of the present century), who believes in almost everything, will not believe in the Cid. He is followed in this pestilent heresy by the judicious and painful Dunham, the English historian. Masdeu refuses to include the Cid among the genuine fighting men of his nation, with Santiago on his white horse, or any of the heroes who gave real help to their country in battle. Masdeu, who accepts the story of St. James the Greater, who, after being beheaded at Jerusalem in A.D. 42, landed at El Padron on the coast of Galicia, to become the patron of Compostella and the champion of his country against the Moors — Masdeu, in his specially "critical history" of Spain, will not allow poor Rodrigo a niche in the gallery of Spanish worthies, holding his deeds to be incredible and his whole story absurd and extravagant. Yet that there was a Cid—a very man, of palpable flesh and blood—who played a very conspicuous part in the affairs of Spain in the Eleventh century, there is now no just ground for doubting. Professor Dozy, the distinguished Arabist, late of Leyden, has re-constructed the Cid's figure out of the old bones which lay scattered in the chronicles, Spanish and Moorish, and in the older poems and ballads (which are not less historical because they are in metre), so that we can now realise what manner of man this was—the great Spanish hero, whose deeds have been the theme of innumerable romances and plays, who has filled so large a space in the drama of the recovery of Spain. The Cid of history is different in character from the Cid of romance. He is less perfect and less pious, though certainly not less picturesque. He is a far truer representative of his age—the fighting age of Spain, as distinguished from the age of heroism or of chivalry. The Cid of the ballads, which were chiefly composed in the Sixteenth century, when the Moors had ceased to be, and orthodoxy was regnant and rampant, was a champion of the faith, the scourge of heresy, a relentless persecutor of the Moslems; who was distinguished above all things for the purity of his life, and the correctness of his principles as a patriot. How good and perfect a Catholic and a Spaniard the Cid had come to be, by process of balladising, in the Sixteenth century, is proved by the remarkable fact that Philip the Second tried hard to persuade the Pope to canonise him as a champion of the faith.

Yet assuredly Philip would have burnt this impious Rodrigo for heresy and sacrilege, if he did not banish or poison him for his liberal opinions, had the Cid lived in Philip's age. Our Cid was indeed of no stuff of which to make a saint. The main secret of his great renown in his own time, and of the ever-green enthusiasm which his name evokes among the Spanish people, is to be read in the true story of his life, which shows him to have been a champion of popular rights, a fearless assertor of the ancient privileges of the commons, an upholder of the old Castilian independence, a redresser of social wrongs—who took his own way, *maugre* King and Pope, and scorned to bow the knee to Christian or Moslem. In his character are united all the best qualities of his race with the worst defects of his age. He was generous, crafty, magnanimous, brutal, merciful, and cruel—in the minor morals austere, but in the large ethics loose—capable of feats of noble self-denial, such as amazed and puzzled that barbarous age, and descending to acts of blood-thirstiness such as shocked even contemporary opinion. He was, on the whole, of an amiable mood; and though he burnt his enemies alive, he was tender of their women and children. Insatiable in his appetite for plunder, he would be liberal of his largesses to the poor and needy. In his relations to the other sex he was a Galahad, never swerving from his fidelity to his faithful Ximena. In his conduct to his bitterest enemy, the Count of Barcelona, he showed a gentlemanly feeling worthy of the purest age of chivalry—an age which had not yet dawned in Spain. His king, Alfonso, his life-long rival and jealous adversary, he would serve and betray by turns, as it seemed good to him; a game of double-dealing in which the king was at least as great an adept as his vassal. And in excuse for the Campeador's breaches of loyalty and offences against patriotism—in those days too common to be severely regarded—we should consider that there was yet no Spanish nation, that Alfonso was a Leonese and the Cid a Castilian, with little claim on the one part for loyalty and small duty on the other to patriotism.

Rodrigo Diez de Bivar, who came of an old Castilian stock, was born in 1026—others say 1040—and was thus a contemporary of William the Conqueror, of England. Diez was his patronymic, meaning the son of Diego (in English James), and Bivar, the village of his birth, near Burgos, where the site of his house is still shown. His name of *El Cid*, the Lord, or *Mio Cid*, which is exactly *Monseigneur*, was given him first by the Moors, his own soldiers and subjects, and universally adopted by all Spaniards from that day to this. Such a title is significant, not only of the relations between the two peoples, but of Rodrigo's position as at once a Moorish and a Spanish chief. *El Campeador*, the name by which Rodrigo is also distinguished, means in Spanish something more special than "champion." A *campeador* was a man who had fought and beaten the select fighting-man of the opposite side, in the presence of the two armies; which points to a custom derived, as much else of early Spanish, from the East. Rodrigo earned the name, not at the expense of any Moor but of a Christian, having when quite a youth slain a Navarrese champion in a war between Castile and Navarre. The first mention of his name occurs in a deed of Fernando I., of the year 1064. In the war between Sancho and Alfonso, the two sons of that king, Rodrigo energetically espoused the cause of the former, becoming his standard-bearer and commander-in-chief of his armies. When the day had gone against Castile in the decisive battle of Golpejara in 1071, it was Rodrigo who (in breach of the laws of honour and of the engagement between the brothers) retrieved the fortunes of Sancho by a night attack on the sleeping victors. At the siege of Zamora Rodrigo took an active part, but was not able to save his master from the treacherous blow struck at him by Bellido Dolfus, nor to avenge his death. When Alfonso was chosen king by the reluctant voice of the Castilians, for want of any other, it was Rodrigo who suggested the condition that the king should publicly swear that he had no hand in his brother's death; and it was Rodrigo who tendered his sovereign that oath, before the select men of the nation, with rough words and scant ceremony, as the ballads have recorded.

There never was after that any good feeling between King Alfonso and his proud and powerful vassal, who never cared to hide his suspicions of the monarch or his repugnance to the Leonese dominion. As a Castilian, Rodrigo's loyalty was due to Castile alone, which is a spirit very characteristic of his age, and, indeed, of many succeeding ages in Spain. Alfonso dissembled for a while, and even married Rodrigo to Ximena, his cousin—daughter of the Count of Oviedo, one of his most powerful nobles. This lady, hereafter the faithful mate and counsellor of her husband—equal to him, according to the chroniclers, in body as in soul—makes a figure in romance only less than that of her doughty spouse. According to the ballads, the match was brought about in a manner far more romantic than the histories allege—Ximena having insisted that Rodrigo should marry her because he had slain her father. The lady thus pleads before King Fernando:—

> "I am Don Gomez' daughter true,
> In Gormaz Count was he;
> Of all the daughters that he had
> I'm youngest of the three.
>
> Rodrigo, with his arm of might,
> My honoured Sire did slay.
> I come to ask a boon, my lord,
> A boon from thee this day:
>
> That Don Rodrigo thou wilt give
> To be my lord and head;
> I'll hold me honoured by the gift
> And think myself well wed."

This more picturesque version of the Cid's courtship, which accords not ill with the character of the age, is confirmed by the *Crónica Rimada*, or Rhymed Chronicle, one of the oldest of the documents relating to the Cid, now admitted to be of the Twelfth century, and mainly historical. The contract of marriage between Rodrigo and Ximena is still extant in the archives of Burgos, bearing a date corresponding to the 19th of July, 1074. This is one of the few authentic memorials surviving of the great Campeador—though if the date is right, the ballads must be wrong, for in 1074 Alfonso, not Fernando, was the reigning king. This, however, is a small matter; and it is pleasanter to believe with Sancho Panza that, "after all, the old ballads are too old to tell lies."

Some time afterwards Rodrigo was despatched by King Alfonso on an errand to Motamid, the Emir of Seville, to collect the tribute due from that prince. Motamid was then at war with Abdallah, the King of Granada, who had engaged the services of several Christian cavaliers, including Garci Ordoñez, of the blood royal, late standard-bearer to King Fernando. Rodrigo intervened as peacemaker, trying to keep the King of Granada from attacking Motamid, but Abdallah, in scorn of his protests and menaces, advanced into the territory of Toledo with fire and sword. He was met by Rodrigo with his own following and the army of the Emir of Seville, who defeated Abdallah with great slaughter, and took prisoner Garci Ordoñez with other Christian knights. Then receiving from Motamid his tribute and many presents for Alfonso, the Cid returned home. Henceforward Garci Ordoñez, a principal man in the state—who seems to have lost nothing of character or influence among the Christians by having served with the infidel king of Granada—was added to the number of Rodrigo's enemies. A tale was brought to Alfonso that Rodrigo had kept back part of the presents which Motamid had sent. The king, who had never forgotten the injuries and affronts put upon him by the Campeador, took advantage of

Rodrigo's attacking the Moors without leave, to banish him from the kingdom.

At this point the story is taken up in the grand old *Poem of the Cid*, which was undoubtedly written not more than a century after the Cid's death. By the general testimony of the best scholars this is entitled to be regarded, not only as the oldest of European epics and an ever-living example of early Castilian verse, but as essentially an historical monument, taking the form in which all history was then expressed. Of the *Poema del Cid*, which ranks above all the *chansons de geste* of that or any succeeding period—which is of an authority as well as of a quality vastly higher than the *Song of Roland*, unfortunately only a fragment remains. What survives, however, is of priceless worth, as a living picture of the age. The poem, as we have it, begins abruptly with the banished Cid taking leave of his native town of Bivar. He looks back upon the towers of his castle, weeping bitterly, lamenting his household goods in disarray, his doors lying open, his chests dismantled, his perches without falcons. Then My Cid sighs, for he has great sorrow, but speaks calmly, thanking the Lord that they were wicked enemies who had done him this scathe. Entering Burgos with his company, the men and women flock to the windows to see him pass, weeping with all their eyes, and saying, "What a good vassal was here had he but a good Lord!" But though they loved the Cid and lamented his fate, they did not, for fear of the king, dare to give him harbourage, or sell him any viand. The Cid, however, who is never wanting for worldly prudence, is found, like other great commanders, to have made provision for his men at the expense of the Jews.

Rachel and Vidas had made him an advance on a chest of gold. As a matter of brutal fact there was no gold there but only sand; but was not the Cid's honour security enough for misbelievers? Promising his men that if he lived he would double their pay, the Cid started for the frontier with three hundred choice companions. It was the resource of every cavalier of broken fortunes in that day to go forth to plunder the infidel—a resource not only not condemned by public opinion but held to be worthy of every man of good descent and a high independent spirit.

Thus did the Campeador, leaving his wife and daughter behind in a religious house, embark on that trade by which he became so famous—the trade of a freebooter or *condottiere*. Having gathered around him a body of well-armed retainers, young men, doubtless of the first families, who were glad to have an opportunity of seeing life under the conduct of so distinguished a leader, the Cid began that new career which, though it divorced him from his country and his fealty to his liege lord, opened to him a path of glory and profit, more suitable to his ambition and character. Henceforth the Cid was a free lance, fighting for his own hand. He offered himself first to the Christian Count of Barcelona, but there being no opening for him there, he went, being always without prejudices, to Saragossa, where Moctadir, the Arab, of the Beni Hud, had lately established his seat. Moctadir engaged Rodrigo's services, but dying soon after, a civil war broke out between his two sons

Moutamin and Mondzir. The Cid took the part of the former, Mondzir receiving the help of Sancho, King of Aragon, and of Berenger, Count of Barcelona. Then commenced that series of adventures which made of the Cid a name of terror throughout all Eastern Spain, among Mussulmans and Christians alike. With a mixed company of Moors and Castilians, trained by himself and doubtless recruited from the choicest of the fighting men of the age, under his famous lieutenant, Alvar Fañez, with the scarcely less renowned Martin Antolinez the Burgalese, and Pero Bermudez, his cousin, and Martin Pelaez, whom he had turned from coward to hero by his instruction and example, the Cid went forth conquering and to conquer—scattering his enemies right and left, devastating the land, burning and spoiling churches and mosques, extending the dominion of the Beni Hud to the gates of Valencia, and spreading the fear of his name throughout the country. The Christian chroniclers, of course, pass over delicately those passages in our hero's career which represent him as strictly impartial in his raids—as never deterred from a fight by any scruple of faith, any more than by a consideration of numbers. Even in the Poem, which is truthful as far as it goes, this side of the Campeador's character is treated with reserve. In the Poem, it is the Moors who administer to the Cid's glory, and lend colour to the fighting. Here is a picture (which loses none of its force and brilliancy in the English of Hookham Frere), of how the Cid rescued his standard, which was nearly lost through the rashness of its bearer:—

Their shields before their breasts forth at once they go,
Their lances in the rest, levelled fair and low,
Their banners and their crests waving in a row,
Their heads all stooping down toward the saddle bow;
The Cid was in the midst, his shout was heard afar,
"I am Ruy Diez, the champion of Bivar;
Strike among them, gentlemen, for sweet Mercy's sake!"
There where Bermuez fought amidst the foe they brake,
Three hundred bannered knights, it was a gallant show,
Three hundred Moors they killed, a man with every blow;
When they wheeled and turned, as many more lay slain;
You might see them raise their lances, and level them again.
There you might see the breast-plates how they were cleft in twain,
And many a Moorish shield lie shattered on the plain,
The pennons that were white marked with a crimson stain,
The horses running wild whose riders had been slain.[1]

But we must leave the poetical Cid to follow the more practical warrior. For seven years the Cid continued faithful to his salt, serving the Emir of Saragossa while using every opportunity to enrich himself and increase his power. He now felt strong enough to start in the kingly business on his own account, setting up what seems to have been a very extensive though loosely defined dominion, got together by conquest from the Moors and encroachments upon his Christian neighbours. He was powerful enough to treat, not only with the outside Christian princes, but with his own sovereign, the King of Castile, on equal terms. He lacked nothing that a king should have. He visited Alfonso in his newly-recovered capital of Toledo, and was received with every mark of honour—Alfonso giving

---

[1] The English closely follows the Spanish text, and the translation is not less faithful than spirited. Mr. John Ormsby has more recently brought out an excellent version of the entire poem. (1882.)

him a charter by which all the lands conquered from the Moors were conferred on him and his posterity for ever. In 1090, when the realm was in danger from the Almoravides, Alfonso urgently besought the aid of the greatest of the Christian warriors, but the Cid was apparently in no great hurry to obey the call. Either the messages miscarried or their tenor was mistaken, for Rodrigo did not arrive on the field in time to prevent the Spaniards from being beaten. Then again the old feud broke out between the king and his over-great and unruly vassal. Rodrigo was deprived of all his patrimonial estates and his wife and children imprisoned. The quarrel was patched up, but there never was any goodwill between the Cid and his king. From 1090 forward, Rodrigo assumed all the state and dignity of an independent chief, throwing off all pretence of fealty, and acting in the character which was really his, of a prince independent of both Christian and Moor—assuming all the state and functions of royalty, and affecting a style which was rather Moorish than Spanish. He preferred to dress, when not in his armour, in the Arab garb, and took delight in hearing recited the deeds of the Arab heroes.

About this period occurred that episode in his strange, adventurous career which illustrates very vividly, not only the Cid's relations to the Christian princes of the time, but his own character for an eccentric and lofty chivalrousness far in advance of the custom of the age, when chivalry was not yet, either as an institution or as a sentiment—at least among the Christians. Raymond Berenger, the Count of Barcelona, was the bitterest of the Cid's enemies, having very good cause for the resentment against the man who had ravaged his territories, defied his authority, beaten his allies, and diverted to himself a great part of the revenue the Count used to derive from the tributary Moorish princes. Burning to avenge himself on the Cid for these injuries, Raymond assembled a large army, and secretly helped with money by King Alfonso, his cousin, marched suddenly against Rodrigo, who, with a small force, was encamped in a small valley hemmed in by mountains. Taking advantage of a dark night, Berenger occupied, without being perceived, the surrounding hills, whence he descended on his unsuspecting and unprepared foe in the early morning. The Cid was caught in a trap. His soldiers had hardly time to arm themselves. Their chief himself, while trying to rally them, was wounded. At last, however, after a desperate fight the Cid, as usual, was victorious. Berenger himself was taken, with his whole camp and a vast booty. Then followed a very dramatic scene between the Cid and his captive, which is given with admirable simplicity and life-like effect in the Poem. The Count Berenger being brought into the Cid's tent, the Cid regarded him sternly, and would not let him be seated. Melting a little at the sight of the rich booty and the Count's distress, he deigned to talk of ransom and to take notice of his prisoner. Setting all the poorer soldiers free to return to their country, when they declared that they had nothing to give, the Cid commanded a table to be spread in his tent, to which Berenger was invited. But the Count was sulky, and would not eat a mouthful for all there was in Spain. "Perish rather my body and soul, since these vagabonds" (*malcalzados*—literally "ill-breached ones") "have vanquished me in battle." "Eat, then, Count, of this bread, and drink of this wine," said My Cid. "If you will do what I ask you, you shall cease to be a prisoner; if not, you shall never in all your life again see the Christian land." Count Raymond replied to him: "Eat yourself, Don Rodrigo, and be glad; but me—leave me to die, for I will not eat." Till the third day they were not able to shake his resolve. While they were sharing their rich spoils, not a morsel of bread could they make him eat. Says My Cid, "Eat something, Count, for if you eat not, you shall not see Christians again; but if you eat, and do my pleasure, I will give you liberty—you and two of your knights." When the Count understands that, he becomes more gay. "Cid, if you do what you have said, I will marvel at you as long as I live." "Eat, then, Count, and when you have dined, I will let you go, you and two others. But all that you have lost and that I have won on the field of battle, know that I shall not give you aught, not even a bad farthing. I will give you naught of what you have lost, for I have need of it, for these vassals of mine, with myself, are necessitous men; I will give you nothing. What is taken from you we have to give to them in payment; we shall lead this life as long as it may please the Eternal Father, as a man who has brought upon himself the wrath of his king and is banished his country." The Count, on hearing this, is overjoyed. He asks for water to wash his hands. They bring him water at once. Together with the two knights whom the Cid has given him, the Count sits down to eat. Heavens! with what a good grace he does it! Opposite to him is seated he who is born in a fortunate hour (*i.e.*, the Cid). "If you do not make a good meal, Count, so as to please me, we shall remain together—we shall not be quit." Then says the Count: "Willingly, and with all my heart!" He dines fast, with the two knights. My Cid regards him, and is content for that the Count Raymond does move his hands so well. "If you will permit it, My Cid, we are ready for the start. Order them to bring us our horses, and we will depart at once. Since the day I was Count, I have not dined with so much appetite. I shall never forget the good meal I have had."

This curious picture of mediæval life and manners, which brings the Cid before us in an amiable light, is made complete by what follows. Count Raymond is mounted upon a palfrey, richly accoutred and provided sumptuously with travelling gear, the Castilian escorting him to the bounds of the camp. He is there set free without ransom, the Cid himself saying he is well repaid in what he has won in booty, and telling the Count that he can be always found when wanted. But the Count has had enough of the Cid, and departs, converted from an enemy into a friend.

It was by these feats of simple generosity and sublime self-denial—as they were then regarded—that the Cid moved the wonder of his contemporaries even more than by his prowess in arms. At last, having extended his conquests to the gates of Valencia, which city was then the richest in Spain, the Cid set the crown upon his achievements by a conquest which must be reckoned as the greatest blow up to this time inflicted upon the Moorish power and prestige. Toledo, it was true, had been recovered five years before, but Toledo, after all, was a military camp to the Moors, whereas Valencia was a colony—their favourite seat, the richest, the most refined, and most luxurious of Arab cities, now that the glory of Cordova had been dimmed. In June, 1094, the Cid captured the city of Valencia after a desperate resistance—to the despair of all Moordom, and the wonder and delight of Christian Spain. In vain did the Almoravides, under their redoubtable chief, Yussuf, attempt the recovery of the city. They came about Valencia with a vast army, and sat before it for ten days. Then the Cid made a sortie, and dispersed them with great slaughter. Rodrigo was now at the apogee of his glory and power. The vastest projects presented themselves to his imagination. He dreamt of nothing less than the re-conquest of the whole Spanish land. "A Rodrigo had lost the country," an Arab heard him say; "another Rodrigo should recover it." The Almoravides came once more against him with a formidable host, but the Cid allying himself with Pedro, King of Aragon, met them on the sea-coast near Gandia, encamped on a high hill, with a powerful fleet of ships defending their flank. Once again the Cid was victorious, chiefly through his personal efforts in the field. Returning to Valencia with an immense booty, the Cid, who felt that his end was approaching, began to make peace with God and with men. He was as magnificent in his benefactions as he had been in his depredations. He who had destroyed so many churches became distinguished for his zeal in church-building. He was already keeping a bishop in Valencia, having turned the grand mosque into a cathedral, which he endowed with everything handsome in the way of furniture and vestments. By these tokens the Cid was clearly sick. The mortal blow was dealt to him by an event which was quite out of his experience. His army which he sent out—he was too ill to go himself—to meet the Almoravides, who had just won a decisive victory over King Alfonso's general—the Cid's old lieutenant, Alvar Fañez—at Cuenca, was cut to pieces close to the walls of Valencia. Rodrigo fell dead when he heard the news, of mingled grief and rage. For two years longer did his widow, the doughty Ximena, hold the city against all the attacks of the enemy. At length, despairing of help from the Christian princes—Alfonso, the king, was otherwise employed, and the others were probably not ill-pleased at the overthrow of a dominion carved out of lands they had marked for their own—Ximena was compelled to abandon the city. The slender band of the Cid's old companions filed out of Valencia with the body of the great Campeador, according to the grisly legend, set on horseback in their midst, in his panoply as he lived, with his famous sword Tizona in his hand. Terrified at the spectacle, and believing that the Campeador had come to life again, the Moors fled in dismay. Thus in death the Cid appeared but to conquer He was buried, with his faithful Ximena, in

CHURCH OF S. PEDRO AT CARDEÑA.

the cloister of the church of San Pedro, at Cardeña, whence his bones, more than once disturbed by the irreverent foreign invader or the ever-curious native admirer, have been removed to the town-hall of Burgos.

With the death of the Cid in July, 1099, there crumbled to the ground the whole fabric of his power. Valencia, which still boasts to be "Valencia of the Cid," fell back into the hands of the Moors—being easily recovered by Yussuf, the Almoravide, who possessed himself also of the greater part of the territory which had been conquered from the Moors. But the example of the Cid and the influence of his character and actions were to be a possession to Spain long after his reign was over. And although the true image of the great Campeador has been greatly altered in the process of the ages, which has transformed him from an honest fighting man and simple freebooter into a champion of the faith and a patriot, yet enough lingered in the memory of the Spanish people of the Cid—the popular hero, the assertor of the liberties of his country, the maintainer of the *fueros*, the tamer of kings and nobles—to make his name one of power in battle, to give hope and encouragement to his nation and assurance of final victory.

IV.

THE PERIOD OF DISSEVERANCE—RISE OF THE SMALLER STATES — CASTILE AND LEON DIVIDED AND UNITED.

DURING the latter half of the Twelfth century Spain exhibited an extraordinary spectacle of dissension, dislocation, and incohesion. The country was split into sections, interspersed and intermixed, without regard to physical, racial, or religious distinctions—a chaos of governments, municipalities, and powers—a huddle of tangled creeds, jarring lusts, and struggling ambitions—a network of war, conquest, and plunder, through which it is difficult to trace the process of national development. The line of cleavage was no longer between Christian and Moor. The Christians were divided into several states, of whom neither their chief nor their highest concern was the extermination of the Moor. After the fall of the Khalifate of Cordova with Hisham III., the last of the race of Omeyya, the Moorish Empire fell to pieces. Every governor of a city, every emir or sheikh who held a hereditary fief or had credit enough in arms to secure a following, called himself king. Toledo, Seville, Granada, Saragossa, set up their own independent princes. These kinglings never ceased to make war upon each other, using the services of Christian mercenaries, as we have seen in the case of the Cid, as freely as the Christians used Moors in their feuds with Christians. Some of the richer cities, like Valencia, in despair of a choice between rival heads of families, took their own government in hand, and started republics, giving the first examples in that kind to modern Europe. By the middle of the Eleventh century there was left no united Mahommedan power in Spain to dispute the sovereignty of the country with the Christians.

Before pursuing the fortunes of Castile and Leon, it is necessary to give some account of the smaller kingdoms which had now risen into existence, which took part in the work of driving out the Moors, though their jealousies and dissensions rather retarded than advanced the cause of Christian Spain. The rise of Navarre is wrapped in a veil of obscurity, which we need not be at much trouble to lift. Whether her kings were more French or Spanish has been always in dispute; and though they played a busy part in the internal affairs of the Peninsula, they were too far removed from touch with the Mahommedans to give material aid in the recovery of Spain. The Navarrese proper, on the southern slopes of the Pyrenees, had a common root with the Aragonese. They had also their Pelayo, in the legendary Don Asnar, who gathered together a remnant of the Goths and established a kind of patriarchal state in their mountain fastnesses—suffici-

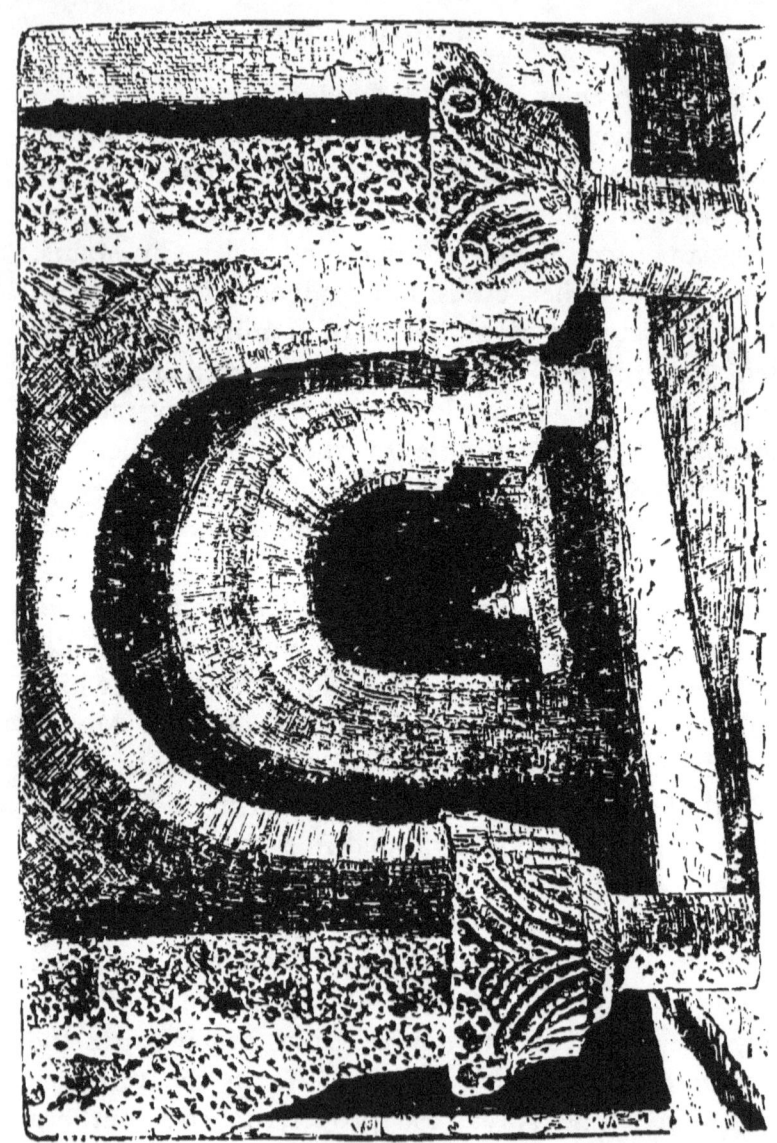

CRYPT OF MONASTERY OF S. SALVADOR DE LEIRE, NAVARRE.

ently developed by 819 to have a code of laws, which, as the *fueros de Sobrarbe*, have served as the source and model of those customs and usages which were the proudest heritage of Aragon. In the beginning of the Tenth century the first of the Navarrese kings who is distinctly visible out of the mists of tradition is Sancho, who is found defending his capital of Pampeluna against the neighbouring Moors or Berbers, and defeating them with the usual expense of blood. He followed up his victory by extending his bounds eastward, reducing the Moorish dominion on the Ebro and carrying his arms even to Saragossa. On the fatal field of Val de Junquera, in 921, Navarre suffered very severely, in concert with Leon, though Sancho managed to hang upon the army of the conquerors as they passed by him into Gascony, cutting up their rear and despoiling them of their plunder in the immemorial Basque manner. He was so successful in winning back some strong places on the frontier that at the close of his reign there remained no Mahommedan in the whole kingdom north of the Ebro. To him succeeded Garcia, oddly surnamed *El Tembloso*, or The Trembler. In spite of his name—due not to any moral but a physical infirmity—the Trembler took an active part in the troubles between Castile and Leon. His son, Sancho the Great, who in right of his wife succeeded to the throne of Castile, and through his daughter became virtual ruler of Leon, we have spoken of in a former chapter. In his time, for a few years, all Christian Spain was united, to be afterwards broken up at his death. His sons fought among themselves, the end being that, from 1076 to 1134, their patrimony was absorbed into the kingdom of Aragon, to be separated afterwards, and again merged, and again created into an independent state—whose history henceforth is of no individual interest. Such part of it as does not belong to France is the history of Aragon.

Aragon, whose origin was a mountain nest at the foot of the Pyrenees in a region inhabited by the ancient Vascones—who may be taken to be represented by the modern Basques—began life in a very humble way as a fief of the Asturian kings. When created into a separate state in 1035, upon the death of the pluralist, Sancho the Great, Aragon fell to the lot of Ramiro, who is entitled to be called the first of her kings. At this period Aragon was but a small section of the country afterwards so named, being limited to one or two valleys in the extreme west, bordering on the Navarre, with the Pyrenees for a base of defence. The Moors still possessed Saragossa, Huesca, and the whole plain country in a straight line thence to the mountains, including all the districts of the east up to the border of the countship of Barcelona. The first care of Ramiro I. on coming to his throne was to take advantage of his brother Garcia's absence in Rome to extend his borders in the direction of Navarre. But Garcia came back in time to repel the attack. Ramiro was more fortunate in his more legitimate enterprises against the Moors, defeating them in several battles, extending his kingdom eastward along the southern base of the Pyrenees, and compelling the Emirs of Saragossa, Tudela, and Lerida to pay him tribute. In respect to the first a difference broke out between the kings of Aragon and Castile, Sancho claiming the tribute of Saragossa for himself, on the ground that his father Fernando had been recognised as lord paramount of that Moorish state. The difference led to a battle between the two Christian kings, perhaps the first of the many which marked the troublous intercourse of Castile and Aragon. Ramiro was defeated and slain, and Sancho his son reigned in his stead, who won some towns from the Moors and carried his standards to the north bank of the Ebro. Being slain at the siege of Huesca in 1094, his son Pedro succeeded in reducing that place, but not until two years afterwards, when a great battle had been fought under its walls between the King of Aragon and an allied Moorish and Castilian army which had been sent to its relief. This battle, which is one of the most memorable in the annals of Aragon, as setting the seal to her independence, was fought in 1096, on the plain of Alcoraz. On one side was Aragon, on the other the Moors of Saragossa with a large contingent of Castilians under the Christian Count of Najera, who represented Alfonso, King of Leon and Castile. The issue was long doubtful, until St. George appeared personally in the field to help the Aragonese, as St. James had helped the Christians at Clavijo. In token of this splendid and valuable assistance the grateful King Pedro—so the national Aragonese historian, Zurita, relates—ordered a church to be built on the spot; the kings of Aragon taking for their device, in memory of the illustrious ally, the cross of St. George upon a silver field.

Having brought down the history of Aragon to the beginning of the Twelfth century, it is time that we should tell how the eastern province of Catalonia, with the great city of Barcelona, came within the Spanish fold, and of the part it played in the making of Aragon. Catalonia, which comprises the north-eastern corner of the Spanish peninsula, had been inhabited from the earliest ages by a fierce, active, turbulent, and fickle people—impatient of foreign dominion, proud of their separate character as of their local privileges, and for ever rebelling against the destiny which made them Spaniards. From their neighbours over the border they have borrowed much, as their language, which is a branch of the Provençal or Limosin, still bears witness. Their earlier history was rather French than Spanish—the Frankish kings, under Charlemagne and his successors, being regarded as lords paramount of the soil, though the people were in perpetual rebellion—sometimes against the dukes of Aquitaine, who were their feudal superiors, and sometimes against the Moors, who more than once succeeded in winning back this province and in establishing their supremacy. In the beginning of the Ninth century Barcelona, the principal town of Catalonia, was reckoned to be a part of the loosely defined dukedom of Septimania.

At what date the countship of Barcelona was first established as a separate and independent fief, belonging rather to the circle of Christian Spain than of France, is not clearly to be made out from the scanty and obscure records. The Moors seem to have been much impressed with the importance of this region, for though it was at the farthest extremity of their European domain, they clung stoutly to its possession. In 852 they retook Barcelona from the Franks, after a great slaughter of the Christians and a wholesale devastation. One Wifredo, or Hunfrido, in 858, is spoken of as the first count who ruled Barcelona as a separate portion of Spain, independent of the Franks, owning the King of France for his feudal superior. Wifredo, his son, named the Warlike, having cleared all Catalonia of the infidels, was the first to throw off the suzerainty of France. His successors, who were concerned in consolidating their possessions, now secure from any foreign enemy, and in works of peace, need not occupy our attention. The Moors had withdrawn from the neighbourhood, and their central power was so far removed from Barcelona as to assure that city, now beginning to be distinguished for its maritime and commercial activity, of undisturbed tranquillity. In 984, however, when the great Almanzor swept the Christian states, Catalonia fell, in her turn, under the conqueror's heel. The native army, under Count Borello, attempted to arrest the Arab general's progress at Moncada, but it was overthrown and destroyed. Barcelona was stormed and taken, the inhabitants put to the sword, and the city fired. On Almanzor's departure, Count Borello came down from the hills, whither he had fled for refuge, and rallied the broken and disheartened Catalans. He laid siege to Barcelona, and drove out the Moorish garrison, eventually expelling the Moors from the land, and restoring it to peace and order.

His successors are heard of as sometimes in alliance

with rebel Moors, and sometimes on their own account, extending their borders at the expense of Christian and of infidel. The second and third Raymundos, who figure most conspicuously in the wars of the Cid, being that hero's most determined and bitter enemies, returned more or less to the French connection, through marriages with heiresses of the fiefs in that country. In the reign of Raymundo IV., an expedition was sent against the Balearic Isles, then a stronghold of the Mahommedan pirates, whose ravages on the coast had caused much loss to the Christians and injury to their commerce. Majorca was taken in 1116 by a combined body of Catalans and Frenchmen, aided by the Pisans and Genoese, and a severe blow inflicted on the maritime power of the Moors. This was the first of those enterprises beyond the sea, in which the people of Eastern Spain became afterwards so conspicuous. In the reign of the next Raymundo, the Fifth, Catalonia became part of Aragon, by the marriage of the Count of Barcelona with Petronilla, the daughter and heir of Ramiro, the last King of Aragon of the old line. From the date of this auspicious event (1135) begins a new epoch in the development of Eastern Spain. The scattered provinces and lordships being consolidated with the kingdom of Aragon, a formidable barrier was raised in the east against Moorish aggression, and a new power added to Christian Spain. It is doubtful, however, whether it did not tend rather to prolong the infidel dominion by the establishment on Spanish soil of two rival and equal states, which henceforth were in perpetual enmity.

Upon the death of Alfonso VI., the King of Castile and Leon, in 1109—his only son, Sancho, having fallen in battle with the Almoravides, on the fatal field of Uclés in 1100—his eldest daughter, Urraca, the third of that unlucky name in Spanish history, succeeded to the united kingdom. (Urraca[1] was married to Alfonso I. of Aragon, her second husband; and thus an opportunity arose for joining the two crowns, had their subjects been disposed to unity. Alfonso, who assumed the title of Alfonso VII. of Castile and Leon, had no right to that designation, and ought not to be numbered among the Castilian kings. He could not even agree with his queen, much less with her people, who at this time hated the Aragonese as much as Leonese and Castilians hated each other. The conduct of Urraca, whether as queen or wife, was such as to cause much disorder and scandal throughout the land; and very soon after her succession the two countries, as well as the two sovereigns, were at open war. Alfonso attempted to extend the Aragonese dominion over Castile, filling all the strong places with his own countrymen, and claiming sovereign power over Castile and Leon. Castilians and Leonese gathered round their own queen, and what is called a civil war—which was really an international conflict—raged between husband and wife and their respective adherents.

After various turns of fortune, the Castilians, who

---

[1] The first Urraca, the daughter of Fernan Gonsalez, was queen of Ordoño III. The second was sister to Alfonso VI. Dunham, in his history, confounds aunt with niece.

QUEEN URRACA.

had taken up arms not so much for love of their queen as for dislike of the Aragonese, became so disgusted with the conduct of Urraca as to seek a reconciliation with Alfonso. A truce was patched up between the rival powers on the condition that Alfonso should take back his wife and share the dominion of the joint states with her. The couple, however, could not agree—Urraca pretending to have scruples of conscience at having her first cousin for a husband, and Alfonso having ample cause to complain of Urraca's misconduct. The king repudiated his wife publicly, and sent her back to Castile. Once more the Castilian nobles took the field in resentment of the insult offered to their queen. A battle took place, in 1111, near Sepulveda, in which Alfonso was victorious. He succeeded in making himself master of the whole country, using his victory so cruelly as to drive the Castilians and Leonese once more into rebellion. By this time a third party was formed in the state, which, disgusted equally by the scandalous behaviour of Queen Urraca and the tyranny of her Aragonese husband, interceded with the Pope to nullify their marriage, so that Alfonso might be deprived of all pretensions over Castile and Leon. The Pope pronouncing the marriage void, Alfonso had no further excuse to meddle with Castile and Leon, and retired to his own kingdom, where he found ample employment of a more congenial and righteous kind in battling with the Moors. Left to herself and to internal discord, Urraca continued to reign in Castile and Leon until her death, in 1126—her evil dominion being marked by an uninterrupted succession of

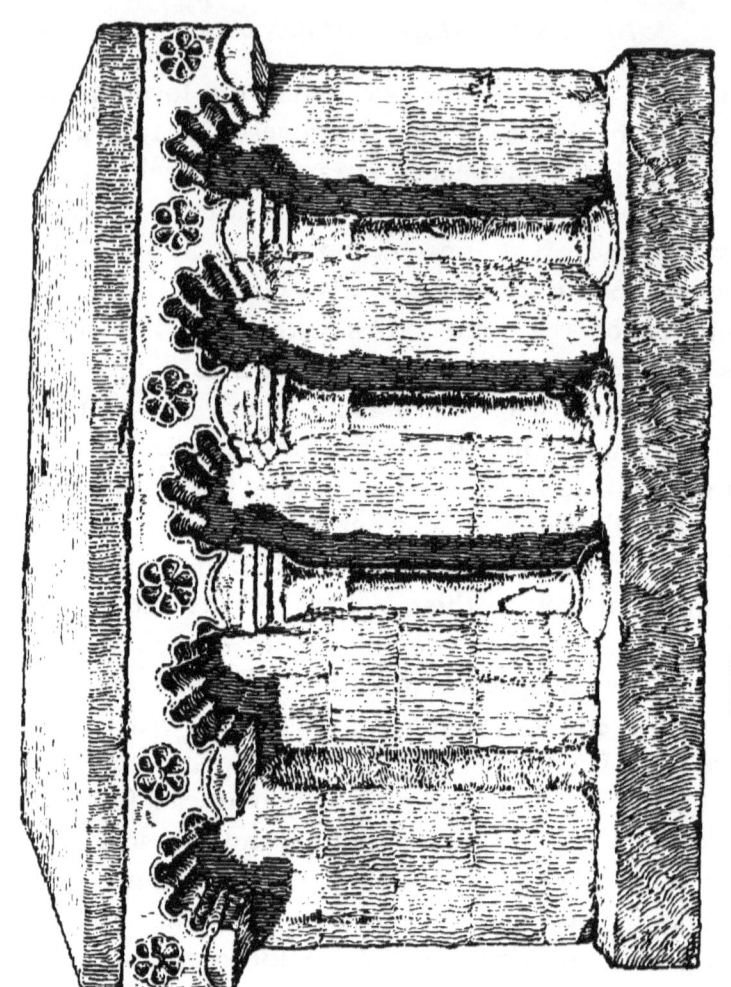

TOMB OF ALFONSO EL BATALLADOR.

troubles, of which civil war and domestic strife were not the worst.

As for Alfonso, the First of Aragon—surnamed, for his incessant wars, *El Batallador* (The Battler) —he survived, when freed from his wife and the ungrateful sovereignty of her dominions, to do much good service for his native country against the infidels. He is to be reckoned among the greatest warriors of the age, who contributed materially to the extension of the frontiers of Christian Spain. Having conquered all the districts north of the Ebro, he laid siege to Saragossa, which important city, a stronghold of the Moors from the earliest days, fell into his hands after a long siege, notwithstanding all the efforts of the Almoravides for its relief. Tudela and other strong places on the frontier had fallen by treachery and force of arms before this. In 1120 Alfonso encountered a large army under a general of the Almoravides, near Daroca, over which he gained a decisive victory; while another army of Africans, under Ali, the Emperor of Morocco, in person, was forced to retreat before Castile and Leon. In the same year Alfonso captured Tarragona and other places on the sea-coast. He then carried his arms south of the Ebro, reducing the strong fortresses of Calatayud and Daroca. He even made a raid into Andalusia, from which country he brought back ten thousand Mozarabic[1] families, the descendants of those who had accepted the conquest

---

[1] Mozarabe (*Mosta'rib*—almost Arab—*pene Arabus*) was the name given by the Moors to the Christian who submitted to their rule and lived under their jurisdiction.

and had remained in their original homes, whom he settled in the lands won back from the Moors. Going hither and thither, sometimes to take up his quarrel with his wife and his affairs in Leon, sometimes ravaging the Moorish territory, and sometimes turning his arms even across his northern border into France, Alfonso fairly earned the name of the Battler by his industry in war. In 1130 he crossed the Pyrenees, to punish the Duke of Aquitaine for injuries suffered at his hands, and captured Bordeaux after a long siege. The next year he was again at work in Catalonia, fighting the Moors. In attempting to reduce the fortress of Fraga, however, he met at last with his fate. The Moors, under the governor of Valencia, reinforced by a large body of Almoravides from Africa, advanced to the relief of the town, and in a desperate battle which ensued outside of the walls, Alfonso and the Aragonese were put to utter rout. The fate of the king himself is left in the same doubt as that of Roderick, the last of the Goths. Some allege that he was slain in battle; others that he lived to fight and fall another day; others that he died in a monastery.

With Alfonso the Battler who is also called *The Emperor* from his wide dominion, fell, as often happened before in Spain, the structure he had raised with so much pains. He was a valiant soldier and conspicuous among the conquerors of the Moors, and though so much of the ground he won so painfully was lost after his death, he is entitled to the remembrance of posterity as the first who set Aragon on her feet, to assume a rank among the

Spanish provinces second only to Castile. He made of his small patrimony a great kingdom—a service perhaps not so great for Christendom as for Aragon, for it led the way to a new series of intestinal wars and postponed the date of the final deliverance of Spain from the Mahommedans. Alfonso left no issue, bequeathing by his will Navarre to the Knights of St. John and Aragon to the Templars—a foolish testament, by which was undone all the work the Battler had accomplished in his life. Neither Navarre nor Aragon would acknowledge the sovereignty of the foreign knights, though they agreed with alacrity to the separation—the Navarrese choosing for their king Garcia Ramirez, a scion of the old royal stock; and the Aragonese fetching Ramiro, the brother of their late monarch, from a monastery, and setting him on the vacant throne. The two kings renewed the old strife between their two countries, and a period of desultory internecine war ensued, in which the Moors were forgotten, or used as instruments by one side or the other. Ramiro returning to his cloister in disgust of the kingly life, the conflict of Aragon was taken up and continued by his son-in-law, Raymundo, the Count of Barcelona, who was lord also of Provence. In this reign the campaign against the Moors was renewed, the Aragonese capturing Tortosa, Lerida, and Fraga, so that by the year 1153 the Moorish dominion was extinguished in all Aragon and Catalonia.

But it is time to return to the main current of our story, and take up again the tale of Castile and Leon, now for a time united. Alfonso VII., who came to his double inheritance in 1126, was the son of Urraca, of evil memory, by her first husband, Count Raymond, of Burgundy. In his early years he was much disturbed by the legacy of bad blood left him by his mother, and by quarrels with his neighbour and kinsman of Aragon for the possession of some frontier places. Profiting by the death of the Battler and on the strength of the help given alternately to Navarre and to Aragon against the Moors, Alfonso claimed the homage of their princes—a claim to which each, for a time and for his own ends, submitted; even the Count of Thoulouse acknowledging him as his superior. Flattered by this access of dignity Alfonso had himself solemnly proclaimed *Imperator totius Hispaniæ* in 1135. How vain was this assumption and how empty the title was shown immediately afterwards, for a new league was formed against Alfonso, in which Navarre and Portugal, the latter recently advanced to the rank of a kingdom and henceforth to take a hand in the internecine war, joined their forces against the Emperor. In the campaign which ensued the Portuguese, now entering for the first time upon the path of conquest, gained some advantages, but they were called back to defend their own territory against the Moors. The great victory which they won over the misbelievers on the field of Ourique was undoubtedly one of the severest blows ever inflicted on the Moorish dominion, which tended materially to abridge its term and hasten its dissolution. But now a new flood of Africans was to be poured over Spain. Just as the Almoravides, fresh from the desert and mountains, had prevailed over the effeminate Andalusians, so a fresh burst of fanatical warriors from regenerate Islam was to supersede the Almoravides, a century after the first coming of Yussuf. The Almoravides, who had won their influence as unifiers of the faith, had made their rule intolerable by their tyranny and their excesses. Under a new prophet calling himself the *Mehdi*, one Mahommed, the son of Abdalla, the son of a lamplighter in the great mosque of Cordova, there arose a sect called the *Almohades*, or Unitarians, which drove out the Almoravides from Morocco, and then poured over into Spain, as their predecessors had done. The Almohades were the fiercest and most fanatical of all the Mahommedan hordes which had yet visited the country, and their coming once more gave unity and strength to the Moslem power. Abdelmumen, the coadjutor and successor of the Mehdi, succeeded in bringing all Moorish Spain within his dominion, which henceforth became a province of Morocco, ruled from Africa. Thus once more was the process of Mahommedan decay arrested, and the Moorish hold on Spain strengthened and renewed. The Almohades were for a time more successful against the Christians than their predecessors had been, and many of the conquests made by the kings of Castile, Aragon, and Portugal, after their desultory and divided victories, fell back into the hands of the Moors.

But even more was the Moorish cause helped by disunion and disruption among the Christian kingdoms than by the new force acquired from Africa. Alfonso VII. could neither beat the Almohades in the field nor keep his two kingdoms together. Although

ELEANOR OF ENGLAND.

he had advanced the frontiers of the Spanish dominion, over the whole interior table-land, from Tagus to the Sierra Morena, by his death this gain was more than lost through Castile and Leon being again divided. Sancho, the elder of his sons, became king of Castile, and Fernando the younger, of Leon. The brothers remained on good terms, their only enemy being their cousin of Navarre. Sancho III., after a short reign of one year, gave place to Alfonso, his son, called the Eighth. Being only three years old when he succeeded, a civil war broke out between the two powerful families of the Castros and the Laras for possession of the king's person and the direction of his affairs. The intervention of Fernando of Leon, the king's uncle, made the confusion worse confounded until the quarrel as to who should be the king's guardian was settled by Alfonso assuming the sovereign power on his marriage with Eleanor, the daughter of the English king, Henry II., in 1170. This was the beginning of that connection between the royal families of England and Spain which was attended with results so happy to both kingdoms—giving to Spain at least two of her best queens, and to England the beloved and worthy consort of the best of the Plantagenets. Alfonso VIII. was only in his fifteenth year when he assumed the crown and a wife. His reign was one so fortunate and memorable for his country as fairly to earn for him the honourable appellation of Alfonso the Noble. It is not always safe, indeed, to accept the distinctions given to the monarchs by the early chroniclers. The only people who could write in those days were the ecclesiastics, and they praised the kings not so much for what they did for the people as for their conduct towards the Church. He who founded religious houses, endowed churches, and benefited the priesthood, was called, whatever his civil character might be, *The Good*. Alfonso VIII., over whose life the chronicler is very effusive, calling him " the best king who had ever been in Christendom—the light of Spain—the shield and sustenance of Christianity—a king most loyal and truthful, in all things straightforward and pious, and perfect in all good manners "—seems to have deserved this flattering character better than any of his predecessors. He was a great benefactor to the Church, and he specially distinguished himself by a decree exempting all ecclesiastics of every order and class from any kind of tax or tribute to the state for ever. He showed his goodness in other and more practical ways by paying more heed than the kings of Castile had been wont to pay to the interests of the people under his care. He seems to have been of a simple, amiable, unaffected disposition, much under the sway of his English wife Eleanor, who would have been untrue to her Plantagenet blood had she been deficient in force or firmness of will.

The chief passages in Alfonso's life were, as usual, those connected with domestic treason or with foreign levy. A civil war with his cousin and namesake of Leon was suspended only by the advance of the Almohades at the head of a formidable army. Alfonso rashly went forward to meet the enemy, without waiting for the promised reinforcements from Leon and Navarre. The battle which was fought in 1195 at

Alarcon, on the banks of the Jucar, is memorable in the annals of Spain as one of the most calamitous reverses ever sustained by the Christian armies—a victory for the Mussulmans so complete as to promise to bring back the days of Almanzor. Alfonso, whose rashness as a general can scarcely excuse his valour as a soldier, was beaten and his army routed—the king being with difficulty prevented by his nobles from plunging into the midst of the Moors and redeeming his lost honour by death. Retreating to Toledo he met his cousin of Leon with reinforcements. From hot words the kings came to war, and a fierce and bloody strife ensued, to the scandal of alarmed Christendom. By the intercession of the bishops, however, peace was at last made—Alfonso giving his daughter Berengaria in wife to her cousin, the Alfonso of Leon. The marriage was afterwards dissolved by the Pope as being within the prohibited degrees, but as we shall see it was fraught with the happiest results for the cause of Spanish unity.

The one exploit of Alfonso which remains to be recorded is of a glory so surpassing and a value so great as more than to redeem his reputation and to justify his name to posterity. After their victory at Alarcon the Mahommedans recovered a large part of the territory they had lost in the hundred years previous—possessing themselves of Madrid, Salamanca, Guadalajara, and other important towns, and filling the Christians with dread of the return of their evil days. An army larger than had yet been seen on Spanish soil was transported from Africa, including contingents from every part of that continent and from Asia—Egyptians, Nubians and Negroes, Persians and Scythians. The terrified Pope, Innocent III., proclaimed a Crusade against the infidel. The Archbishop of Toledo, as distinguished in war as in letters, went about the courts of Europe to solicit aid from the Christian princes. A large number of foreign knights, chiefly English and French, took the route to Spain to engage in this new holy war. Navarre and Aragon suspended their quarrels, and even Portugal promised her assistance. The Almohades, who seem to have been badly led, wasted their strength in laying siege to fortified towns, and gave time to the Christians to concentrate their forces. Some loss of men and greater scandal were caused to the latter by the desertion of a large body of their foreign allies, who returned home disgusted at the small opening for plunder. But at length King Alfonso, with the two kings of Aragon and Navarre and their joint armies, came up with the Mahommedans, who had occupied the defiles of the Sierra Morena. This range of mountains, dividing Castile from Andalusia, rises from the high plateau on the north by a gentle ascent to its crest, then dips suddenly to a level nearly two thousand feet lower to the plains, thus giving to an army attacking from Castile the better position to one defending the steep and abrupt declivities on the Andalusian side. The chief scene of the battle, which was decided on the 16th of July, 1212, was certain small upland valleys, girt by trees and rocks, called *Las Navas de Tolosa*.[1]

[1] Nava is an old word, signifying a small plain among the mountains. It is contained in the name of Navarre.

The King of Navarre commanded the right wing of the Spanish army and the King of Aragon the left, while Alfonso himself, with the flower of the Castilian cavaliers, led the van and the centre. Among them figured several fighting prelates, the celebrated Rodrigo Ximenez, Archbishop of Toledo—

> turning his tongue divine
> To a loud trumpet and a point of war;

Arnaud, Archbishop of Narbonne, the Papal Legate; the Bishop of Nantes, with other native bishops. The vast army of the Moors, comprising all that was best of Andalusian chivalry—with contingents from all the Mahommedan states, and a strong body of Africans, the immediate followers of the Emperor—was led by Mahommed himself, the Miramolin (as the Spaniards called him), or *Amîr-al-Mouminîn* (Commander of the Faithful), with a scimitar in one hand and the Koran in the other. The battle raged furiously all day, and for a time the issue was in doubt. The Christians were on the point of giving way to the vastly superior force of the infidels. The Templars and the knights of Calatrava, who were in front, were overborne and destroyed. King Alfonso himself, who showed himself here, as before, a better soldier than a general, was in despair, and calling out to Archbishop Rodrigo, "Let us die here, prelate!" made ready to throw himself into the enemy's ranks. The Archbishop, however, to whom the chief glory of the day belongs, was of a cooler head, and himself fighting in the van restored the battle. The Andalusians were the first to flee. Entangled among the rocks and woods, fighting on ground the least suited to their tactics, the very numbers of the enemy were a hindrance to their rallying and an impediment to their flight. An enormous multitude of the Moors was slain. The king himself, in his letter to the Pope, giving an account of his great victory, estimated the slaughter at more than a hundred thousand of the enemy, besides many who were taken captives. Of the Christians, according to the same authority, there died only twenty-five or thirty in the whole army. The Miramolin himself fled from the field, and did not rest till he was safe in Morocco, whence the Almohades or any other sectaries never afterwards came over in any combined body to the relief of their fellow-religionists or the disturbance of Spain.

Not content with the honour won by their countrymen in this famous fight, the early chroniclers, with Archbishop Rodrigo at their head, insist upon claiming the victory of Las Navas de Tolosa as due to the miraculous interposition of Heaven. It is related, with the usual circumstantiality, that when the Christians came up to the enemy they found them strongly posted along the ridges of the Sierra Morena. At this critical moment there appeared before King Alfonso a rustic, clad in the garb of a shepherd—*missus a Deo*—who showed the king how that by taking a narrow path across the hills he might come between the vanguard and the rear of the Moorish army. This was no other than Isidro himself, the holy shepherd, who for this and other good deeds was canonised in the Seventeenth century at the instance of Philip III., to become the patron saint of Madrid. His stone image, set up in token of his patriotic service, is still to be seen in one of the chapels of the cathedral of Toledo. Moreover, as though this victory was not miracle enough, it is related that at the crisis of the battle, when the Christians were beginning to despair, there appeared in the air a great sign of the Cross in red, which inspired the Spaniards with fresh courage and filled the Moors with consternation. But this, though a report credited and celebrated throughout Spain for generations after, is not to be traced to any authority earlier than the middle of the Fourteenth century, and probably rose out of the actual standard carried before the martial archbishop in the battle, which was a gigantic red cross, fortified in the lower part with a shield of iron for the defence of the bearer.

The battle of Las Navas de Tolosa was the most glorious ever fought by the Spaniards against the Moors; and though not followed up, it broke for ever the power of the Mahommedans. From that day forth they can no longer be said to have disputed on equal terms with the Christians for supremacy in the Peninsula. Excepting some desultory raids the Moors never afterwards attempted anything against Castile proper, but confined themselves to Andalusia and the districts adjoining, where the air and soil were more congenial to the children of the south. The whole country from the Bay of Biscay to the Sierra Morena and from Lisbon to Barcelona was now recovered, after a tedious and

QUEEN BERENGARIA.

troublous process of five hundred years. Even the divisions among the Spanish princes, though they delayed, could no longer render doubtful the final result.

Alfonso VIII. survived that great day which is his title to the gratitude of his countrymen only two years, leaving an only son, Enrique, to inherit his kingdom. This prince was but eleven years old on his accession, so that his sister, Berengaria, was appointed regent of the kingdom. Berengaria, for wisdom, goodness, and prudence, was a princess whose only rival in the annals of Spain is Isabel, of the same English blood. The two queens much resembled each other in character, and it is no less to the good fortune of Spain to have possessed as to the honour of England to have contributed, at two passages perhaps the most critical in Spanish history, two women strong enough and virtuous enough to preserve the state. Berengaria, though beset by the unprincipled and ambitious nobles, and especially by the turbulent house of Lara, who seem to have pretended to a hereditary right of guardianship over royal minors, discharged her duty with fair success. The premature death of Enrique, by an accident, led to a renewal of the civil strife. According to the law of Castile, Berengaria was now queen in her own right; but, with a mixture of prudence and self-denial rare in those days, she resigned in favour of her son Fernando, who was also, in right of his father, heir to the crown of Leon. Fernando was acknowledged King of Castile in 1217. Thirteen years afterwards, by the death of Alfonso IX., King of Leon, Fernando became king of both countries; and thus once more, never afterwards to be separated, were united the two states which up to this time and henceforth played the leading part in the restoration of Spain.

V.

UNITED CASTILE AND LEON—RISE OF ARAGON.

(1217-1254.)

FERNANDO III., better known in Spanish history as San Fernando—owing his promotion to a saintship less to his goodness, which was much, than to his austerities and his piety, which were more—mounted the throne under happier auspices than any of his predecessors, coming to a dominion which, thanks to his excellent mother, was peaceful and prosperous—reigning over a kingdom in which, Leonese and Castilians, weary of their quarrels, were for the first time really united—having nothing to fear from any domestic rival or foreign enemy. The empire of the Almohades in Spain was broken to pieces. Of the once powerful Moorish kingdom there survived only the governments of Seville, Cordova, Jaen, Granada, and Valencia, each under a separate chief. Castile had for her only competitor for supremacy in Spain her sister of Aragon, with whom she was presently at peace.

Relieved from all cares at home Fernando was able to resume those schemes of conquest from the Moor to which his predecessors had been so often

SAN FERNANDO.

impelled by political ambition or by religious zeal; from which they had been so constantly diverted by civil dissension. The victory of Las Navas de Tolosa had laid open to the Christians an easy passage into Andalusia. The ancient capital of the Moors, Cordova, lay at their feet. Almost immediately upon his accession to the throne in 1230 Fernando prepared for a campaign in the south. At this time a descendant of the Moorish Emirs of Saragossa, Mahommed Ibn Hud, profiting by the feebleness of the Almohades and of the divisions among the smaller Mahommedan states, by his courage and address had gained the adhesion of the native Moors, and had possessed himself of the sovereignty of the greater part of Andalusia. Aben Hud even aimed at restoring the former glories of the Cordovan empire, taking advantage of the despair and alarm which now had seized the Moors at the near prospect of their total extermination. Murcia, Granada, Cordova, and Seville were brought into one dominion. The attempt to preserve the wreck of the Moorish power came, however, too late. The differences among the Moors and the jealousies of the rival kinglings were but partially healed when the troops of Fernando poured down into the plains. The important frontier cities of Ubeda and Baeza— the former of which had been sacked and destroyed by Alfonso VIII. after his victory, and reconquered and rebuilt by the Moors—were finally recovered. Another Castilian army had already defeated Aben Hud on the banks of the Guadalete, avenging after five hundred years the fate of Roderick. In 1235 a still more valuable prize was made by the Christians, the fame of which resounded through Europe. The great city of Cordova, which had been the pride and glory of Spanish Mahommedanism—the seat of the highest civilisation to which Islam had ever attained—the centre of light and learning—the second Mecca to the faithful—fell easily into the hands of Fernando. Cordova, indeed, was no longer what she had been. The famous capital of the Omeyyad Khalifs, which had been a light to Europe when all around was darkness, had fallen greatly from its old splendour. Still it was a name held in reverence throughout Islam. The fall of the sacred city, with its great mosque, the wonder of the world—its treasures in art, in science, and in letters, was regarded as a presage of the impending final doom.

The consternation among the Moors at Fernando's rapid march and easy conquests reached its culminating point in the news, which came almost simultaneously to the remnant of the faithful in Andalus, of the capture of Valencia by the King of Aragon—Jayme (James), known in his own Catalan tongue as *Lo Conqueridor*. Aragon, since last we took up the thread of her story, had increased steadily in power and in importance. The incorporation of Catalonia and the accession of the wealthy and industrious city of Barcelona had tended to the promotion of internal peace and the cultivation of that spirit of commercial and maritime enterprise for which Eastern Spain was always conspicuous. Pedro II., the grandson of Petronilla, who brought Aragon to be one with Catalonia, was a prince who contributed greatly to the development of Christian Spain, though renowned rather for courage than for wisdom or goodness. After loyally helping his kinsman, Alfonso of Castile, in the great battle of Las Navas de Tolosa, in which he took a conspicuous and very active part, King Pedro was moved to intervene—less perhaps from sympathy with their religious views or zeal in the cause of free opinion than from motives of state policy—in the quarrel between the Albigenses and the Papal Crusaders. Inspired by his allies, the Counts of Thoulouse and of Foix, who hoped to use him as an instrument in working their own ends, Pedro led an army of Aragonese and French across the border into Western Gascony, where the Albigenses were besieging the fortress of Muret, near Thoulouse. To the relief of the beleaguered town came Simon de Montfort, the elder of the two foreign Earls of Leicester so conspicuous in the history of England, at the head of a body of Papal Crusaders. In the battle which ensued the Aragonese, though greatly superior in numbers, were utterly routed. The victors, inflamed by religious fury, gave no quarter, and in the wholesale massacre King Pedro was slain, fighting manfully. "Thus died my father," says his son and successor; "for such has ever been the fate of my race, to conquer or to die in battle."

Pedro being slain, his son, then six years old, was left in the hands of the bitter enemy of his house, Simon de Montfort. De Montfort, who wanted to keep the young Jayme to marry him to his daughter, was persuaded by the Pope to give him up to the Aragonese. Jayme, upon his release, was taken charge of by the Templars. In his early years he was subject to much trouble from his two uncles. Gaining possession of the throne at last he began to distinguish himself by his vigorous efforts to enlarge his dominion. Of his enterprises against the Moor, and of his dealings with his refractory subjects we have a full account in a record which is unique in history, being a memoir of the king by himself, in the Catalan language. This is written in a simple, manly style, with obvious sincerity of purpose, and regarded either as a monument of literature or an historical document, is a very striking picture of a busy and troublous period. It passes over lightly King Jayme's notorious coarseness of life and personal misdeamours, but on the other hand it speaks with a modesty of his exploits in war and a *naïveté* of some questionable public actions, which entitle it to favourable consideration as a true piece of history. King Jayme, who towers over all the kings of Aragon by his conquests as high as he towered over common men by his stature—he was nearly seven feet high, and of a bulk to match his inches—having subdued all his enemies turned his thoughts to the increase of his kingdom at the expense of the Moors. His first achievement was to recover the Balearic Islands, which, conquered by a former Count of Barcelona, had since fallen back into the hands of the Mahommedans, who by their depredations had become the terror of the narrow seas. In 1228 an expedition in a hundred and fifty vessels was despatched against Majorca, which succeeded in wresting that island from the Moors. The other islands were captured during the next three or four years. Flushed with the glory of this exploit, King Jayme next meditated the conquest of the Moorish kingdom, with its capital, of Valencia. Valencia, the city of the Cid, had been recaptured, as we have seen, by the Almoravides on the death of that hero. It was now one of the chief strongholds of Moorish dominion in Spain. King Jayme, whose discretion was at least equal to his valour, before making his attempt on Valencia, sought counsel of one of his nobles, Don Blasco de Alagon, who was reported to "know more of war than any man in the world." Don Blasco gave his opinion thus shrewdly: "Valencia is the best land and the first in the world. My lord, I stayed two years or more in it, when you drove me from your country. There is not in these days so desirable a place as the city of Valencia and the surrounding region; the land is seven days' journey long; if it be God's will that you conquer it, I can assure you that no land of more fertile and luxurious plains and stronger castles is to be found in the whole world." The king being advised that there were many strong castles in the land, with five or six thousand cross-bowmen and men so numerous "that they will not allow an army to approach the walls of their city," proceeded cautiously to his work; first taking the outlying places which guarded the sources of supply to Valencia, and blocking the access to the city by sea. Several years were spent in thus gradually drawing closer the chain around Valencia. At length, his generals having beaten the enemy in several engagements, the Moors were closely invested within the city. In vain did a fleet from Tunis attempt to throw in reinforcements and supplies. The Valencians were starved into surrender. On the 25th of September, 1238,[1] King Jayme entered the city, thus achieving a bloodless conquest—having, to the mortification of some of the zealots in his camp, agreed to let the Moorish king depart safely, with as many as chose to go with him, and giving him five days to take away their families. The king himself, when he saw his standard hoisted upon the tower, writes: "I dismounted from my horse, turned myself towards the east and wept with my eyes, kissing the ground for the great mercy that had been done to me."

Thus was Valencia, one of the remaining strongholds of the Moorish power, finally taken by the King of Aragon, to the great enhancement of his fame and the grief of the Mahommedans. The conquered land was divided among the Christians, such of the Moors as preferred to remain being guaranteed security of life and property and the free exercise of their religion—a guarantee afterwards broken, whenever convenient, as were all such guarantees given by the conquerors.

Having subdued all Valencia, with very little more trouble than came of the jealousies of those among whom the spoils were distributed, King Jayme then

---

[1] King Jayme himself says 1239, but Gayangos in a note to the passage (Royal Chronicle of King James of Aragon, vol. ii. p. 403), proves that the date was 1238. There is much confusion of dates in the early Spanish histories, owing to the difference of Eras. Some reckon by the Spanish Era, some by the Incarnation, and some by the Nativity. The Era of Spain, abolished in Aragon in 1350 and in Castile in 1393, requires thirty-eight years to be subtracted from—the Era of the Incarnation, nine months added to—the common Era.

marched westward towards Murcia. That kingdom, which was now the most northern of those possessed by the Mahommedans, lay on the frontier between Castile and Aragon, and was an object of ambition to both these Christian powers. The King of Castile at this time was Alfonso X., who was King Jayme's son-in-law, being married to his daughter Yolande (Violante). Some jealousies ensued between the two kings in respect of Murcia, a collision between them being warded off for the time by King Jayme's singular, and for that age most unusual, moderation and some clever family diplomacy on the part of Alfonso. The latter sent his wife to plead with her father, ostensibly to seek his aid against the Moors who were threatening him with a fresh invasion of Africans from beyond the sea. At this time there ruled in Granada, which had now become the centre of the Mahommedan power in Spain, Mahommed-ibn-Alhamar, the founder of a new dynasty—a man, like all founders of dynasties, of brains and pith, who aimed at absorbing the whole Moorish dominion, and even of restoring the glories of the Khalifat. He had made an alliance with the Emperor of Morocco, who was to send over a large force of Africans to help to recover the land from the Christians. According to King Jayme, "the Granadine had besides laid his plots in all the towns and castles of the King of Castile, wherever there were Moors still, as well as in Seville, where a great number of them were living. All together they were to rise on a given day, and attack the Christians everywhere, so that the King of Castile and his wife should be taken prisoners, and the lost towns and castles recovered at one blow." A formidable rising did take place, so that in less than three weeks the King of Castile lost three hundred large towns and castles. Such was the situation which the Queen of Castile came to report to her father, who was then preparing for an expedition against Murcia. She prayed King Jayme " for God's sake, for our kindred, and for our own credit, not to let her be disinherited. They had no one to consult how to assist them. The Moors had taken possession of all their country, except perhaps a little." In this state of things, which was not without some consolation to Jayme, then at the height of his power and renown, the King of Aragon, before seeing his daughter, took counsel with his barons and prelates. Their opinion was that, though the king could not very well deny his daughter's suit nor refuse to give help to his son-in-law in his present strait, now was the time to get amends for the wrongs which the King of Castile had done him—that at least he should ask for an indemnity, since the expedition of help would be an expensive one—that the king should give no aid until he had got back the castles he had so often demanded from Castile. In his reply to his Cortes, King Jayme admits that this advice is not unpalatable to him, and declares his resolution in terms which prove him to be at once a prudent ruler in his own interests and a dutiful father-in-law. He avers that he cannot decline to render the aid sought of him by Castile for three reasons: first, because he cannot absolutely desert his daughter and her children when it is sought to take their heritage from them; secondly, because, even if he were not obliged by honour and duty to help the King of Castile, still he should wish to do so "owing to his being one of the most powerful men in the world," who, if he were not now helped and ultimately managed to extricate himself from his difficulties, would regard the King of Aragon as his mortal enemy hereafter, and certainly seek to do him harm; thirdly, that if the King of Castile should lose his land, the King of Aragon would hardly be safe in his own. Therefore it was resolved by the nobles of Aragon that aid should be given to Castile. In appealing to the States of Catalonia, however, the king was less successful. They even sought to make that an opportunity of seeking redress for certain wrongs of their own. They answered the king so "ill and basely"—even the clergy, whom he could not persuade of the danger of losing their churches and having the name of Mahommed proclaimed therein—that Jayme went away angry to his own house. Afterwards terms of accommodation were arranged with the Catalans, ever stubborn on a question of their privileges, by which, in consideration of charters being confirmed, they promised the necessary supplies. The King of Aragon met the King of Castile, and after that, the city of Murcia having been encompassed about by Jayme's knights so as to be isolated from its neighbours, fell without a blow. There was some difficulty about the great mosque, which the Moors were reluctant to give up, saying, "it was the best place they had for their prayers." But the king insisting that, for the same reason, he wished the place to be a Christian cathedral, and making a demonstration with his knights and cross-bowmen,

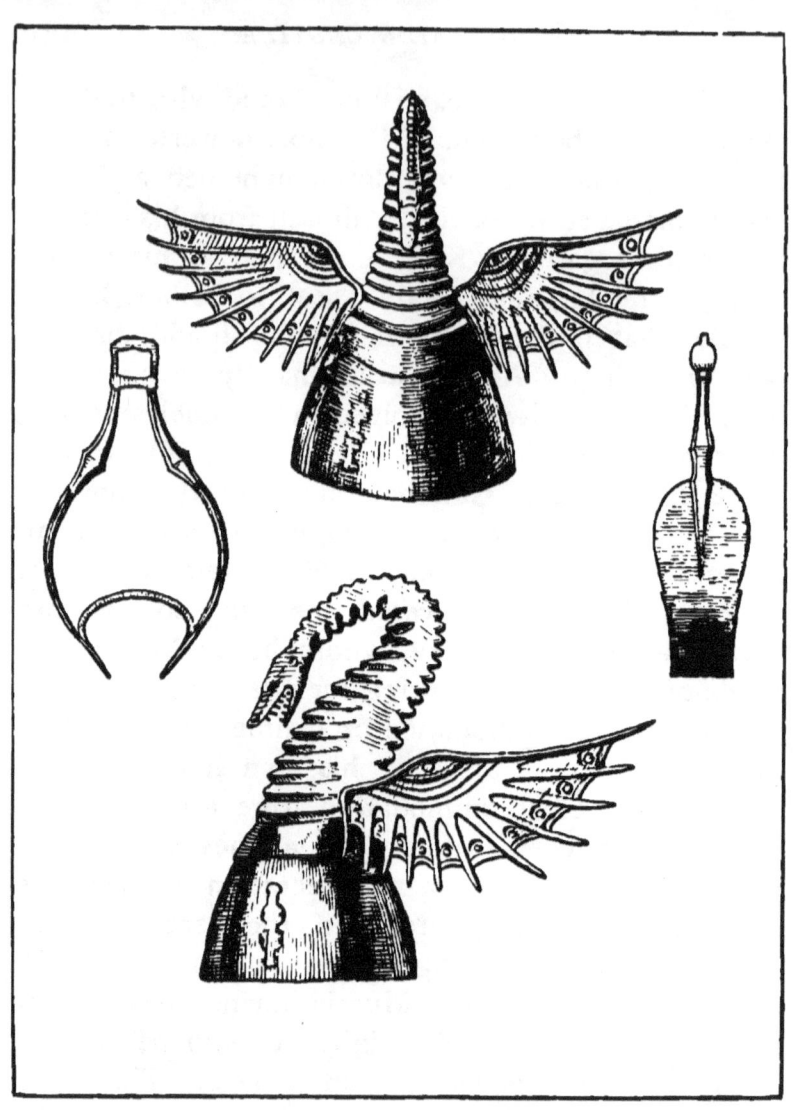

HELMET AND STIRRUPS OF KING JAYME, EL CONQUISTADOR.

the mosque was given up—the Moors being secured in the enjoyment of all the other mosques and of their liberties, such as it was usual to grant them. Murcia and the adjacent territory were given up, in fulfilment of some pact with Castile, to King Alfonso. Further, that king received advice from his father-in-law as to seven things he was to observe in the conduct of affairs—advice which proves Jayme to have been a shrewd man, whose name for wisdom should have stood higher with posterity than it does. Among these seven things Alfonso was advised that, " if some only were to be kept in his grace, and he could not keep the others, he should keep at least two parties— the church, and the people and cities of the country ; for they are those whom God loves more even than the nobles and the knights, for the knights revolt sooner against their lord than the others ; if he could keep with him all of them, well and good ; if not, he should keep these two parties, for with their help he could easily destroy the others."

The character of King Jayme, if closely examined, is less admirable than would appear by his own account of his conquests and his dealings with his people. He was perfidious, dissolute, and cruel, abusing even the privileges of his time and rank. For the conquests which won him his proud appellation he was indebted as much to his craft as to his valour. He broke all his promises to his own people as well as to the Moors. He violated with impunity the laws of his states, artfully setting up Aragon against Catalonia or Catalonia against Aragon, whenever convenient for his own safety. He was magnanimous by calculation and merciful only out of self-interest. When his favourite confessor reprimanded him for his profligacy, he caused the prelate's tongue to be torn out by the roots—an offence for which the Pope excommunicated him and placed his kingdom under an interdict. To make atonement for his many sins he undertook, in his old age, to go on a crusade to the Holy Land. He started from Barcelona with a thousand knights, but the wind and waves were contrary, and after buffeting about for nearly two months, the bishops decided that it was not the pleasure of heaven that the party should touch the Holy Land, so they returned to a port in the South of France. In 1276 King Jayme ended his long reign of sixty-three years, leaving his realm greatly developed and Aragon advanced to a rank equal with Castile.

Meanwhile the older kingdom, under Fernando III., was steadily growing in greatness. The capture of Cordova in 1255 was followed up by attacks on the outlying places in Jaen and Murcia. One by one the cities were taken from the Moors, and either merged into the territory of Castile or reduced to vassalage. The city of Jaen itself, the frontier stronghold of Aben Alhamar, the King of Granada, was invested; and the Moors defeated in a great battle outside of the walls. Alarmed for the safety of his own kingdom, the King of Granada took a step which, while it proves how low the ancient Moorish prestige had fallen, seems to throw a not unpleasing light upon the relations which the kings of the opposite faiths held to each other, and upon the honourable allegiance of both Moors and Christians to the laws

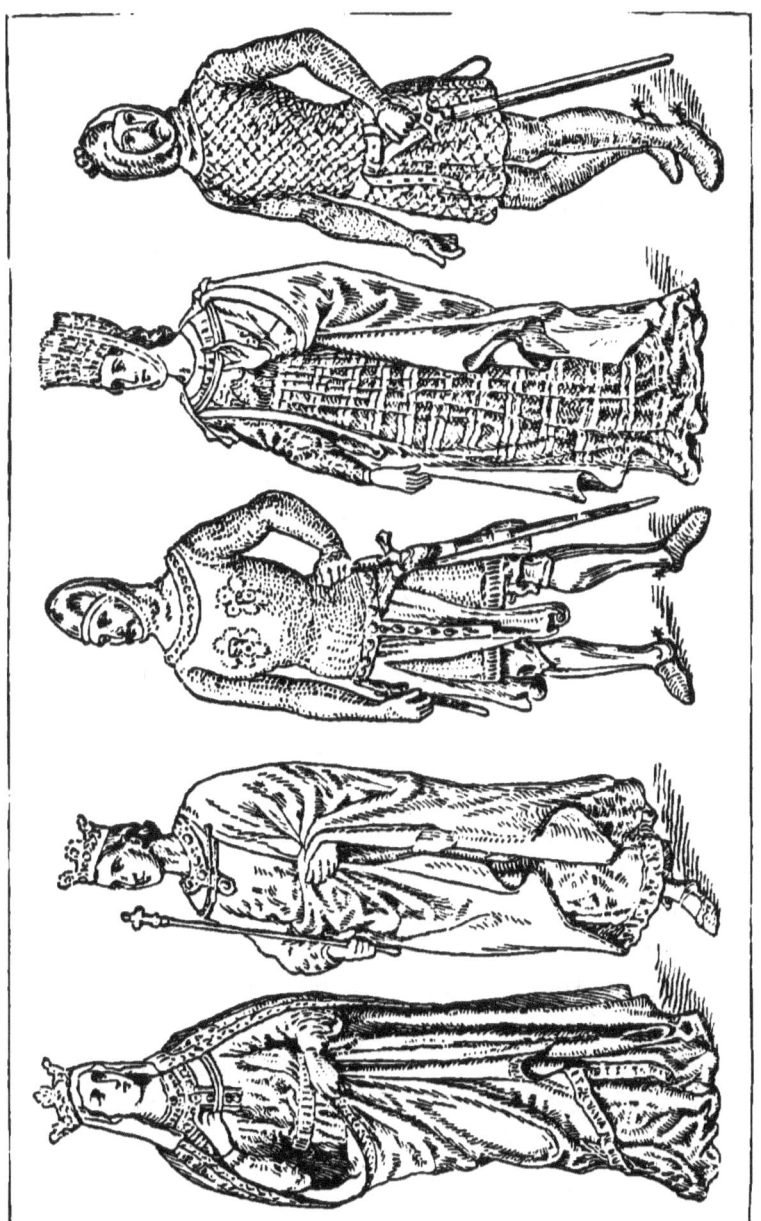

COSTUMES OF THE THIRTEENTH CENTURY, KINGS AND NOBLES.

of chivalry. Mahommed-ibn-Alhamar went in person unattended to the camp of King Alfonso, declared his name, and submitted himself to the king's pleasure —offering to become a vassal of Castile. Fernando proved himself equal to the Moor in generous feeling, receiving him cordially with all honour and respect, and calling him his dear friend and ally. Terms of peace and mutual support were agreed upon between the two kings. Jaen was surrendered to the Christians. Aben Alhamar agreed to pay tribute to Alfonso and to furnish him with a contingent of Moorish knights when he went to war—engaging, which appears to be the most singular condition of all, considering the deadly strife which had raged between Moor and Christian for more than seven hundred years, to attend the Cortes at Toledo, when summoned as a feudatory of Castile.[1] Aben Alhamar, on his part, was confirmed in his possession of the Kingdom of Granada, and promised assistance against his enemies.

It was not long before the King of Granada was called upon to render service to his Christian suzerain. Fernando's next enterprise was the capture of Seville. Having made himself master of all the intervening towns and fortresses on both banks of the Guadalquivir, with the assistance of his Moorish ally, Ferdinand advanced to the siege of Seville—then the largest and richest of the cities remaining to the Moors, and the centre of their traffic with Africa and the East. A strenuous defence both by sea and land was made by

[1] The attendance of Moors, as vassals, at the Cortes of Castile was not unusual in the Twelfth and Thirteenth centuries. At the great Cortes of Toledo, summoned in 1135 by Alfonso VII., to confirm his title of Emperor, there were Moorish princes.

the besieged. Finding that it was impossible to take the city so long as the mouth of the Guadalquivir was held by the Moorish fleet, Fernando had a number of ships built in Biscay, and sent round to the entrance of the river, which is the first mention in history of the Castilian navy. The Christians having triumphed in a sea battle, and a relieving army of Mahommedans coming from Algarve being beaten by land, the city surrendered on the 23rd of November, 1248. The conduct of Fernando to the vanquished, who had made a very brave resistance, was conspicuous at once for clemency and good policy. Such of the Moorish inhabitants as chose to remain were guaranteed the security of their lives and property, under a tribute equal to that which they paid to their own princes. Those who elected to depart to Africa or elsewhere had free permission to go, and were furnished with means for the journey. The greater number of the Mahommedan citizens chose to take refuge with their fellow-countrymen in Granada, which now remained the sole refuge of the Moors under their King Mahommed-ibn-Alhamar.

Fernando made his entry into the city in December 1248, proceeding to the great mosque which, purged and sanctified, was turned as usual into a Christian temple. The conquest of Seville was one of great importance, not only because of its intrinsic worth as a rich and populous city, but because it gave the Christians of Castile, for the first time, a secure port and harbour for their ships in the south—the river Guadalquivir being navigable up to Seville for the largest vessels then in use in those seas. The rich

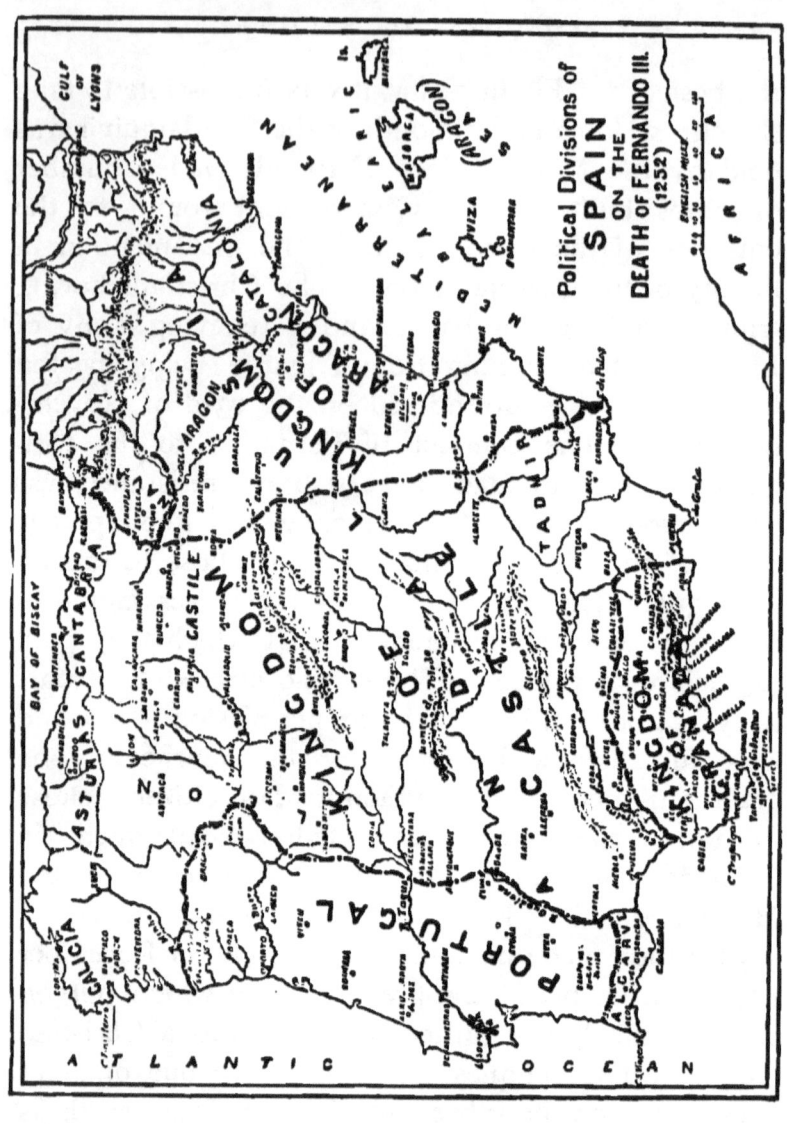

lands adjoining, together with the houses in the city, were divided among the conquerors—the deed of partition, or *Repartimiento*, being still extant, and testifying at once to the value of the spoil, and the names and characters of the participants. Fernando did not long survive his conquest. Worn out by the hardships of the siege, as well as by the austerities he was accustomed to practice on his person by way of devotion, he died on the 30th of May, 1252, leaving to his son Alfonso a heritage greatly enriched and enlarged, and a character which, in 1671, was thought good enough by Pope Clement X. to merit canonisation.

Alfonso X.,[1] surnamed *El Sabio*, or *The Sage*, deserved that epithet less by his wisdom than his learning. His character may be likened to that of our James I. While deeply versed in books, with a taste for literature and a capacity for science far in advance of the age, he was shallow in himself, vain, frivolous, ostentatious, feeble, and irresolute—for ever aiming at greatness beyond that of a King of Castile, but devoid of all the strength and skill needed for its achievement. His misdirected ambition and his extravagant follies brought on himself many humiliations, and involved

---

[1] There is much confusion among the many Spanish Alfonsos, the name being common to the kings both of Castile and of Leon, as well as of Aragon. In the western kingdom the enumeration follows the line of Leon as the most ancient. Thus Alfonso, the grandson of San Fernando, is called the *Tenth*, the Ninth Alfonso being his father, who was king of Leon only. Dunham, following some native historians, rejects this intercalary Alfonso, making the numbering straight by calling Alfonso of Aragon, *El Batallador*, Alfonso VII. But this Alfonso has no business to be in the line of succession, having never been acknowledged as king, either of Castile or of Leon.

him in endless quarrels with his neighbours and with his own people. The first of his many projects for exalting his name in the eyes of Christendom was a scheme for the acquisition of Gascony, which province he claimed on the strength of its having been promised by the King of England as a marriage portion to his great-grandfather, Alfonso VIII. Gascony was then held for the English king, Henry III., by Simon de Montfort, Earl of Leicester, as governor. Obtaining the aid of some of the discontented barons, such as the Counts of Béarn and Limoges, the Castilians laid siege to Bayonne. But with his usual fickleness Alfonso was led to withdraw from the enterprise, upon condition of giving his sister Eleanor in marriage to Prince Edward, son of the English king—the bride to take with her as dowry all the rights of Castile over the disputed territory. The marriage, which turned out notably happier than most of the marriages arranged by state policy, was celebrated with great magnificence in the monastery of Las Huelgas, near Burgos—Prince Edward receiving knighthood at the hands of his brother-in-law, and performing his vigils in the chapel. Alfonso's next ambition was to be Emperor of Germany—resting his claim on being the son of Beatrix, who was a daughter of Philip, the late emperor. For some twenty years the King of Castile urged his rights, vexing Pope after Pope for his support and expending large sums of money upon the electors, out of the treasure which had been amassed by his frugal father. The electors passed him over with scant respect, choosing on the first occasion his rival,

Richard, Earl of Cornwall, brother of our Henry III.; and on the next, in 1273, when Alfonso was able to secure but one vote, Rudolph of Hapsburg. In the end Pope Gregory I., wearied by Alfonso's importunities, ceased to correspond with him and excommunicated his supporters.

These follies, for which the country had to pay in the unwonted form of direct taxation, made Alfonso very unpopular at home. The discontent of the nobles came to a climax when Alfonso, in marrying his natural daughter, Beatrix de Guzman, to the King of Portugal, gave away with her the Castilian rights over the province of Algarve. A league was formed against the king, headed by his brother, the Infante Felipe, and supported by the ever-rebellious family of the Laras, which was joined by the Moorish King of Granada. Alfonso temporised with the insurgents, whose demands went to the extent of claiming exemption from taxation and from fixed military service for the nobility. The Cortes were summoned at Burgos to treat of the matter between the king and the nobles, who, although favourably disposed to support the former, were by Alfonso himself induced to concede nearly all the arrogant demands of the nobles, with whom he sought to be reconciled with most unkingly alacrity. Another cause of quarrel arose out of the succession to the throne. In 1275, the king being absent in France, his eldest son Fernando, known in history as the *Infante de la Cerda*,[1] died,

---

[1] So called from a tuft of hair (*cerda*) growing out of a mole on his face.

leaving two sons of tender age by his wife Blanche, sister to Philip IV. of France. According to the old Visigothic law, the second son of the king, if of age, was recognised as heir in preference to any infant child of the eldest son, on the abstract ground that he was one degree nearer in blood, but perhaps for the more practical reason that he was better able to maintain his state and dignity. To settle the question the Cortes were convoked at Segovia in 1276, who decided in favour of the native as against the foreign law. King Alfonso's second son was Sancho, who was thus proclaimed heir to the throne. The decision of the Cortes offended the French king, who demanded that at least his sister's dowry should be restored, and herself and her children permitted to return to France. These demands being refused, war was declared by France against Castile. The transactions which ensued were complicated by the flight of Alfonso's own queen, who had taken the part of the Infante de la Cerda, into Aragon, and the murder of Prince Fadrique, his younger brother, by order of the king.

All these things together, with sundry petty acts of oppression, of vindictiveness, and of greed, tended to aggravate the temper of the people and to fill up the measure of their contempt and hatred for their sovereign. His son Sancho was induced to lead the malcontents, who quickly gained possession of Toledo, Cordova, and all the important towns. Alfonso, reduced to despair, even besought aid from the Emperor of Morocco—while applying at the same time, by a curious double policy, very characteristic of this king, to the Pope to excommunicate his rebellious son. Some kind of reconciliation was come to at last. The last act of Alfonso's life brings his reign to a dramatic close. He died of grief and anxiety, because his penitent son Sancho had fallen suddenly sick.

Of those acquirements which earned Alfonso X. the name of *The Learned*, we may speak with greater respect than of his conduct as a king. Making every allowance for the not very high standard by which the accomplishments of a reigning prince are measured, in an age when most princes could scarcely spell, Alfonso, by what he has left behind, is proved to have been a man in culture and in knowledge far in advance of his time. He has left us, as proof of his attainments in astronomy, the *Alphonsine Tables*, in which doubtless he was assisted by the Arab mathematicians. He compiled the *Siete Partidas*, which are a digest of the laws in force in ancient Spain, derived from the Roman and the Visigothic Codes. He wrote, or rather caused to be written, and edited, the *Crónica General*, the first great history of Spain, which, in spite of its abundant faults and fables, deserves to be ever remembered because it is the first prose writing of any importance in the Castilian tongue. He was a poet, and wrote Canticles to the Virgin oddly enough not in the Castilian but in the Galician dialect—a proof among many that up to this time the national language was still in process of formation—that there was a doubt whether the language of Castile or of Galicia (which is akin to Portuguese) would prevail. Many other works, of philosophy, history, and poetry, are credited to Alfonso, which prove that though a bad king he was a man of considerable general intelligence and culture. He was the first monarch of modern Europe who was also a man of letters. In happier times and in more favourable circumstances, he might even have risen to a respectable rank among the minor poets of his nation.

VI.

LAWS AND GOVERNMENT OF CASTILE AND ARAGON—THE CORTES AND THE FUEROS—PROGRESS OF ARTS AND LETTERS.

THE mention of the Cortes in the previous chapter suggests that this is the proper time and here the proper place to describe the laws and institutions under which the people lived, of whose kings and conquerors only we have been hitherto treating. The early Christian Spaniards inherited from the Goths a very elaborate and complicated code of laws, founded partly on the system of jurisprudence which was introduced by the Romans, but deriving its most characteristic features from that Northern stock of which the Visigoths claimed to be a scion. For three hundred years at least after the revival of the Spanish monarchy under Pelayo, the Christians of Leon and Castile were subject to the Visigothic code, called anciently the *Forum Judicum*, which became corrupted during the barbarous age, when very few remained who used the Roman tongue, into *Fuero Juzgo*, whose origin goes back to Euric, a Gothic king of the Fifth century. This code was, indeed, never formally superseded, but continued to be quoted in the acts and decrees of the Cortes and the kings up to the end of the Eighteenth century, being the basis of all Spanish jurisprudence. Under the *Fuero Juzgo*, consisting, as revised and extended in the version

CHURCH OF S. MIGUEL DE LINO.

ordered to be translated and promulgated by San Fernando, of nearly six hundred laws, arranged in twelve books every act and function of life, every relation of citizen to citizen, every duty of subject to state, or of men to one another, every right and every obligation, is minutely defined, prescribed, and provided for. Beginning with the celestial system and citing the obedience rendered to God by the angelic host, the Code goes on, in a descending series which in the higher stages is axiomatic rather than statutory, to tell what every man should do, and what, in default of his duty, is to be his punishment; to enumerate each several offence of which a man in any of the orders can be guilty, to arrange the process of trial; and to fix the penalty, varying not only according to the nature of the crime, but according to the degree of the offender and the rank of the injured. So minute and searching are the distinctions and the grades of offending, so particular the penalties, and so precise the terms and conditions of justice, that scarcely any transaction in which a man could be engaged remains omitted from the schedule. The first thing to remark in this code, as illustrative of the character of the people and their condition under the early kings, is that the offence was prescribed with due regard to the degree and standing of the offender, and of him against whom it was committed. Such a principle as equality before the law was unknown and could not have been understood in old Spain. The privileged classes were the clergy and the nobles, especially in the earlier days the former, when the prelates were at once the chief possessors of wealth and of learning and the most prominent fighting men. The nobles who, as an order, did not rise into prominence until the Eleventh century, were not so much favoured by the laws as by the circumstances which enabled them to set those laws at defiance. There being no proper feudal system such as prevailed in Western Europe, and the noble's property being what he conquered for himself from the Moors, or what was given to him by the king as a share of the general spoil, there is no social distinction to be traced in the *Fuero Juzgo*, except between freeman and slave. An offence by a freeman against a slave was deemed less than an offence against another freeman. If a freeman killed a slave he paid only half the penalty he would have paid had the victim been free. If a master punished his slave so that desertion ensued, he had only to show that the punishment was more severe then he intended, to be acquitted of all blame. The slaves were of three classes—those born so, those captured in war, those condemned to be such by justice. As for slavery, it was a recognised institution in the Visigothic period, and it seems to have been maintained for at least three or four hundred years later. There being no record of its formal abolition we may presume that it was suffered to die out, at least in name, and to lapse into villeinage.

Under this code, which probably had ceased to be obligatory, as its provisions could not but have been impracticable, in the disturbed condition of old Castile and Leon, long before its re-publication by Fernando III., the people could hardly have been content, in the times when they were at perpetual war with the Moors. It was formally superseded, or rather supplemented, by the *Siete Partidas*, or *Seven Sections*, compiled by order of Alfonso X., which appeared in 1258. The *Siete Partidas*, which are still the basis of

Spanish common law, was an adaptation of the *Fuero Juzgo* to a more advanced state of society. The jurists employed by Alfonso to draw up this celebrated code seem to have been inspired by a greater respect for Roman than for Visigothic law. As in the *Fuero Juzgo* the whole fabric of society was dealt with in the abstract and in detail. Whatever men do—whatever they suffer—is here provided for. It is a whole body of morality and of religion. The scope of the new code was even more comprehensive than of the old. In some points we may perceive an advance to a higher civilisation, as in the abolition, as a legal process, of the trial by ordeals and in the mitigation of torture. In other points there is a very perceptible growth of the prerogatives and privileges of the kings. Treason against the sovereign is made the greatest of crimes, involving death and confiscation of the traitor's substance. By many ingenious ways the royal authority, for which the sanction claimed is nothing less than divine, is fortified and extended. On the other hand, there is an obvious design, carefully disguised as it is in the *Siete Partidas*, to lower the knightly order, and to reduce the privileges of the nobles, by exalting at their expense the Church and commonalty. This last order had been much strengthened in political importance by the number of new settlements which had been created in the lands conquered from the Moors, and was beginning to be a formidable power in the state.

The people, long before Alfonso X. had issued his new code, which at first did not get much acceptance among any order in the community, had already secured many valuable privileges from their kings in the shape of local *fueros* or charters, wrung from the necessities of the sovereign or won as trophies of war. By degrees there arose the *comunidad*, which was originally a colony planted on the border, in lands recovered from the Moors, which was endowed with special privileges, as being exposed to the enemy and a barrier against invasion. On condition of defending the land and of cultivating it, the settlers were exempted from the jurisdiction of the nobles. They were empowered to elect their own magistrates, to form municipalities, to raise and spend a great part of their revenues on themselves. These *comunidades* became so rich and flourishing as province after province was recovered from the Moors, as to excite, we are told, the jealousy and the greed of the nobles, some of whom were even tempted to renounce their own caste and to enrol themselves among the commoners, in order to be qualified for places in the community. Sometimes a *comunidad*, in the belief that it was richer than plebeians ought to be, was subject to predatory excursions by the neighbouring count, just as though it had been Moorish territory.

In this way insensibly the commoners increased in wealth and in power, so that in the Thirteenth century they had begun, even in Castile, to be a power in the state, on which the sovereign was accustomed to lean when hard pressed by his nobles. At what precise period the voice of the people, such as it was, began to make itself heard in the state, it is not easy to decide. Councils in which the nobility, the prelates, and "the people," were represented are spoken as

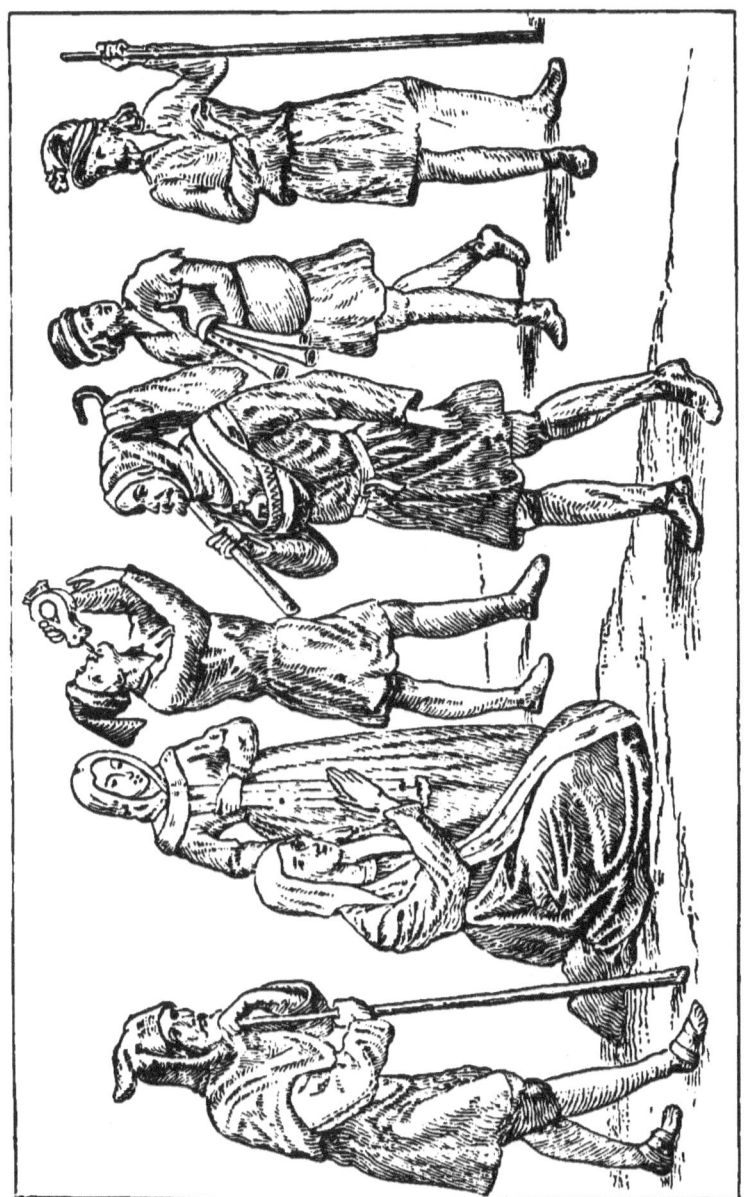

COSTUMES OF COMMON PEOPLE, THIRTEENTH CENTURY.

having been held in Leon even before the close of the Tenth century. But these could only have been occasional assemblies, summoned to consult with the king in some extraordinary crisis. From the plural term *Cortes (Courts)*, which came to be used to signify a parliament, we may assume that these representative bodies deliberated not in one general assembly but separately—the clergy apart from the nobility and either distinct from the cities—to meet together perhaps, formally, to register their final decision. The early authorities speak of the great Cortes which was summoned at Toledo to acknowledge Alfonso VII. emperor as having been attended by vassal princes, prelates, and *ricos hombres*—noble men, including not only the men of title, who were few in those days, but those possessed of estates. At this council the people were present, but only " to see, to hear, and to praise God "—according to the chronicler. The first Cortes in Castile which can properly be called a parliament were held at Burgos in 1169. Here, besides the two privileged orders of the clergy and the nobles, were present delegates from many cities and towns, each of whom had but one voice, irrespective of their rank or importance, though not an equal number of representatives. They deliberated in common with the other orders, but consulted apart on domestic affairs, such as taxation and local administration. Afterwards, except on great occasions such as the accession of a new king or the settlement of the throne, the clergy and nobility were not present, nor was their sanction needed to what may be called the legislative acts of the Cortes. From that time forward, as long as a native dynasty kept the throne, the Cortes were recognised as an authority in the state, whose special functions were to control the public income and expenditure, to help the king to money when he wanted it, and generally to maintain the old *fueros* and the privileges of the communes. Such a body of course was very far from being a popular assembly in the modern sense. There was no system of representation. The deputies were chosen arbitrarily, sometimes by lot, from such towns as the king might select. They met only on the king's summons, who we may suppose, did without them as long as he could, calling them together only when he needed a buffer against the growing power of the nobles or money for his wars. Lastly, there was no recognised right of voting or process of election. Such power as the Cortes had grew, as it did elsewhere, out of the necessities of the times, the expansion of territory, and the development of wealth and civilisation. Yet even at an early period the Cortes seem to have exercised a real authority in the correction of notorious abuses in the state, and enjoyed much freedom of speaking. By the middle of the Thirteenth century they had begun to concern themselves with the public morals—a branch of their prerogative in which they were ever afterwards very zealous. They remonstrated with their weak King Alfonso X. on his personal extravagance, requiring him not only to diminish the expenses of his table, but to bring his appetite within a more reasonable compass. They took advantage of the quarrel between Alfonso and his son to assume a much higher tone in political matters—claiming to interfere in the administration of justice, in the making of treaties with foreign powers, in deciding war or peace, and even in the settlement of the title to the crown.

It does not lie within the scope of this work to pursue this investigation into the nature and business of the government in early Castile. Suffice it to say, that by the closing years of the Thirteenth century there had grown up a civil polity in the kingdom which was perhaps on a level with that of any European state. The king was still absolute in theory, and, according to his temper and ability, absolute in fact; but the communes had attained to a substantial power, and were able to exercise, at times, a degree of influence in the affairs of state such as was unattainable under the two first kings of the Asturian dynasty.

If the possession of old charters, or at least the assertion of ancient rights, be admitted as a proof of liberty, then was Aragon even freer than either Castile or Leon. The *fueros de Sobrarbe*, which date from some early year of the Eighth century, are supposed to be the foundation of Aragonese freedom; but though often appealed to they have never been seen and perhaps never had a real existence. The laws and customs of Aragon, as of Catalonia and of Navarre, were always different from those of Castile, and may be said, partly through the circumstances of their political growth, and partly from the more independent and stubborn character of the Eastern races, to have developed at an earlier period into what may be called a settled constitution. There has been doubtless much exaggeration, arising from over-trust in some native authorities, as to the degree of liberty anciently enjoyed by the Catalans and the Aragonese. The statement of the historian Robertson that the government of Aragon, though monarchical in form was in its genius and its essence purely republican, is absurd. The *fueros* were not so much charters of freedom as customs expressive of the independent character of the people. The genius of the Aragonese was undoubtedly one tending to impatience of authority and to self-rule. There was at all times, up to the date when their native laws were violently trodden under foot and their privileges abrogated by Philip II., much more individual liberty in Aragon than in the neighbouring kingdoms. As to popular rights, in the modern sense, they can scarcely be said to have existed. It is true that the Aragonese *cortes* were more of a real parliament than the *cortes* of Castile. The several orders were more sharply distinguished, and their powers more precisely defined. The communes, who seem to have been admitted into the Cortes as early as 1133—that is to say, earlier than in Castile, had a real and distinct authority. In Catalonia, where commerce and industry occupied the people rather than war or conquest, there was a strong democratic spirit, which, from first to last, gave much trouble to the kings. In the internal administration the Cortes of Aragon and of Catalonia were far more prominent and active than in the neighbouring states, as we perceive by the constant attention paid by the early kings, even by King Jayme the Conqueror, to the wishes and feelings of the nation. One peculiar feature of the Aragonese administration was the *Justicia* or Justice; a functionary of very high and solemn character, who may be said to have combined in his own person the powers of the Lord Chancellor of England with those of the Supreme Court of the United States. He was the highest interpreter of the law, the keeper of the king's conscience, and the final referee in all disputes, not only between subjects, but between the subjects and the sovereign. He could interfere, of his own authority, in any cause, and remove it to his own jurisdiction. He could review the royal decrees, and declare whether they were agreeable to law or not. He could exclude any of the king's ministers from the conduct of affairs, and call him to account for mal-administration. He was *ex officio* a permanent counsellor of the king, and had to accompany him wherever he went. He was regarded as a power between the king and the people—the controller of the one and protector of the other.

It is true that he owed his appointment to the king, removable for "a just cause or some considerable crime"; and in this limitation lay his defect, which was a very serious one in those days, when a good cause for the Justice's removal could so easily be found, and the temptation to fasten a crime on him was so great. There is no doubt, however, that the *Justicia*, whose very existence under that name is a proof of the liberty claimed by the Aragonese, did exert a powerful influence in the government, superior to that of the Judges in Castile, and of a kind which is without parallel in any cotemporary European state. This was all the more necessary, seeing that the Aragonese aristocracy, though less formidable in numbers than that of

Castile and of Leon, was of a specially turbulent and arrogant sort. The great barons, who affected to be peers of the king, claimed to derive their descent from twelve principal nobles who, sometime in the middle of the Ninth century, elected a king of Aragon upon his swearing to observe certain rules limiting his authority—being entitled, according to the letter of the compact then made, "to substitute any other ruler in his stead, even a pagan, if they pleased." These powerful barons were called *ricos hombres de natura*—noblemen by nature—to imply that they had not been created by the sovereign, and to distinguish them from the ordinary *ricos hombres*, advanced to that dignity by the king, who were called *de mesnada*, or of the household. No superior baron could be deprived of his fief except by the *Cortes;* and it was among these, the "nobles by nature," that the king was obliged to distribute the lands conquered from the Moors. In return the barons were required to render him military service; so that the feudal system may be said to have existed in Aragon and Catalonia before it prevailed in Castile, if it ever did so in the latter kingdom. According to the law, these barons had other privileges peculiar to themselves, and in excess of those enjoyed elsewhere by their class. They were allowed to throw off their allegiance to the king on certain conditions. They had the right of making war on each other without interference; and they did so frequently, with a zest and ferocity which tended not a little to spoil the otherwise excellent system of the Aragonese domestic administration. One other feature is to be noted in the government of Aragon, that, up to the Thirteenth century at least, the clergy had less power than in the other states—not so much because the people were less devoted to religion, but because of their strong and abiding jealousy of the temporal power of Rome. A large portion of the bishops and dignitaries of the eastern kingdom were drawn from Aquitaine and Provence, a fact which would alone account for the smaller influence exercised by the Church in the civil and political affairs of Aragon.

This independence of Rome was a characteristic of the people throughout Spain, and was a more important factor in shaping the national destinies than some native historians, in their zeal for orthodoxy, are willing to allow. From the date of their first conversion to Christianity, the Spaniards were among the most disobedient of all the nations to the central religious authority. The Goths, for the greater part of their reign, were Arians—scarcely admitted to be Christians. Even after they were restored to the Catholic fold under Recared I., they claimed and exercised entire liberty in their own country, using for centuries an independent ritual, which differed in some essential points from that of Rome. This, called the Mozarabic ritual, from the Mozarabes, who retained its use throughout the period of their subjection to the Moors, is characterised by the simplicity, beauty, and earnestness of the prayers, and especially by the absence of any mention of auricular confession. It was in force throughout all Christian Spain until the reign of Alfonso VI. That uxorious king, at the instance of his wife, Constance of Burgundy, who was under the influence of the Frenchman Bernard, the first Archbishop of Toledo, was induced, in spite of the protests of the native clergy, who were unanimous in favour of the ancient service, to insist upon the Roman missal being used in all the churches in place of the Mozarabic. But before that decision was arrived at the matter was submitted to what was called "the judgment of God," that is, trial by battle. As a concession to the people, a champion was appointed on the Mozarabic side to fight against the Roman. The duel took place in the presence of the king and court, with all the usual formalities. After a severe fight, the Mozarabic representative, to the delight of the populace, overcame his antagonist. Still the king was unconvinced. A second trial was arranged, this time, of two bulls, one baptised "Toledo," and the other "Rome." Again the national champion was victorious, the Mozarabic bull slaying the Roman. Once more the king refused to abide by the result, demanding the ordeal by fire. A fire was kindled in the king's presence, and after being duly consecrated, the two missals were cast into it, the king declaring that the one which was unconsumed should have the preference. The Roman was scorched by the flames; the Mozarabic came out whole and sound; when the king, in a passion, flung it back again, and insisted, in spite of all these clear indications of its lesser sanctity, that the Roman missal should be universally adopted; and adopted it was accordingly, everywhere but in one small chapel of Toledo Cathedral, which still preserves the daily use of the ancient Gothic ritual.[1]

These stories, gravely reported by native historians, usually jealous of the honour of their Church, throw a curious light, not only on the relations of the king to the ecclesiastical establishment, but on the attitude of the people to both. It is eminently characteristic of the age when the religion was nothing if not national, when the struggle for the faith was also a contest for independence, when truth as well as liberty was promoted by hard blows, and patriotism and orthodoxy were one—that a bull-fight should decide a question of breviary, and a liturgy be determined by single combat. Up to this date, at least, that is, in the latter half of the Twelfth century, the claims of the Pope of Rome to universal dominion over the churches was not acknowledged by the Spaniards— not even by the Aragonese and the Catalan, whose connection with Rome, through France, was closer than in Castile. But though the temporal jurisdiction of the Pope was resisted both by king and people, as indeed was the case up to the last—even in the reign of Isabel, specially designated *The Catholic*—there was no country in which the national Church was so closely linked to the national sentiment and so intimately allied to the national policy as in Spain. It mingled in every transaction of life; it was the abiding spirit and moving influence in the great transaction of all, which was every man's business, the recovery of the land from the Moors—the business

---

[1] From this incident is said to rise the old proverb, *Alla van leyes a donde quieren reyes*—" The laws go where the kings will."

which, however interrupted or suspended for other matters, never ceased to be the chief concern of every Castilian. It was the bishop whose voice called to war, who led the fighting. Thus piety went hand in hand with patriotism, and the true nationalist was he who was the good Catholic. Amidst these conditions and these environments, when the daily care of every man was to keep his store with his strong hand, and the only hope of increase was by taking from the infidel, the people and their faith grew together in that indissoluble connection which ever afterwards gave its peculiar character to the Spanish nation.

In those early ages, when Leon and Castile were battling for existence, there was small space for the development of the arts of peace. The Christians were a rude, unlettered people, doubtless far behind their Arab conquerors in civilisation. As they advanced from a small band of rustic mountaineers into a settled nation, the contact with their more refined and luxurious neighbours led to a higher civility. Even the competition in arms was fruitful of good, for out of it came chivalry, and the good manners which war teaches—the sense of mutual respect, the spirit of generous emulation, the cultivation of the sentiment of honour, which was carried afterwards to so great an excess as to become a national infirmity. By the Thirteenth century the dawn of a brighter day had begun to appear.

The long darkness, which lay for centuries like a pall upon Christendom, when art after art had gone out in Europe, and the lamp of knowledge flickered dimly in a few monastic cells, was perhaps more intense and of longer duration in Christian Spain than elsewhere. The people, engaged in continuous warfare, had small time for learning or literature. What little the Goths had possessed of letters, inherited from the Romans, had perished amidst the confusion and trouble of the Moorish conquest. In the mountains of Asturias, where every man was a soldier, the only art which could be safely practised was that of fighting.

It was not until the Spaniards had recovered their hold over the greater part of the country, and until the struggle for supremacy among the Christian states had resulted in the assured predominance of Castile in the north and centre, and of Aragon in the east, that the national genius began to assert itself in works of peace. By the middle of the Thirteenth century the long and doubtful conflict of the tongues born of the Latin—which was perhaps never a spoken language in the Peninsula after the Gothic conquest—had resolved itself into the victory, happily for literature, of the Castilian. The rival dialects of the Galician (from which descended the Portuguese) and the Catalan, or Valencian, the off-shoot of Provençal, were confined to the districts of the north, west, and the east respectively. Latin continued, indeed, to be the language of the Church, of the law, and of the official decrees up to the Twelfth century; but few, even among the most learned of the clergy, were able to write it with purity after the Eighth century. The speech of the people had come, by corruption and phonetic degradation, by the influence of physical, social, and political causes, by the nature of their occupations and the character of their surroundings to take a shape of its own—nearer Latin in genius than any of the children of Latin, but considerably modified in structure, with large additions to the vocabulary from the Arabic as from the Gothic. The nouns ceased from declension. The preposition was called in to help the case, just as the verb had to invoke an auxiliary. The final *us* was universally rejected for the final *o*. The infinitive dropped its tail vowel, and the noun got itself fitted with the article. According to the best authorities the Castilian language was fully formed, pretty nearly as it is now written and spoken, by the middle of the Twelfth century, though it was not perhaps until a century later that it came to be adopted as the universal speech of central Spain, the dialect of the court and of society.

The beginning of the national literature in Spain, as probably everywhere else, was the ballad. This eldest born of the poetic progeny rose quickly in the Peninsula to a stature and a dignity such as were attained in no other country of Europe. The ballads extant number nearly two thousand, and though for the greater part they are of a date subsequent to the period of which we are speaking, many of them retain the spirit and even the form of older compositions, transmitted from mouth to mouth, and all are characteristic of their age and their nation. They form a body of verse which is to be regarded as more than poetry. In the language of Richard Ford: "They are not merely ballads, but historical and national poems; they record events and popular notions; they speak out for the whole nation what lies in every man's heart; they are the means of expression to those who want words not feelings." It is the ballads which are the basis of all Spanish history; and in Spain at least there are no other literary documents so trustworthy. Handed down from mouth to mouth until the Sixteenth century, when they were first reduced to print, it is certain that the ballads have lost much in the process of oral transmission; but enough remains to furnish much valuable aid in reading the character of the people of old Spain.

Of the famous *Poem of the Cid* we have already spoken. It is the beginning of literature proper in Castile, and though intended to be rather history than poetry, it deserves to rank, for its poetical merit alone, as the first of European epics. The best authorities fix the date of the Poem at 1200; which would make it a generation older than Gonzalo de Berceo—the first known poet, avowedly such, who wrote in Castilian—chiefly devotional verses. But with Alfonso X. may be said to have been born the age of Spanish literature. He was a king, as Mariana says, "more fit for letters than for the government of his subjects; he studied the heavens, and watched the stars, but forgot the earth and lost his kingdom." He was a wise man, only in an abstract sense, to whom may be applied the saying of Tacitus—*capax imperii nisi imperasset*. He contributed greatly to the advancement of Castilian prose; and though his poetry was chiefly written in the inferior Galician dialect, he shows himself a master of the art of rhyming and of metre. As a lyricist Alfonso may probably claim to be the first who introduced into Spain that form of composition—a form not natural to the Castilians, and marking a higher degree of culture than that to which they had then reached. That the accomplishments of the tenth Alfonso can be safely taken to reflect the temper and spirit of the age, may be greatly doubted. By his subjects the king was held in undisguised contempt for his effeminate arts, and by his more knowing contemporaries chiefly regarded as a magician of supreme powers, who owed his science to unholy inspiration.

Of arts, industrial and useful, except such as administered to war or to religion, the early Spaniards had but little knowledge. From the beginning of the Eighth to the middle of the Eleventh century, when the kingdoms were yet in the process of making and battle with the Moor the one all-engrossing business of life, the condition of the people was perhaps ruder than that of the corresponding age in any country of Western Europe. Such civilisation as the later Visigoths had inherited from the Romans had expired. There was scarcely any intercourse with the outer Christian world. From Cordova came but a pale reflection of the light, touching but the highest souls—received with a resentful impatience, when admitted at all. The science taught by the Arabs had something suspicious to the mind of the true believer. Such learning could not be conceived as coming from aught but an unholy source. The luxuries created for the Arabs by their superior taste and skill in art were detested, even more than they were envied, as being the product of a reprobate and ungodly creed—the creed of the usurper and conqueror. The pride of the native Spaniard was to make himself as different as possible from the Moor. The flesh of the swine became to him the sweetest of meats, because it was rejected by the unfaithful. That the Moor loved frequent ablution was to the true Spaniard "old and rank," reason enough to eschew baths. In everything the Christians aspired to be unlike the Mahommedans—in their mode of life, their dwellings, their dress, their pursuits, exercises, and amusements.

Yet in spite of their national and religious antipathies there was much, as we have shown in the foregoing pages, that brought Christian and Moor together, and perhaps the real feeling between the peoples was less unfriendly than the chroniclers would have us believe. The larger and more catholic spirit such as shone in the relations between that good Catholic, Sancho Panza, and his fellow townsman, the Morisco Ricote, probably reflects the tone of the commerce between Moor and Spaniard, as to which there is much reason to believe that it was less bitter in the Tenth than in the Seventeenth century.

That the Moors had early attained to a very high degree of excellence in the arts, the monuments which they have left behind throughout all the country which they ruled sufficiently attest. Their palaces, mosques, castles, bridges, and aqueducts—of which the best are those of the period when Cordova was the centre of Arab civilisation—were works far beyond the capacity of the native Spaniards of that age. As builders, engineers, mechanics, and handicraftsmen the Moors were unrivalled. Their proficiency in all the industrial arts, their excellence in taste as in skill, made them the wonder as much as the envy and the scorn of their opponents, who yet were compelled to use the talents they affected to despise. To the true Spaniard it was a degradation to put his hands to these base mechanical uses—war being held to be the only trade of the good cavalier, and fighting the sole pursuit worthy of an honourable Castilian. Art and handicraft, even the cultivation of the soil, were relegated to the lowest of the people. In the early days the Mahommedan slaves were put to these disgraceful callings, from which, as far as possible, every Christian gentleman removed himself.

A curious proof of the extent to which all industry and art were monopolised by the Moors is furnished by the fact that, even in the building of their churches, the Christians had recourse to the skill and the knowledge of the infidel workmen. It was the *mudejar* [1] who drew the design, a *mudejar* who laid the stones, a *mudejar* who painted the walls. As seen in the two or three churches of the Tenth century which are still extant, as that of Santiago de Peñalva in the Vierzo, it is Moorish art throughout, with the horseshoe arch and the tracery and the capitols, as in Cordova, and of the same school from which came the glorious Mosque. Nor must these buildings,

---

[1] *Mudejar* was the name originally applied to the Moor who lived under Christian dominion—derived from the Arabic *moudeddjan*, a tributary.

ROMANESQUE CAPITALS.

which probably were more numerous than their few and scanty remains would seem to show, be taken to be Moorish places of worship converted to Christian uses, such as is the great Mosque itself, but churches designed and built for Christians by Mahommedan hands. Even when the Spaniards, in a later age, came to have a style of their own, or at least a style imported from Christian Europe, it was still the Moorish artist and the Moorish mason and carpenter who raised the walls and did the hewing and the carving.

It was not until the reign of Alfonso VI., in the later half of the Eleventh century, that the architecture borrowed from the Moors gave way to the Romanesque, introduced from France. Alfonso, the first to whom may be applied the name *Afrancesado*, as being the first who cultivated that connection with France which is held by patriotic Spaniards to have been so calamitous for their country, took from France, with his Burgundian wife, much ecclesiastical apparatus—including, besides the Roman missal, the Romanesque style, then dying out in Western Europe, though new to Spain. In the train of Queen Constance came Bernard, who was made Archbishop of Toledo — a Frenchman, who brought into his adopted country all the ardour of building which then distinguished the prelates of the age. Of his works in the Romanesque style, which replaced those edifices of Moorish art with which, till then, the Spanish kings had been content, very few entire specimens now remain. The next century witnessed the introduction of the Pointed or Gothic style, of

PORCH OF CATHEDRAL OF LERIDA.

which one of the purest and most beautiful examples is Leon Cathedral, which was begun in 1181 though not completed till 1303. In this latter style are most of the cathedrals and churches of Spain, with variations introduced by native architects, which have been overlaid since, in the process of ages, by much inferior modern work, so that it has become difficult to recognise, in any one building, the true Spanish-Gothic. The most perfectly finished specimen of the mixed style, and one of the most glorious remains of Christian art, is the famous *Portico de la Gloria*, on the western front of the Cathedral of Santiago, executed by *Maestro Mateo*, or Master Mathew, about 1168–1188.[1] In this, as in other works, there were employed, by the close of the Twelfth century, native architects and native builders, but they derived their inspiration and their teaching from France.

In all the common work of the building, as in the mechanical and industrial arts generally, the Spaniards were undoubtedly much indebted to the Moors, who, either as hired workmen or in after years as slaves captured in war, contributed greatly by their industry and skill to the development of the comforts of life and the wealth of the country.

[1] Of which a fac-simile is in the South Kensington Museum.

INTERIOR OF S. ISIDRO, WITH TOMBS OF KINGS.

VII.

THE REIGNS OF SANCHO IV., FERNANDO IV., AND ALFONSO XI. IN CASTILE—VICTORIES OVER THE MOORS—AFFAIRS OF ARAGON.

(1284–1387.)

UPON the death of Alfonso X. the Cortes, acting on behalf of the nation, set aside the provisions of the king's will, under which the dominion of Castile would have been once more sundered, and recognised Sancho, his eldest surviving son, as king—to the exclusion of the Infantes de la Cerda, the children of the deceased Fernando. Thereupon ensued a long train of intestinal troubles, fomented by the partisans of those who were disappointed of their expected heritage. Sancho IV., called *El Bravo*, though deficient in filial virtue, was a man of vigorous character, who had acquired popularity by his success in the wars against the Moors. Among the foremost of his enemies at home was his younger brother Don Juan, to whom the late king had bequeathed the city and territory of Seville. The province of Murcia had already been assigned in Alfonso's life-time to the La Cerdas. This kind of bequest, so common in the early history of Spain, which implied that the king's domain was but a parcel of properties which could be disposed of at the owner's will, proves how loose and unsettled was the kingdom of Castile, in which the idea of a nationality was hardly yet engendered. But for the select men of the country in the Cortes, who more than once interfered to save the integrity of the realm, the domain so painfully recovered from the Moors would have fallen in pieces, just as the Moorish Empire had done. The Infante Don Juan, prevented from seizing Seville, went into permanent rebellion, having for his chief adherent the powerful Count Lope de Haro. These two in the west, with the partisans of the La Cerdas in the east, involved the country in a perpetual disturbance as long as Sancho IV. reigned. The King of Aragon was induced to side with the rebels. Alfonso, the elder of the Infantes de la Cerda, was proclaimed King of Castile and Leon, and engaged in return for the support of Aragon to surrender Murcia to that kingdom. A desultory war between the two countries, in which each did much damage to the other without either obtaining any decisive advantage, continued for some years. At length a peace was patched up by the intervention of the King of France. Murcia was abandoned to the Infante Alfonso. The king's daughter Isabel was given in marriage to her cousin King Jayme of Aragon. Don Juan, the king's rebellious brother, was driven to take refuge with the Moors in Africa—sometimes engaged in their civil wars, sometimes joining with them in their attacks upon Christian Spain.

King Sancho, the Valiant—who earned that title by his prowess in the field—in the brief intervals of legitimate war allowed him by his Christian kinsmen and competitors, gained some important places from the Moors in Andalusia. He conquered Tarifa in 1292—a strong frontier town on the coast, at the furthest extremity of Spain—which dangerous post, fronting Murcia, was committed to the charge of Alonso de Guzman, the first of that noble name so famous in Spanish history. His story is connected with a deed of exalted virtue worthy of the classic ages of old Iberian and Roman heroism. Don Alonso, who had pledged his honour to the king that he would hold Tarifa for a twelvemonth, found himself beleaguered by an overwhelming host of Moors, serving with whom was the recreant Prince Juan, the king's brother. Being unable to overcome the stout resistance made by the governor, the besiegers brought out Don Alonso's eldest son, a lad of nine years, who had been entrusted to Prince Juan's keeping as a page, and threatened to slay him before his father's eyes if the town was not surrendered. But Don Alonso made answer that he held the town for his lord the king, and would yield it to none else. Then drawing his dagger he threw it to the Moors from the top of the wall, crying: "Kill him with this if you will, for I would rather have honour without a son than a son without honour." Whereupon the traitor Prince Juan plunged the dagger in the boy's throat, in a rage at being foiled in his base purpose. When the king heard of this deed he honoured Don Alonso with the name of *El Bueno* or *The Good*, which was borne henceforth by all his posterity—however little the Guzmans, in after years, who came to be Dukes of Medina Sidonia, were deserving of the epithet. It is curious to read in the ballads that this same patriotic hero Alonso the Good was, shortly before this date, in the employment of Aben Yussuf, the Moorish king, at the "customary wages"—distinguishing himself, in a service evidently not considered unbecoming a Christian knight, by slaying a terrible serpent and training a fierce lion, so that he filled all the land with wonder and envy of his singular prowess.

After a distracted reign of eleven years, Sancho IV. gave place to his eldest son Fernando, who being only nine years old at his accession in 1295, the regency of the kingdom was entrusted to the queen-mother.

The crown rested as uneasily on Fernando's head as it had done on his father's. A new crop of pretenders to the throne and claimants of the king's estates sprang up, greatly favoured by the disorder into which the country had fallen during a long course of civil war. The irrepressible Don Juan, the king's uncle, aided by the Moorish King of Granada, asserted his claim to the crown. The Count de Haro laid his hands on Biscay as being a family estate. The King of Portugal took advantage of his neighbour's helplessness to seize some frontier places. The ever-disloyal Laras, commissioned by the queen-regent to recover Biscay and furnished with moneys for the purpose, went over, with characteristic perfidy, to the rebels. Amidst all these troubles the hapless queen-mother found a new enemy in her partner in the regency, the Infante Enrique, the young king's grand-uncle. The climax of the country's misfortunes seemed to be reached in 1296, when a league was formed between the La Cerdas, the Laras, the rebel princes, and Aragon, under the sanction of France, Portugal, and Granada, to divide the patrimony of Fernando IV. among them. The Infante Juan, the king's uncle, was to have Leon, with Galicia and Seville; to Alfonso de la Cerda was allotted Castile; and to the King of Aragon, the province of Murcia.

The fortunes of Fernando IV., himself a man of small ability and of feeble character, were now reduced to their lowest point, and with treachery in the innermost circle of the king's advisers in the person of the co-regent, the Infante Enrique, who diverted the money voted by the Cortes for the defence of the state into his own pockets, there seemed to be no way of safety open to the distracted country. Don Juan was proclaimed King of Leon, and Don Alfonso de la Cerda, King of Castile. While the Aragonese invaded the kingdom from the east, the Portuguese seized several fortresses on the frontier, the Moorish King of Granada profiting by the opportunity to ravage all Christian Andalusia. The kingdom was saved by the fortitude and devotion of the queen-mother, aided by dissensions among the king's enemies. The Pope intervened to draw Aragon away into the Sicilian war; while Portugal was induced to desert her allies and make peace with King Fernando, which was cemented by a double marriage between the royal families. The troublous and inglorious reign of Fernando IV. came to a sudden end, with a moral which the pious chroniclers love to point. Two knights of his court, being accused of the murder of one of the king's nobles, were put to a summary death, without proper trial, in spite of their protestations of innocence. Before their heads were laid on the block they cited their false

RUINS OF MONASTERY OF S. JUAN DE DUERO AT SORIA.

king to appear before the judgment seat of God within thirty days. Before that time had elapsed King Fernando was found dead on his couch. He left an only son, Alfonso XI., who being but a few months old on his accession, there ensued another long period of confusion and trouble. There were, first, disputes about the guardianship of the infant king. The post was sought by the king's uncle, Don Pedro, and his grand-uncle, Don Juan; as well as by the two queens, his grandmother and his mother.

The contest was attempted to be settled by the Cortes, in 1313, but the deputies voting equally between the rival rulers, they fell to war. Eventually they agreed to govern jointly. The two regents then engaged in a war against Granada, which began auspiciously; but falling out with each other through jealousy their end was disastrous. In a great battle fought near Granada, in 1319, Ismail, the Moorish king, won a decisive victory over the Christians, the two princes being slain. Once more there was a struggle for the guardianship of the young king, which ended in the office being shared by two members of the royal house—Don Felipe, the king's uncle, and Don Juan Manuel, a direct descendant of San Fernando. Then a third claimant for the office appeared in the person of another Don Juan, surnamed *El Tuerto*, or The Crooked—son of the prince of the same name who had been so great a disturber of the realm in the previous reigns. Fernando de la Cerda also again appeared on the scene;[1] and once more there was a general hurly-burly, till Alfonso, in 1324, summoned the Cortes at Valladolid and assumed the sovereignty,

---

[1] The La Cerdas, as representatives of the elder son of Alfonso X., never ceased to urge their claims to the crown. Long after they had become reconciled to the throne, the head of their house, the Duke of Medina Celi, on the accession of a new king, would put in an appearance and formally claim the title, for which offence he would be fined in a nominal sum. The farce was kept up down to the accession of Fernando VII., in 1808.

being then in his thirteenth year. Juan *el Tuerto* continuing to disturb the kingdom, he was got rid of at last by assassination. Juan Manuel, who made for himself a name in letters as the author of a collection of tales called *El Conde Lucanor* and as a munificent patron of learning, and was also conspicuous as a soldier, winning many battles over the Moors, remained for some time longer in open rebellion, but was reconciled to the king at last and died in his service.

Alfonso's campaign against the Moors in Granada is almost the only distinctive episode of his reign. He was one of the most warlike of the kings, and his victories, though hardly earned and barren of results, were honourable to his character as a soldier and contributed no little to the final deliverance. The fortress of Gibraltar, whose importance seems scarcely to have been realised in these times, had been taken from the Moors, in 1309, by Alonso *el Bueno*. It was recovered by Mahommed IV., the King of Granada, to the great scandal of Christian Spain—the commander of the force sent to its relief diverting the money which should have paid his soldiers to his own uses. Alfonso XI. thereupon set out with a large army to attempt the recovery of the lost fortress, whose value seems to have been new, for the first time, recognised. Although he defeated the Moors in a great battle, Alfonso was compelled to retire from the siege, being recalled to the affairs of his own kingdom, which was now being exposed to the attacks of his neighbour of Navarre. Having beaten the Navarrese, Alfonso then turned his arms against Portugal, ravaging the southern provinces of that kingdom, while the Portuguese king was doing the same to Alfonso's northern province of Galicia. The Pope at last having intervened to make peace between the two Christian kings, Alfonso resumed his more legitimate work of fighting the enemies of the faith. The Moors, having been reinforced by a large body of Africans sent by the Emperor of Morocco, thought fit to violate the truce which had been made between Castile and Granada by an invasion of the territory of the former. At this time the city of Xeres was the furthest outpost of the Christian dominion towards Granada, while Algeciras, in the bay facing Gibraltar, was regarded as the key of the Moorish position—being strongly fortified and garrisoned by a large army under Abu-Melik, son of Abu-l-Hassan, the Emperor of Morocco, with the flower of the Moorish chivalry. Abu-Melik opened the campaign by sending out a body of horse from Algeciras to ravage the country of the Christians, following up his advance guard with his whole army, and taking town after town until he had reached the suburbs of Xeres. In a skirmish which took place near Alcalá de los Gazules, Abu-Melik was surprised and died of exhaustion— or, as the chronicler says, of fear—which inflamed the wrath of the Moorish Emperor, his father, and made him more than ever resolved to clear the land of the Christians. In a great battle at sea, Alfonso's fleet was destroyed and the Castilian admiral slain, by a superior Moorish armament. The Emperor of Morocco himself in person, with a vast army, laid siege to Tarifa, a frontier town, which had been in possession of the Castilians since 1290. King Alfonso summoned all his principal noblemen and prelates to a solemn council at Seville, in 1340, and seated in state, with his crown on one side and his sword on the other, made a speech to the assembly, in which he laid before his estates very candidly the whole situation, asking their advice as to what he should do, "for he was but one man, and without all of them could do no more than one man could do." And some of them, the king being absent, said that Abu-l-Hassan had a very great force of men, and that it was certain the King of Granada would aid him with all his power; and that those who were with the King of Castile were not so many as the fourth part of the Moors; and that they should take care not to put their lord the king into a peril so great; for were he beaten, so great was the host of the Moors, and so strong, so cruel, and so stubborn was the King Abu-l-Hassán, that in a very little time a very great portion of the Christians' land would be subdued; therefore, it was better to make some composition with the King Abu-l-Hassan and give him up that town of Tarifa; and if they could so arrange with the Moors, it was better than fighting with such a multitude of people. The manlier counsel, however, prevailed, which was for giving succour to Tarifa, inviting the Kings of Aragon and of Portugal to render their aid to preserve the town from the infidels. The King of Portugal responded to the appeal in a manner worthy of his reputation as a loyal and faithful knight, coming in person to Seville. The King of Aragon sent his ships, under his admiral, to cruise off the coast. The allied army, under the two kings, encountered the Moorish host on the banks of the Salado, a little river near Tarifa ; and here was fought, on the 28th of October, 1340, one of the most important battles which ever took place between the Christians and the Moors, in which the latter were defeated with enormous loss. Cannon are said to have been used in this battle, for the first time in Europe. One of the sons of the Moorish Emperor was slain, and his whole *harem* captured. Abu-l-Hassan himself might have been taken had the Aragonese admiral done his duty ; but though the fleet was maintained, as the Castilian chronicler avers, with the moneys of Castile, the Aragonese not only would not stir out of his ship, but refused to let any of his crew give aid to the Christians.

The fame of this great victory, which finished the work began at Las Navas de Tolosa in 1212, was blazed throughout Christendom, to the great increase of King Alfonso's glory. Great numbers of Christians from all parts of Europe came to swell Alfonso's host, somewhat to the inconvenience of his quartermasters and his commissariat ; for, as usual, but insufficient provision had been made for the support of the army, so that the victory could not be followed up. King Alfonso sent news of this triumph of the true faith to Pope Benedict, at Avignon, together with some living trophies of the day—a train of Moorish captives, with the flags taken in the battle, and the horse he had himself bestridden, with the pennant which had been borne before him—asking the Holy Father for some aid towards his maintenance. To the last point there seems to have been no response, though great rejoicings were made and thanksgivings offered for the signal triumph which the Cross had won over the Crescent.

The next enterprise which engaged King Alfonso was the capture of Algeciras, which had served the invading Moors for a landing-place ever since the days of Tarik. Being situated within a day's journey of the opposite port of Ceuta, it was of enormous value to the enemy in Africa, as the Spanish end of the bridge across the Straits. The Moors being still masters at sea, the Africans could land at their pleasure in aid of their fellow-religionists. King Alfonso seems to have had some difficulty in persuading his estates of the advisability of attacking the enemy at Algeciras, so formidable were the defences of that place, which was furnished with all the newest engines of war. At last, in 1342, the king was enabled to gather an army to encompass Algeciras on the land side. The King of Aragon withdrawing his fleet caused much inconvenience, for the Moors were enabled to draw supplies from the other side of the water. The siege, if it can be so called, lasted for over twenty months, and is one of the most memorable in the annals of Spain. The besiegers seem to have been exposed to privations and hardships quite as great as those suffered by the besieged. The defence was as obstinate as the attack was valiant, and so great a noise did the fighting make throughout Christendom that numerous gallant knights from all parts of Europe came to Alfonso's camp, to be exercised in the art and mystery of battle.[1]

Even the restless Don Juan Manuel laid aside for a time his schemes of sedition for the more attractive pursuit of Moor-baiting. Among other distinguished gentlemen who came from foreign parts to help the Christian enterprise, the ancient chronicler especially records " el Conde de Arbi et el Conde de Solusber " (the Earls of Derby and Salisbury), men of high class in the kingdom of England (Edward III. was then the English king), who came to the Moorish war " for the salvation of their souls and to see and know King Alfonso." The two Earls being in Spain, and hearing of the great fight to be fought, took horse and made such great haste to reach the camp as that they left all their companions behind. Of the Earl of Derby it is said that he was of the royal family of England,[2] while the Earl of Salisbury had lost an eye in one of the many battles he had fought. There came also some nobles from France, such as the Comte de Foix and his brother Roger Bernal, " Viscomte de Castiel-

---

[1] Chaucer's " verray perfight gentil knight " is distinguished for that—

" In Gernade atte siege hadde he be
Of Algesir."

[2] This must be Henry, nephew of Thomas of Lancaster beheaded in the Barons' war of 1312, who was son of Edmund, brother to King Edward I. Both the English earls were men of great experience in war. Among the other allies of Alfonso in his wars with the Moors was the good Lord James Douglas, who being on his way to the Holy Land with the heart of Robert Bruce, stopped to do some fighting in Spain. It was in the battle of Teba, in 1328, that Lord James Douglas threw the silver casquet in which he wore the Bruce's heart into the thickest of the fray, saying : " Pass first in fight, as thou wast wont to do, and Douglas will follow thee ! "

bon," with several companies of Gascons, to whom the king assigned quarters apart from the Englishmen, seeing that their two nations were then at war. Presently came also the King of Navarre with a small following, but a welcome supply of meal, barley, wine, and bacon. Of some of these foreign auxiliaries the chronicler gives no good report, being especially severe on the Comte de Foix and his brother, who being with difficulty persuaded to head a party which was sent against the walls under cover of a shield— "for up to that time they had essayed no feat of arms since their arrival before Algeciras"— bore themselves so tamely as to give the Moors an occasion for triumph and cause much scandal in the camp. The Comte de Foix, it is complained, was fonder of giving private counsel to the king than of fighting; while his brother would set them laughing by his silly boasts, "without shame and ever to his own enhancement." At last the Comte de Foix declared he would serve no longer unless he was paid, to which the king consented, fearing to lose his contingent of Gascons, assigning two hundred *maravedis* a month for his mess and fifty to his brother. The Comte de Foix and the Viscomte abode but a small time in the camp, departing without beat of drum on some pretext that they had to look after their vassals at home. The King of Navarre also went away on a plea of sickness. The Christians suffered very severely in the last months of the siege from want of food, and though generally successful in their combats in the open field, seem to have been unable to achieve anything against the walls owing to the superiority of the Moorish archers and engineers. At sea it was with great difficulty that the Genoese were persuaded to remain with their hired ships, which were not strong enough to intercept the passage of reinforcements across the Straits.

At last Algeciras was starved into surrender, Abu-l-Hassan ordering the place to be given up, which was done on March 24, 1344, to the great joy and relief of the Spaniards. A truce of ten years was made between Castile and Granada, which was broken by Alfonso on the pretence that the Moorish king had violated his promise to do him homage. A Castilian army invested Gibraltar, but a plague broke out in the Christian camp of which the king died in 1350, leaving as his heir his only legitimate son Pedro, of whom, if one of his historians is to be credited, his dying father said that he "grieved very bitterly to leave such an inheritor as lord of the kingdom."

The transactions in the neighbouring state of Aragon during this period now demand our attention. King Jayme the Conqueror left as heir to his greatly extended kingdom the favourite of his many sons, Pedro, whose mother was the Hungarian princess, Yolande. Pedro III. was married to Constance, the daughter and heiress of Manfred, the Norman king of Sicily, out of which connection flowed great and troublous issues for Aragon and for Europe—paving the way as it did for the entrance of a Spanish state within the Italian system and the development of the Aragonese dominion by foreign conquest and annexation. Pedro's first years as king were spent in bringing his turbulent barons into obedience and

TOMBS OF KINGS OF ARAGON IN MONASTERY OF POBLET.

in settling the quarrels regarding the succession which had broken out during his father's time. How he came to extend the power of Aragon beyond the sea is an episode which, however romantic and notable, belongs rather to the history of Europe than to the story of the Spanish nation. Aragon, having no Moors to subdue within her bounds, being now bordered by Christian states on every side, with Murcia, a province of Castile, as a buffer between her and the sole remaining Mahommedan state of Granada, could expand no otherwise than by those maritime adventures for which her Catalans had always a strong taste. An opportunity was shortly afforded for the entrance of Aragon into the quarrel between the Guelfs and the Ghibellines of Italy, the outcome of which was the conquest of Naples and of Sicily by Charles of Anjou, brother to the King of France, who was aided and abetted by the Pope. Sicily was occupied by the French in 1266. The people of the island, groaning under the tyranny of their conquerors, appealed to Pedro, King of Aragon, for protection, regarding him as their liege lord in virtue of his being the husband of Constance, the daughter of their late king Manfred. Pedro prepared to assert his rights in spite of the fulminations of Rome and the threats of France. Then occurred in 1282 that rising against the French, accompanied by the wholesale massacre known in history as the Sicilian Vespers. The way was thus cleared for the King of Aragon, who got ready a great armament at Barcelona and set sail for Sicily. In order to disguise the real object of the expedition from the Pope, he pretended that it was directed against the Barbary states. Landing on the Sicilian coast Pedro was enthusiastically received and proclaimed King of Sicily. The siege of Messina, then closely invested by the French, was raised, and in a naval fight the fleet of Aragon was victorious over that of France. Charles had to fly from his newly-acquired kingdom, in spite of the support of the Pope, who excommunicated the Aragonese and proclaimed a crusade against King Pedro. The King of France retaliated on Pedro by invading Catalonia at the head of a large army, and taking Gerona and some other strong places—being joined in his enterprise by King Pedro's brother Jayme, the King of Majorca. The invaders were ultimately repelled by land, and the French fleet shattered off the coast by the Aragonese under their famous admiral, Roger de Lauria.

King Pedro III. died in 1285, soon after these events, and was succeeded in Aragon by his eldest son, Alfonso—the crown of Sicily being left to his second son, Jayme. Alfonso was engaged in putting down his uncle, the King of Majorca, when his father died, and he gave great offence to his nobles by not coming back at once to have himself duly proclaimed by the Cortes, before assuming the functions of king in the Balearic Islands. His short reign of five years was chiefly remarkable for an extraordinary development of the power of the great nobles, who insisted upon appointing not only all the king's ministers but his domestic servants, and at whose instance the office of the great Justiciary was elevated into supreme importance. Alfonso was compelled to submit to these encroachments on his authority for fear of losing the support of the nobles in the war with France and Rome. In his negotiations with his foreign enemies regarding Sicily Alfonso had the assistance of Edward I. of England, whose daughter Eleanor was promised to him for a wife. An interview took place between the two monarchs and the French pretender to Sicily at Conflans, with a view to adjusting all difficulties with the Pope; but the Pope was obstinate, and nothing came of it except that Sicily was confirmed in the possession of Jayme, the King of Aragon's brother.

King Alfonso III. died suddenly soon after, in 1291, and leaving no issue, the double crown of Aragon and Sicily went to Jayme, the second of that name. At the instance of the Pope and the French king Jayme was persuaded to give up his kingdom of Sicily to Charles of Anjou, now King of Naples, receiving in exchange the hand of Charles's daughter and restoration to the favour of Rome. This base bargain, one of the terms of which was that Jayme should use all the forces of Aragon to coerce the people of Sicily who had been so faithful to him, was carried out to the letter. The Sicilians refused to submit to the yoke of Charles of Anjou, and chose for their king Don Fadrique, Jayme's brother. Jayme then collected a large force, with which he passed over into Italy. In the war which ensued between the two brothers the Sicilians bravely maintained their independence; and though the Aragonese were victorious at sea they could gain no footing in the island. Jayme at length abandoned the unnatural and disgraceful contest, and left the King of Naples to fight his own battles with the Sicilians, upon the pretence that he was wanted at home. Nor in his domestic affairs was he any happier. He joined with the Castilian malcontents in taking up the claim of the La Cerdas, with a view to acquiring Murcia for himself. Afterwards he was reconciled with Fernando IV., the Castilian king, who gave his daughter to be wife to Jayme's eldest son. But the strange behaviour of this young prince very nearly led to a breach between the two crowns. He protested violently against being married to any one, and declared that he would rather give up his right to the crown and enter a cloister. He was dragged almost by force to the altar, and ran away from his bride after the ceremony. It does not appear that his aversion to the marriage state, which gave great scandal to both the courts, arose from any other cause than an unconquerable propensity to the lowest forms of vice on the part of this graceless prince; who, according to his own wishes, was formally deprived of his rights, which were bestowed on his next brother, Alfonso. There is no other event worthy of mention in King Jayme's reign, except that he acquired, at the instance of the Pope and by way of recompence for Sicily, the sovereignty of the islands of Sardinia and Corsica.

This possession involved the next king, Alfonso IV., in much trouble. Instigated by the Genoese, who were jealous rivals of the Catalans in commerce, the Sardinians rose against their new masters. A desultory war between Aragon and the Genoese at sea continued to rage during all this reign, which was marked by nothing of more importance than a quarrel in the king's family—his heir, Prince Pedro, falling out with his step-mother, who was Leonora, sister to Alfonso XI. of Castile.

Pedro IV. succeeded on his father's death in 1336. His reign was notable for nothing else than a long-continued struggle between the sovereign and the great nobles. The quarrels respecting their several powers were complicated by a dispute between the Aragonese and the Catalonian deputies about the place where the king should be crowned—not the first as it was not the last of the many jealousies between Saragossa and Barcelona. A question also now arose in regard to the succession. Pedro had only a daughter by his Queen Maria of Navarre, and he wished to secure the throne to her, in exclusion of his collateral male heirs. Pedro had contrived to add the clergy to the number of his enemies, by crowning himself instead of receiving the crown from the hands of the Pope's delegate. At a convocation of the estates at Saragossa there was a furious scene of disorder, the hall being filled by the confederate barons and their retainers, who were opposed to the king, and Pedro narrowly escaped with his life. A civil war then devastated the kingdom, which ended after various changes of fortune in the triumph of Pedro, the people suddenly turning round from the side of the nobles, and in consideration of ancient rights being confirmed rallying to the king's party. Pedro, who was as perfidious and cruel as his namesake and contemporary of Castile, lived to reign for more than fifty years, in perpetual strife either with his subjects, his kinsmen, or his neighbours. His foreign wars were conducted with equal recklessness and unwisdom. He was involved in a struggle with the Genoese for the possession of Sardinia. He tried to regain the island of Sicily, which had passed out of the dominion of Aragon, and he even sent an expedition to the Morea, where a colony of Aragonese was established, to secure the country for himself. But these outside transactions of Aragon have little to do with our story. They rather retarded than assisted the development of Spain. Pedro III. ended his tumultuous and chequered career in 1387.

VIII.

REIGN OF PEDRO THE CRUEL—THE GREAT CIVIL WAR—ENGLAND AND FRANCE IN SPAIN.

(1350–1369.)

WITH Alfonso XI. ended the warrior kings of Castile. Thenceforward, for a hundred years and more, the history of Spain is one of political development rather than increment by conquest from the outside enemy. Under Alfonso's successors, until Isabel the Catholic took up and ended the crusade, the war with the Moors, who were now concentrated within the narrow bounds of the territory of Granada, was suspended, or only fitfully and intermittently waged, in desultory frays and frontier skirmishes. The great design which had never wholly been lost sight of during six centuries and a half—the recovery of the Spanish soil from the Mahommedans—ceased to occupy the attention of the Kings of Castile, who now began to enter into the general field of European policy, as those of Aragon had done some two generations before.

Pedro I., who on his accession to the throne was only in his sixteenth year, was not long in justifying the gloomy forebodings of his dying father, and in giving proof of the temper which has earned for him his evil name. His first business was to pursue his father's mistress Leonora de Guzman and her eldest son Enrique, whom Alfonso had been with difficulty dissuaded from making his heir. Leonora fled for refuge to her own city of Medina Sidonia. Thence she was drawn, by the treacherous assurances of Albuquerque the king's minister, to Seville, which Pedro had made his capital. Here she was imprisoned, and after being transferred from one fortress to another, was put to death by order of the queen-mother, her rival. Her son Enrique narrowly escaped falling into the same trap. This was the first of a long series of murders, perpetrated in cold blood and with circumstances of perfidy and brutality such as shocked even the hardened sentiment of the Castilians, accustomed as they were to see human life held in light estimation. The *adelantado* of Castile, an officer of the highest rank, was the next of Pedro's victims. He was brought into the presence chamber and there butchered before the king—his body being thrown out of the palace window. The Cortes suggesting that Pedro should take a wife from the royal house of France, the king, who had already become enamoured of the beautiful Maria de Padilla—whose love was the one bright spot in all his life—made choice of Blanche of Bourbon, niece to the French King John. Pedro went to meet his bride at Valladolid, where the marriage was celebrated with much splendour; but left her after two days to return to his mistress Maria de Padilla, in spite of the remonstrances of his mother and aunt. Poor Blanche, of whom an idle story is told in one of the chronicles that she was bewitched by a certain Jew magician her enemy, who turned her girdle into a great and terrible serpent when the king went to visit her, never had any more of her graceless husband's company. She was shortly afterwards shut up in the fortress of Arévalo where no one was allowed to see her—to the scandal of the whole realm and the great indignation of her people in France. The favourite Albuquerque now fell into disgrace, being replaced by a member of the family of Padilla. To indulge a passing fancy for a beautiful widow, Juana de Castro, Pedro's next freak was to insist upon marrying her—silencing the scruples of the bishops of Avila and Salamanca by declaring that his marriage with Blanche of Bourbon was invalid, and that as king he could marry whom he pleased. Out of the great fear which we are told they had of him the bishops did as they were ordered, and the wedding with Doña de Castro took place publicly at Cuellar, the lady being proclaimed as Queen Juana. After a short time she was abandoned for ever, Pedro mocking her with the trick he had played upon her.

Up to this time Pedro was playing with his half-brothers, the sons of Leonora de Guzman, like a cat with mice—pretending to entrust them with important missions, but laying his schemes for catching them in some act of treachery. The brothers, on their part, were not unequal to the contest Being despatched to Portugal to inveigle Albuquerque from his retreat in that kingdom, they formed a secret league with the disgraced favourite in their own interest. Don Fadrique was Master of the Order of Santiago, by virtue of which office he held many strong castles, of which the king vainly tried to possess himself. A desultory civil war now raged throughout the kingdom provoked by Pedro's freaks of tyranny, at the head of which, though not openly in arms, were Don Enrique and his brothers. On the pretence that Queen Blanche was not safe in her prison of Arévalo Pedro ordered her to be taken to the Alcázar of Toledo. On Blanche's arrival in that city she was the object of an extraordinary demonstration on the part of the citizens. They rose in a body against her guards and formed themselves into a league for her protection, joining hands with the malcontent nobles, and sending for Don Fadrique, Fernando de Castro (the brother of Pedro's victim Juana), and Albuquerque to help them with their companies. Even the Queen-mother Maria, who had hitherto sided with her son, took part with the leaguers. Many important cities sent their adhesion to the cause of the insurgents, which was actively favoured by the Infantes of Aragon. The main object of this rising, though it was probably not the sole one, was to compel Pedro to acknowledge his lawful wife Blanche of Bourbon, whom he had treated so foully. Finding his opponents too powerful for him, Pedro resorted to his usual shifts of lying and dissembling, until he had got supplies from his Cortes at Burgos, on the promise of living with Queen Blanche. Then he managed to obtain an entrance into Toledo, the citizens being persuaded that he desired to fulfil his duty to Queen

Blanche; when his first act was to send her away under a strong guard to a safer prison at Siguenza.

Once more master of Toledo Pedro began a general slaughter of all those who had lately opposed his will, including the principal citizens and the followers of Don Enrique and Don Fadrique. Afterwards the king went to Toro the chief seat of the leaguers, which through the treachery or the weakness of the townsmen was given up to him, and there, in the presence of the queen, his mother, and of the wife of Don Enrique, he commanded a number of gentlemen to be butchered one after another, so that the queen, at the sight of the blood, fell into a dead faint with her ladies. On recovering, seeing the mutilated corpses round her, she began to cry out loudly, cursing her son the king and declaring that this deed would shame him for ever. And then she got leave to go to her father in Portugal, and so parted mother and son. Many of the barons whom Pedro could not seize, fled into Aragon and joined the king of that country in a war against Castile, which endured for many years.

Don Enrique, the king's eldest half-brother, had fled to France, and thenceforward was at open war with Pedro. But Don Fadrique, another brother, the Master of Santiago, had made his submission to the tyrant and was apparently in his good graces. Having returned to Seville from an expedition against the king's enemies in Murcia, Don Fadrique went to pay his respects to the king, whom he found playing at backgammon in his private chamber in the Alcázar, and was well received. His assassination by the king's guards in the very presence of the king is a sample of Pedro's way of ridding himself of those whom he feared. Suspecting nothing, the Master went to the apartments of Maria de Padilla, who being, as the chroniclers all agree, tender-hearted and of a good disposition and knowing what was the fate to which he was destined, put on so sad a look that all could guess that something evil was impending. Other hints Don Fadrique received, but either would not or could not profit by them. Going up to where the king lay with other gentlemen of the Court, he found Pedro within shut doors, who presently, appearing at a wicket, called out to his guards to "seize the Master"; then to his archers, "Kill the Master of Santiago!" Then they set upon Don Fadrique, who tried to defend himself, but could not draw his sword, so they slew him with blows on the head. His squires and attendants, who were waiting outside, were also taken and slain. One of them flying for his life sought shelter in the room where Maria de Padilla was with her daughters, and catching hold of the lady Beatrice, tried to interpose her between himself and his assassins. But the king caused Doña Beatrice to be taken from his arms, and himself struck the man with a poniard, and left him to be butchered by one of his guards. Then the king returned to where the Master was lying, and finding that he was still breathing, drew his dagger and gave it to a servant, and made him deal the death-stroke.

Many other individual murders did Pedro order, of those who had opposed his will, especially in the matter of Queen Blanche, throughout the towns which had been most disobedient. He sent an emissary to Biscay to kill Don Tello, another of his half-brothers, whom he even followed in person in a ship, when Don Tello took a fishing-boat and escaped to St. Jean de Luz, in the district of Bayonne, which was then English territory.

An attempt was made in succeeding ages to clear the memory of Pedro the Cruel—to prove at least that though he robbed and murdered the nobles he spared the people, that he was a lover of justice and a defender of popular rights. Philip II., who can hardly be said to be altogether a competent witness of what constituted a just and clement monarch, complimented Pedro with the name of *El Justiciero*. The balladists and the dramatists, including Calderon, have also taken a favourable view of Pedro's character. He might have been given to blood-letting on too light occasion, but he was the mildest-mannered man, when all was said, who would see no murder done by others. Allowing that Pedro de Ayala, his chief chronicler—who was however an eye-witness of most of the deeds he records—was not entirely without prejudice as being afterwards a servant of Enrique of Trastamara, it is impossible to clear Pedro's memory of a load of iniquity, of base perfidy, meanness, and wanton and inhuman brutality, greater than belongs to any other monarch in modern history, except Ivan the Fourth of Russia. Unfortunately for the theory which seeks to whitewash this monster, who seems to have shed blood for the animal gratification it gave him, every part of his history is consistent with his taste for cruelty. He was as devoid of generosity as of pity, as reckless of the truth as of life, as greedy of gain as of blood—a false knight, a perjured husband, a brutal son—not even loyal to the love which was the one bright gleam in his dark history—the love for the hapless Maria de Padilla, of whom there is none to speak a word of ill. He has been likened to our Richard III., but the comparison is most unjust to the Plantagenet, who never killed but on provocation and out of deep policy.[1] Some of Pedro's actions are indeed scarcely consistent with a belief in his sanity. Returning from his fruitless chase of Don Tello to Bilbao, he sent for Don Juan, his cousin, who claimed the lordship of Biscay in virtue of his wife, and had him butchered out of sheer wantonness—setting his servants to take away Don Juan's dagger as in a joke, and the chamberlain to embrace him so that he might not approach the king, while an archer struck Juan on the head with a mace. Then the corpse was cast out of the window, while the king cried out aloud to the Biscayans, "There take your Lord of Biscay whom you asked for!" He then caused to be murdered his own aunt Doña Leonora, of Aragon, mother of the above Don Juan, for nothing but because Aragon would not make peace with him—being compelled to get Moors to do the job, as no Castilian could be induced to undertake it, says King Pedro IV. of Aragon in his memoirs. A certain priest coming before him to say that St. Domingo had ap-

---

[1] Richard III. was a direct descendant of King Pedro, being the great-grandson of Edmund of York, who married Isabel, Pedro's daughter.

peared to him in a dream and counselled him to tell the king that he would meet his death at the hands of his brother Enrique, Pedro insisted that the priest must have been prompted by Don Enrique himself, and so ordered the poor dreamer to be burnt alive. The murder of the Archbishop of Santiago, when the king himself was at the lowest ebb of his fortunes and his subjects at the height of their disgust and rage at his tyrannies, was an item of almost inconceivable brutality in this tale of horrors. For no other motive apparently than because the Archbishop held some important castles which Pedro desired for himself, he caused the prelate to be treacherously slain at the door of his cathedral. But the climax of Pedro's iniquities—a crime of incredible meanness and brutishness, for which there is no parallel in the annals of Moordom itself—was his betrayal and murder of the Moorish king, Abu Said, of Granada, who came to implore Pedro's help against his rival Mahommed-ibn-Yussuf. Having his richest jewels with him (among which was the famous ruby now the chief gem of the English regal crown), the Red King, as he was called, took his way as a suppliant to the court of Pedro at Seville, attended by three hundred courtiers and two hundred footmen. The king received the Moor with fair words, and ordered him and his suite to be lodged handsomely. Then learning of the rich jewels which they possessed, Pedro sent a party of armed men, who seized the persons of the Red King and his attendants, and relieved them of their jewels and money. The King of Granada was despoiled even of his raiment, and then, meanly clad, was led out into the plain adjoining the city and mounted upon an ass, and with him thirty-six of his Moors, who were then severally done to death, on the pretence of having betrayed King Pedro in his war with Aragon. Abu Said, when he received the first blow and recognised his doom, cried out to Pedro in his Arabic, "Oh, what a scurvy chivalry is this thou hast done!"

In truth, in all the history of the transactions between Christian and Moor there is to be found no deed so foul as this, which has left an indelible stain on Spanish knighthood. But there was no crime from which the tyrant recoiled. The innocent Blanche of Bourbon, whose young life he had already blighted and abused with every conceivable outrage, was among his victims. Jealous of the sympathy she had won from his subjects, Pedro resolved upon her murder. The governor of the castle of Medina Sidonia, in which the queen was imprisoned, was directed to "give her herbs so that she should die." But the governor, Don Iñigo Ortiz, to his great honour, refused to do the king's will, and paid with his life for his loyalty. Another agent was found of a more pliable conscience, who either by poison or by steel rid the young queen of her life, she being then but twenty-five years old, and as beautiful as she was devout. But neither age nor sex had any power to stay the tyrant's hand when he was in the mood for killing. Shortly after the death of Queen Blanche, Maria de Padilla herself died, who alone of all human beings seems to have had any power over Pedro's heart. Of her, whom the king declared to be his true and lawful wife before the Cortes of Seville, recognising her children as his only heirs, it must be said that all tongues report well. She alone of all Pedro's numerous mistresses is without reproach—a gentle and pious lady whom all men regarded, whom the king himself treated, as his real wife. In his offences against the sex, the *Justiciero* was no more burdened by scruples of delicacy than in his murders. One lady, Urraca Osorio, for refusing his addresses, was burnt alive in the market-place of Seville. Another disfigured herself in order to escape his attentions.

A kind of stupor seems to have possessed the people at these reckless doings of their king, which was brought to a climax by the murder of Queen Blanche. The nobles fled for their lives to Aragon to take part with the Count of Trastamara, though they loved him little more than they loved his brother. The towns fell away from Pedro one after another; even the communes whom the king favoured being revolted by the mad deeds, which threatened not only to dismember the state and destroy all law and liberty, but to bring down the wrath of foreign nations upon Spain. The King of France was furious at the outrage offered to a member of his royal house in the person of Blanche. Although Charles V. could not openly espouse the cause of Enrique, being occupied at home in looking after the English, he permitted his soldiers to serve in the expedition against Castile which was organised in Aragon under the celebrated Constable Bertrand du Guesclin and other French leaders. After various turns of fortune in the civil war which followed, Pedro—who had hitherto been successful, less because the cause was his than because it was a national one against Aragon—was driven by the allies from place to place until all Castile was lost, and the cities of Burgos and Toledo had recognised his brother Enrique as king. In vain did King Pedro, who now had lost his only son Alfonso and had procured his eldest daughter Beatrice, by Maria de Padilla, to be acknowledged his heiress, seek for help from Portugal, sending Beatrice there with a large marriage portion to be wife to the Portuguese heir-apparent, Fernando. He himself, compelled to quit Seville by a rising of the city—the last which had clung to him—took refuge in Portugal. But the Portuguese would have none of him, his daughter, or his treasure—returning the two latter with an uncivil message that neither were wanted, Castile having proclaimed Enrique as her king. It was with difficulty that Pedro obtained leave from his uncle, the King of Portugal, to pass through his territory into Galicia, which some of the nobles still held for him. Stopping at Santiago to murder the Archbishop (who had been one of the first to invite him to the province) in the manner already related, Pedro took ship at Coruña, to sail for Bayonne—there to entreat the help of Edward, Prince of Wales, who was Governor of Aquitaine for his father, King Edward III.

Then followed a remarkable change of fortune for Pedro, and a romantic episode in the story of Spain, the subject of some of the most stirring chapters in the chronicle of Froissart. The Black Prince, England being then at truce with France, having heard of the entrance of the redoubtable Du Guesclin and the hereditary enemies of his country into the quarrel on the side of Enrique, naturally embraced with ardour the cause of Pedro. He could not be expected to be a very severe judge of Pedro as a ruler. He had probably never heard of all his misdeeds. He knew him only as the legitimate King of Spain, who had been driven out of his land by his bastard brother with the help of the French free lances. The adventure was in every way most tempting to a warrior of Prince Edward's temperament and renown in arms. The swords of his good knights were rusting for want of use; and it was more than ten years since Poitiers was fought. The King of Spain bestowed on him the lordship of Biscay (having sent secret orders to the Biscayans not to admit the foreigner), besides half a million of golden florins for the support of his army, and the great ruby he had feloniously taken from the person of the Red King for the prince himself. Doubtless the prospect of "Castles in Spain" to be won by the sword was not without its influence on the English and Gascon knights, who formed the Court of the Black Prince. Don Enrique had already been most liberal of his donations on the other side. To Bertrand du Guesclin, who by virtue of his great renown in arms was chosen captain of the free companies, was assigned Don Enrique's own Countship of Trastamara, with the town of Molina and other valuable fiefs. To Sir Hugh de Calverley, an Englishman who found himself by some strange chance on that side, was given the lordship of Carrion; to every man-at-arms of note, some of whom were of distinguished lineage and rank, including a Marshal of France, some town or castle, so that from this time men began to speak of *chateaux en Espagne*, to express the goods of fortune in expectancy.

The Black Prince crossed the Pyrenees by the pass of Roncesvalles in February, 1367, halting at Logroño, where he expected to find the supplies which had been promised by King Pedro. But he was disappointed, as have been all who relied upon Spanish succour, which comes, according to the national proverb, "either late or never." The English army suffered greatly from want of food, but were encouraged by their leaders to hope that they would be able to furnish themselves at the expense of the enemy. On the 2nd of April the two armies met in battle array near the village of Navarrete, within a few miles of the spot where Wellington beat the French under Joseph Bonaparte and Marshal Jourdan, on the 21st of June, 1813. The forces were most unequal, for while the Prince of Wales had under him no more than 30,000 men, hungry and footsore (Mariana says 20,000), the Count of Trastamara had 80,000 French, Castilians, and Aragonese. The Englishmen, though few in number, were highly trained and exercised in war. "There was not in the Prince's army," says Chandos Herald, in his metrical story of the fight, "one who was not as hardy and as bold as a lion; nor might men compare with them Oliver or Roland." The leaders on each side were men of the highest renown in war, the Black Prince being regarded as the greatest warrior of the age, the "mirror of chivalry," who by his valour in arms, no less than by his prudence, wisdom, and good generalship, had earned an extraordinary reputation throughout Europe. With him were his brother, John of Gaunt the Duke of Lancaster, Sir John Chandos, the Constable of Guienne (who acted as chief of the staff to the Black Prince), Sir Oliver de Clisson, the Count of Armagnac, and many other captains of note, English and Gascon. On the side of Don Enrique were Bertrand du Guesclin, the Captal de Buch, Count Gaston de Foix, and the Marshal d'Andreghen, with Enrique's two brothers, Tello and Sancho.[1] Finding themselves exceeded in number by more than two to one, the adherents of Don Enrique disregarded the prudent advice of Du Guesclin, which was to draw the English farther into the interior so that they might perish of famine, and attacked the Prince of Wales with great fury. The Spaniards under Don Tello were the first to attack and the first to fly. The Aragonese slingers and cross-bowmen caused much destruction in the English ranks, and the French companies made a stout fight. By midday, however, the Black Prince had gained a great victory—the enemy losing, according to Froissart, 17,500 men, including many chiefs of note, French and Spanish. Bertrand du Guesclin himself with the Captal de Buch, Don Sancho (the Count of Trastamara's brother), the Marshal d'Andreghen, the Master of Santiago, and a great number of the principal nobles of Castile and of Aragon, were

---

[1] Sir Hugh Calverley, like a good liegeman, preferred his duty to his Prince to his countship of Carrion, and went over with four hundred lances to join the English before the battle.

taken prisoners; some of whom fell into the power of King Pedro and were at once put to death. Don Enrique himself with difficulty escaped with a few followers into Aragon, not deeming himself safe till he had reached Avignon, where he sought shelter with the Pope Urban V. The Pope however would not see him, " for they all," the Spanish chronicler says, " feared to anger the Prince of Wales, so powerful did they hold him then."

The first act of King Pedro, after the battle was over, was to demand his captives of the Black Prince, so that he might put them to death—offering to pay him a ransom for them. But the English Prince refused, saying that for all the money in the world he would not give up his prisoners taken in lawful war, though if the king named any who had been properly sentenced to death before the battle, he would deliver them up. King Pedro replied, that if he had known this was to be he would rather have lost his kingdom, for now he had lost his treasure and given his help to the Prince for nothing. To which the Prince retorted angrily in this manner: "Sir cousin, to me it appears that you have now a method of recovering your kingdom more forcible than you had when you possessed it; and hast ruled it such wise that you had to lose it. And I counsel you to cease from compassing these deaths, and to search for some way of gaining the good will of the lords, the cavaliers, and gentlemen, the cities and towns of your kingdom; for should you govern otherwise, as you did before, you stand in great peril of forfeiting your kingdom and your person, and of arriving at such a pass that neither my lord and father, the King of England, nor I, shall be able to serve you." King Pedro departed in great wrath at his scheme of vengeance being thus frustrated, and thenceforth there seems to have been no good will between him and the Black Prince, especially as the king tried to evade all his pledges respecting the moneys to be paid to the Prince's troops, and the castles to be bestowed on Sir John Chandos and other of the leaders of the army which had restored to him his throne. The Prince of Wales went no farther with his host than Burgos—some say to Valladolid—whence he turned back home to Bordeaux, to die of the distemper which he had caught in Navarre, as a consequence of his privations and hardships in the campaign.

It is pleasant to turn from this ill-conditioned king, his barbarities and perjuries, to an episode of true chivalry, illustrative of the relations between the Black Prince and his honourable enemy. According to the usages of war Bertrand du Guesclin was a prisoner at ransom—the sum to be fixed by his conqueror; but the Prince sent him a complimentary message averring that so great was the value of this illustrious knight, and so signal had been his services to his country, that it were better to retain him in captivity, during the prospect of war between France and England, than receive any sum of money for his deliverance. Du Guesclin replied, acknowledging the Prince's courtesy in holding him at so high a price, and declaring that since it was so, he was more honoured in his confinement than he would be in his deliverance. Upon this the Prince returned an answer that Bertrand was at liberty to ransom himself, and in regard to the amount of ransom, it might be such as the prisoner himself chose to fix, for however small it was he would demand no more; for Sir Bertrand should understand that he was not detained for any fear of him the English had. Then when all supposed that the Constable would name some small sum for his ransom so that he might gain his freedom at once, Bertrand replied, that though a poor knight, without gold or money, he would name a hundred thousand gold francs for himself, and give good security for the payment. At which they all marvelled, the Prince at Sir Bertrand's greatness of heart, and they at the confidence the prisoner had in his king and fellow nobles. So Bertrand was released and the ransom was duly paid—to the glory of chivalry and the exaltation of the honour of both these illustrious knights.

Pedro recovered his kingdom as quickly as he had lost it, but disgusting his allies by his perfidy and his cruelty, they left him to fight his own battles in future. Enrique, when he heard of the Black Prince's departure, once more entered the field against his rival, and aided by supplies of money from the Pope and the King of France, invaded the Castilian territory—the troops sent against him secretly conniving at his enterprise. He was joined by all his old supporters, and quickly made himself master of Burgos and some of the principal towns of the North. Once more we are told that the communes stood by Pedro, in spite of his flagrant misdeeds, while the barons and the gentry were for Enrique; but it is probable that this was less through affection than fear. In order to recapture Cordova, which city had declared for his brother, Pedro was compelled to seek the aid of the Moorish King of Granada, who sent a large force to his assistance. The enterprise failed, through lack of confidence in each other on the part of the allies. Toledo still remained loyal to the king, and it was while he was engaged in collecting a force for its relief that Pedro met his doom. Bertrand du Guesclin had now returned from France with six hundred lances, and was once more in the service of Enrique. Pedro was shut up with a scanty following in the castle of Montiel in La Mancha. Here one of his knights opened a secret correspondence with the French leader, offering him, on behalf of his master, a large bribe in land and money if Du Guesclin would help Pedro to escape. The proposal was communicated by Du Guesclin to Enrique, at whose suggestion a plot was arranged by which Pedro was to be drawn into Du Guesclin's tent, on pretext of arranging the terms of a treaty. The transaction can hardly be regarded as otherwise than disgraceful to the memory of Du Guesclin, whatever may have been Pedro's faults and whatever the temptation to Enrique. Nor does the famous French knight come out any better in the scene that followed upon his treachery, whichever version of the story is to be believed. Pedro accompained by some of his knights went out of his castle of Montiel at night, relying upon the assurances of safety given him by Du Guesclin; and dismounting from his palfrey entered the tent of the Breton knight. While waiting for Du Guesclin there entered, doubtless by a preconcerted scheme, his brother Enrique, fully armed. At first, it is said, Enrique did not recognise Pedro. One of the Frenchmen calling out, " Look, this is your enemy ! "—still Enrique doubted, until Pedro cried, " I am, I am ! " Then Enrique knew him and struck him with his dagger in the face, and they fell to the ground together in a close embrace. Then Enrique stabbed his brother several times in the body till he died. Froissart gives another, and more particular and picturesque account of the scene, making the two brothers fling scandal each on the other's mother, after which they grappled, and Pedro being the stronger got Enrique down upon a couch, and drawing his poniard would have killed him if the Vicomte de Rocaberti had not seized the king by the leg and turned him over, so that Enrique got uppermost, who then drew a long dagger and plunged it into Pedro's body—the bystanders helping him to the mortal stroke. Two English gentlemen who were with Pedro, Sir Ralph Holmes, called the Green Squire, and James Rowland, in defending Pedro were also slain—the Spaniards making their jokes upon their king's body, and leaving it for three days unburied. A third account, in the ballads, which we would fain not believe as it is the most discreditable to Du Guesclin, makes the Constable himself interfere in the struggle, turning Pedro over so that Enrique might kill him, while he stood aside and said, " *Ni quito rey ni pongo rey, pero ayudo á mi señor*" (I neither make king nor mar king, but I aid my master)—the first part of which saying has passed into a common proverb.

Thus miserably perished by a shameful fratricide—a fate not unfitting the man whose hands were red with the blood of his own kin—Pedro, who is branded of all posterity as *The Cruel.*

IX.

THE DYNASTY OF TRASTAMARA — ENRIQUE II. — JUAN I.—ENRIQUE III.—AFFAIRS OF ARAGON.

(1369-1412.)

UPON the death of Pedro the Cruel Enrique was freed from all native competitors for the crown of Castile, though being of illegitimate birth he had no just claim to the throne. The lawful heirs were undoubtedly the three daughters of Pedro who had been legitimised by the Cortes—one of whom, Costanza, was married to John of Gaunt, the Duke of Lancaster, and another, Isabel, to Edmund, Duke of York, his brother. After them came Fernando, the King of Portugal, who was a grandson of Beatrice, the daughter of Sancho IV. But the Castilians were not likely to choose a stranger, above all a Portuguese, for their king, however little they loved Enrique, and hereditary rights were of small value in those disjointed times unless backed up by superior force. By the aid chiefly of his French mercenaries, a large number of whom he had retained in his pay, Enrique—who was not wanting in energy of character though otherwise almost as cruel and perfidious as his predecessor—

managed to secure the adhesion of the principal cities of Castile, though Galicia and a great part of Leon declared for the King of Portugal. In the war which ensued with Portugal, backed up by Granada and by the ever-changeful Pedro IV. of Aragon, who claimed some frontier towns as payment for his services in the late civil war, Enrique obtained some advantages, recovering the towns on his western border and driving back the Portuguese on Lisbon. The important fortress and seaport of Algeciras, however, which had cost his father so much trouble to take, was recovered by the Moors, who took advantage, as usual, of the dissensions among the Castilians to extend their conquests, regaining much ground in Andalusia which had been lost in the previous reigns.

Despairing at last of securing the succession for himself, and his fleet being destroyed at sea by the Castilians, King Fernando of Portugal retired from the field in favour of a new competitor, the English Duke of Lancaster, who claimed to be King of Castile in virtue of his wife Costanza. At this time Enrique was in close alliance with France, and it was perhaps as much to divert him from intervening in the French interest in Gascony as with any serious idea of obtaining Castile for himself that the Duke of Lancaster prepared to assert his pretensions in person. Enrique had sent a force to besiege Bayonne, then in the English possession, and, moreover, had joined his ships to the French in ravaging the English coasts, harrying various seaports in the Channel, and desolating the "Isla Duyc" (the Isle of Wight). It does not appear that the Duke of Lancaster was much in earnest in his claims; for though he assumed the title of King of Castile and of Leon, and bore their arms on his shield, and signed deeds in that name still extant, under the date 1372, the preparations he made for the invasion of Spain were found to be required for the defence of the English dominion in Guienne. In 1375 a truce was made between France and England, to which the King of Castile was a party. In the next year died the Black Prince, the hope and strong arm of the English and the terror of their enemies. Enrique, now secure on his throne, retained peaceful possession of it till his death in 1379—occupying himself in his last years in confirming his dynasty by marriage with the neighbouring families of Portugal and Aragon. It had been his intention, says his chronicler, had he lived, to have equipped a great armada, with which he would have recovered the mastery of the Straits from the Moors, after which he would have invaded the Moorish kingdom by land with three great armies, one under himself and one under each of his two sons, Juan and Alfonso, and so made an end of the Moors. But death prevented the execution of this great enterprise, for which Enrique never found time in his life, having lost during his turbulent reign more ground than he gained for the Christian kingdom.

Juan I., who succeeded his father, came to the throne under happier auspices than most of his predecessors had done—there being none to contest his right, and the nobles, worn out and impoverished by the long civil wars, being at rest. King Juan renewed the alliance his father had made with the French, and aided them in their wars against England, vexing the English greatly by sea, and sending his galleys even up the Thames, where never till then had an enemy's ship been seen. As a consequence of this unfriendly disposition to the English, the claims of the Duke of Lancaster to the crown of Castile were revived. A treaty was made between the English and Portugal by which the latter power agreed to co-operate on behalf of the Duke of Lancaster. Edmund, Earl of Cambridge, the Duke's brother (who was himself married to the youngest daughter of the late King Pedro), landed at Lisbon with a thousand men-at-arms and as many archers. Discord, however, soon broke out between the King of Portugal and his allies, whose behaviour, according to the native authorities, seems to have been of the rudest. King Fernando was persuaded to patch up a peace with King Juan, giving his daughter in marriage to the Castilian monarch. Among other conditions of the treaty was one that the English force under the Earl of Cambridge should be sent home in King Juan's ships at the expense of Castile. Another condition, significant of the jealousy between the two kingdoms, was that the King of Castile should have no share in the administration of Portugal in right of his wife. Fernando dying soon after without sons King Juan, oblivious of his engagements, proceeded to take possession of Portugal in his own name. He was at first supported by the queen-mother and by some of the nobles, but the people would have no Spaniard for their king, and declared for Don Joam (Juan) the Master of Avis—the illegitimate son of their king, Pedro I., by the celebrated Iñez de Castro. He was at first proclaimed Protector of the kingdom, and vigorously repelled an invasion by the Castilian king. Succeeding in recovering most of the fortified places from Juan, whose incapacity in the field was as conspicuous as his imbecility and faithlessness in the affairs of state, the Master of Avis was made king by the voice of the Cortes assembled at Coimbra. Under the title of Joam II. he became the second founder of the Portuguese Monarchy. While engaged in assembling a great army to conquer Portugal the Castilian king received an urgent message from his ally, King Charles VI. of France, saying that he was preparing to pass over with all his force to the island of England, and praying for ships and men to aid him in that enterprise. Juan made answer that as soon as he had recovered the kingdom of Portugal he would come to the help of France. But the destinies did not favour any such conjunction. The Castilians found plenty of employment in endeavouring to possess themselves of Portugal. Marching into the country at the head of an army of thirty-four thousand men, among whom were two thousand French knights of the highest quality, the King of Castile encountered the Portuguese—only ten thousand strong, with a few English knights and archers—who were strongly posted under the direction of some skilful men-at-arms among their foreign allies near the village of Aljubarrota, a little way within the Portuguese frontier. The battle which ensued, on the 14th of August, 1385, is the most glorious in the records of Portuguese chivalry, and may be said to have established the independence of Portugal for ever. The Castilians were utterly defeated, their French allies, who had borne the burden of the fighting, suffering most severely. Froissart suggests that the Spaniards kept aloof out of pique, because of their king's partiality for the foreigners. Thus said the Castilians of the French: "They have obtained the honour of the van, and hold us so cheap they will not invite us to make a part. They are now drawing themselves up separately. Well, we will do the same on our part, and, by God, let them combat and fight by themselves. Have they not boasted that they are sufficient to vanquish the Portuguese? Be it so then; we are contented." The Spanish historians favour this version of the story, as the least unpalatable to the national self-love while undoubtedly true to the national character. On the other side it is admitted that the handful of English knights, by whose advice the army had been placed in a strong position, had contributed greatly to the Portuguese victory—the small body of archers having performed their accustomed function with signal effect on the mailed horsemen of the enemy. King Juan, who had been too weak to mount a horse, was borne on a litter by the squires of his body, who when they saw their people retreating set the monarch on a mule, much lamenting, and led him away from the field. Eventually he reached the shores of the Tagus, and got away in a boat to Lisbon, where he embarked in a ship for Seville.

Thus ended an expedition almost the most discreditable to the king which had ever disgraced the annals of Castile, from which Juan emerged with damage so great to his honour and estate as to make us wonder how his dynasty remained unshaken. The Portuguese now proceeded to carry the war into Spain. To strengthen himself on the throne the King of Portugal sent messengers to the Duke of Lancaster to report to him the victory of Aljubarrota, inviting him to reassert his claims to the crown of Castile. The aspiring Lancaster, who had never given up his pretensions, encouraged by Pope Urban VI. to this great enterprise, landed at Coruña with his wife and daughters, and a select body of fifteen hundred English knights with as many archers. At Santiago he was solemnly crowned King of Castile and Leon. Meeting the King of Portugal on the frontier, he entered into a league for mutual support, giving his eldest daughter, Philippa, in marriage to King Joam, from which auspicious union sprang that celebrated family of brothers who in the next generation raised Portugal to the height of her glory and greatness. On the other side, the King of France and the anti-Pope Clement VII. declared for King Juan of Castile—the former contributing two thousand lances, with money for their support, a hundred thousand francs in gold, under the Duke of Bourbon, his uncle, while Clement sent his blessings and his consolations. The war was renewed by the invasion of Castile. A few towns were captured. Then a pestilence broke out in the allied camp, which carried off great numbers of the English and the Portuguese, so that they were compelled to retire into Portugal. By this time (1387) his own growing infirmities and the losses he had sustained in the campaign, together with the small encouragement he had met with in Castile and the condition of affairs in England, made the Duke of Lancaster, whose political aspirations were always tempered by a large amount of practical discretion, anxious to close an enterprise which seemed to promise small profit or honour. Accordingly he listened to one of those proposals for accommodation through marriage which were so frequent in that age and so much in unison with his own humour, which ever ran to advancement by politic wiving. King Juan offered to take the Duke of Lancaster's daughter, Catherine, for a wife to Enrique, his eldest son, then under age. Such a union, though the bride was three years older than the bridegroom, was all the more desirable for King Juan, seeing that it would confirm the dubious royal title in the next generation, by joining the dynasty of Trastamara to the legitimate line of Castile—Catherine being the grand-daughter of Pedro the Cruel. The conditions of the match were that the Duke of Lancaster and his wife should resign their claims to the Castilian crown ; that the Duchess should receive certain towns in fief, besides a fixed revenue ; and her husband six hundred thousand francs in gold for the expenses of the war.

Thus was settled a troublesome dispute to the advantage of both parties, the King of Castile obtaining peace and a renewed assurance of his dynasty, while John of Gaunt, who seldom came off the worse of his many matrimonial bargains, got one daughter settled as Queen of Portugal and the other as bride to the heir-apparent of Castile. From both resulted issues most fortunate for Spain and for Portugal. This controversy being happily closed, King Juan, being weary of the troubles of state, wished to abdicate in favour of his son Enrique—retaining only a certain portion of his domain, including Seville and Cordova, and the kingdom of Murcia. But the great council which was summoned at Guadalajara to discuss this matter strongly dissuaded the king from his purpose, citing the many evils which had accrued to the kingdom from the frequent partitions of territory by the old kings; whereupon Juan spoke no more of the project. Shortly afterwards the king ended his short, inglorious reign, in 1390, by a curious accident, in which the Moors, who had remained unmolested for some years, are for the first time mentioned, and in a manner which shows that there was settled peace between the two races. The king being at Alcalá de Henares, there arrived there fifty Christian knights—descendants of those who had lived in Moorish territory since the conquest—called *Farfanes*, with their wives and families, who had been permitted to return to the land of the Christians by favour of the Moorish king. King Juan going out to receive them, his horse stumbled in a ploughed field and threw him, and by the fall he died. His son Enrique, the third of that name, succeeded him in 1390, being then just over eleven years of age. As usual, the question of a regency was the first to disturb the public peace. The late king had named in his will twelve persons, six of whom were either prelates or nobles, and the other six representatives of as many of the large cities, to be of the regency. Such an arrangement could result in nothing but wrangling and confusion. The unruly and ambitious Pedro de Tenorio, Archbishop of Toledo, sought to be sole tutor to the king, and made war with those who opposed him. At last the Cortes of Burgos decided, in 1392, that the regents should rule alternately in two batches of six each. In this year took place the great tribulation of the Jews, who were harried and robbed in all the great cities, on grounds identical with those which have furnished every anti-Semitic crusade from first to last—namely, that the Jews were overrich and their way of life a scandal to Christendom.

Enrique put an end to the dissensions respecting the regency by assuming the reins of government himself in 1393, when barely fourteen years of age—his first act of sovereignty being to revoke before the Cortes at Madrid all that had been done by his tutors. During all this time an intermittent war was carried on with Portugal, waged with a ferocity which neither treaties nor family alliances seem to have had the power to abate. As for the hereditary feud with the Moors, a strange, romantic episode of this time shows that the feeling of enmity against the infidel usurpers of the soil had already degenerated into individual bursts of fanaticism, in which religious zeal had more part than patriotism or policy. The Master of the military order of Alcántara, on his own account—out of love, as he averred, for Jesus Christ—sent to the Moorish King of Granada two of his squires to tell him that the faith of Jesus was holy and good and the faith of Mahommed false and a lie; and should the King of Granada assert the contrary he, the Master, would do combat with him, giving him the odds of two to one; that is to say, with one hundred Christians he would fight with two hundred Moors. Blind to all sense of courtesy, the King of Granada, instead of accepting this fair proposal for settling the religious controversy, clapped the two squires in prison and used them dishonourably. Whereupon the Master writes to King Enrique to say that he had determined to start at once for the kingdom of Granada and carry his challenge forward. Enrique and his counsellors, when they heard what the Master of Alcántara had done, agreed that this business did not belong to the king's service, for he had made a treaty with the King of Granada, which treaty would be broken if the Master, a vassal, were to go with his company to execute his threat. Moreover, the king was aware that the Master had no more than three hundred lances under him, with which to do battle with the King of Granada. Therefore, messengers were sent to the Master of Alcántara to turn him from his purpose. But the royal commands had no effect upon the zealous Master, who, while professing respect for the king his lord, declared that this was a work of faith—that it would be a great dishonour to turn the Cross back nor carry it forward as he had begun to do. And he would not be stopped on the road, even though the knights and the officers of the city of Cordova tried to block his way over the bridge, for the people rose and murmured so loudly, saying that the Master was going on the service of God and for the faith of Jesus, that they had to let him pass with his three hundred knights, besides a few hundred footmen. In vain did other two nobles whom he met on the road point out to the Master, not only that there was peace with Granada, but that the force with him was wholly inadequate to fight with the Moors, who were very numerous and powerful, and had given great trouble in former wars, slaying many Christians and doing much damage to the land. But the Master was a man who believed in all his imaginations—who inquired of the stars and of omens, and kept a hermit, who had told him he would prevail and conquer all Moordom; and his men on foot were simple folk, who heeded naught but said: "*We go in the Faith of Jesus Christ.*"

Crossing the frontier into the territory of Granada the Master and his small company encountered an overwhelming force of Moors, who hemmed in the deluded Christians, and slew them, every mounted man and most of the footmen, making prisoners of the rest, except a few who escaped across the border. On the King of Granada complaining of this breach of treaty, King Enrique was able to satisfy him that it was committed contrary to his will and in defiance of his authority; and so the matter ended.

In the conduct of his domestic affairs Enrique seems to have been more successful than his immediate predecessors, being credited with the passing of many good laws for the benefit of his people, and attending to their just administration, in a spirit of benevolence out of character with the age. He was no great warrior any more than his father had been, and lost some frontier towns to the Portuguese, while, as we have seen, he discouraged those forays into Moorish territory which, in spite of treaties, had been a habitual exercise to Castilian manhood out of employment. The king himself was of a weakly constitution, and lived only to his twenty-eighth year—leaving, on his death in 1407, one son by his English wife Catherine, who succeeded him as Juan II.

The affairs of Aragon during these last reigns in Castile were of little moment in themselves, nor much concerned with the making of the country. Pedro IV. outlived his namesake of Castile, his competitor in perfidy, greed, and bloodthirstiness, as well as the two first kings of the house of Trastamara. He was succeeded by his son Juan I., whose chief trouble during his short reign was on account of the over-gay disposition of his French wife Violante, who was a patroness of all those frivolities, the off-shoot of a decadent chivalry—the Courts of Love, with their appendages, the troubadours, the *jongleurs*, the professors of *Lo Gai Saber* (the Gay Science), which had been imported from Provence. The queen's fondship for these diversions, which were as little to the taste of the solid and sombre men of Aragon as abhorrent to the shrewd and practical Catalans, gave much offence and caused much scandal to the people. The states remonstrated with the king on these indulgences of his Court, and insisted on the foreign professors of the arts of love and of song, the fiddlers and the dancers, the *trouvères* and the *jongleurs*, being expelled from the country. King Juan resented, at first, this interference with his wife's amusements, but was compelled to give way—purchasing peace for himself and immunity for his own pleasures, which were those of the field, at the expense of the softer delights of his ladies, who were left to lament the loss of their troubadours, minstrels, and dancing-masters.

Dying early of a fall from horseback while hunting, Juan was succeeded by his brother Martin, to the exclusion of his daughters, one of whom, through her husband, the Count de Foix, laid claim to the throne. The Aragonese, however, though they had not formally adopted the Salic law, would have no woman to rule them, especially one married to a foreigner ; and the Count de Foix could gain no adherents. Martin was in Sicily helping to recover the island for his son, who, in right of his wife, was king of that island, when he succeeded to the throne of Aragon. His reign was distinguished by nothing worthy of record in internal affairs. His ambition, like that of his immediate predecessors, was confined to extending his dominion over the islands of Sicily and Sardinia, both of which gave him ample occupation—to the disgust of his native subjects, who grudged the money which was spent on foreign expeditions. The dispute about the possession of the two islands was embittered about this time by the quarrel between the rival Popes of Rome and of Avignon. The Aragonese having acknowledged Benedict, the anti-Pope, who was Pedro de Luna, their countryman—the legitimate claimant to the chair of St. Peter, Boniface, took his revenge by setting up a pretender to Sicily and Sardinia, and inciting a party among the islanders to resist the Aragonese dominion. After one of the battles which ensued between the Aragonese and the insurgent Sardinians, the king, who was also heir to the throne of Aragon, died of a fever through overexertion. His death led to a long series of troubles in Aragon, Martin having no other son to inherit the kingdom. A civil war, which began before King Martin died in 1410, raged for two years after his death. The chief rivals were the Count of Urgel, who was directly descended in the male line from Alfonso IV. of Aragon, and the Infante Fernando of Castile, the brother of Enrique III. of that kingdom, who claimed through his mother Leonora, the eldest daughter of Pedro IV. of Aragon. Don Fernando, the Castilian claimant, had the worse title. He was not even the elder son of Leonora, so that if that were his only claim his brother Enrique III. of Castile, and next after him his nephew Juan II., had clearly the better right. But this would have been to recognise the King of Castile himself, as King of Aragon ; and neither country was as yet ripe for that union. The Infante Fernando was a man of character and ability superior to his rival, and was undoubtedly preferred by the people of Aragon, even though he was assisted by money and troops from Castile. After much desultory fighting, in the course of which the country suffered greatly from the disorders committed by the partisans of the rival leaders, the two principal competitors joined in a pitched battle in which Fernando was victorious. At length the three states, Aragon, Catalonia, and Valencia, agreed to meet in a general assembly to decide upon the choice of a king. The meeting was held at Alcañiz in 1412. The deputies from Valencia not being present, owing to their being equally divided between the two parties, Aragon and Catalonia proceeded to the election. Nine arbitrators were chosen, three for each state, in whom was vested the right of electing a king. Out of these, six voted for Fernando and three for the Count of Urgel. Thus Fernando, of the blood royal of Castile, was elected to the throne of Aragon. The unsuccesful competitor, the Count of Urgel, made some attempt to dispute King Fernando's right, obtaining aid from the English Duke of Clarence. But his troops were defeated in the field and himself taken prisoner—declared by the Cortes to be a rebel and a traitor, and retained in prison during the remainder of his life. Thus the throne of Aragon passed, with tolerable ease, into the hands of a prince of the house of Castile—a transaction which heralded, as doubtless it prepared, the subsequent auspicious union of the two crowns.

X.

THE REIGN OF JUAN II.—THE AGE OF CHIVALRY.

(1407-1454.)

THE long reign of Juan II., though marked by no extraordinary incidents at home or abroad, and by little or no progress in the great work of freeing the land from the Moors, was not without importance in the making of Spain. It was a period of transition in the national history—the middle age between the rough, heroic struggle for existence and the more courtly times which succeeded, when the battle with the Moor was over. With the feeling that their dominion was safe was quickened in the people the germ of that broader life now slowly tending to its full accomplishment. To fight the Moors was no longer the first duty of the good Spaniard. The infidels were suffered to remain in peace in their shrunken domain. Nay, their land was no longer the chosen field of adventure even for the soldiers of the faith. Cavaliers of spirit preferred to seek glory on foreign ground, and traversed Europe in search of fighting. At home the kingly power, though almost for the first time clearly recognised and firmly established, was beginning to be subject to limitations

A KNIGHT ON HORSEBACK (GALA ATTIRE).

—not rising, as heretofore, only from the turbulence of a class but from the growth of something like a popular opinion. A taste for luxury and splendour was spreading through the country, as the cities increased in wealth and importance. The nobles, without relinquishing their claims to independence each within his own domains, were grown more orderly, if not more honest, seeking their diversion in the practice of the fantastic rites and the ordinances of chivalry. King Juan himself, a man of feeble character, impatient of the cares of state, was an encourager of letters and of learning. He was a patron of poets and a poet himself. Under his auspices literature and art became established at Court, and admitted to be pursuits not unworthy of princes. "He was very free and gracious," says the chronicler, "and gave himself much to the reading of philosophy and poetry. He was skilled in matters of the Church, fairly learned in Latin, and a great respecter of such as had knowledge. He was a lover of music; he played, sang, and made verses, and he danced well." A king so accomplished in the humanities had not been seen in Spain since Alfonso the Sage. Juan had even a taste for the new art of painting, then first imported from Italy, and is fairly entitled to the glory of being the earliest of the Spanish kings who sought distinction by their patronage of artists. In this reign was the true beginning of Castilian literature. Don Enrique de Villena may claim to be, if not the founder of Castilian poetry, the first who gave it form and regular structure. His friend and kinsman, the celebrated Marquess of Santillana—the first of that noble race of Mendoza who won such high distinction in war, in statesmanship, and in letters—was a still better poet and a man of wider culture and sympathies, not the least of whose services to literature is that he gave permanent life to that most characteristic product of the national genius —the proverbs, in which the force and beauty of the ancient language of Castile are so admirably preserved. After him Juan de Mena and many others, learning art and refinement from Italian models, gave shape and grace to Spanish verse. These softer pursuits, in harmony with the spirit of the king, now beginning to be adopted by the people, mark the character of this reign as the first in which the Castilians raised their thoughts above what had hitherto been the engrossing occupations of war and conquest.

During the early years of his minority Juan II. had the good fortune to have his affairs directed by his uncle, the able and loyal Don Fernando, and by Catherine, his mother, of English descent, who were co-regents of the kingdom. The ambitious nobles were held in check with a firm hand, and a war with Granada, carried on with vigour, was closed with some increase of territory. In 1410 Don Fernando, as we have related in the last chapter, was elected King of Aragon— leaving the administration of Castile to be conducted by a council of regency, under the queen-mother, Catherine. He continued to give his advice on the government till his death in 1416, which was followed two years afterwards by that of Catherine. Juan was now left alone in his sovereignty. Nor was it long before the young king displayed that tendency to lean upon a stronger nature, which was his chief characteristic. He was one of those monarchs who, like our Edward II., could not govern but through a favourite. The man to win that dangerous name, who exercised that ungrateful office with singular constancy on the one part and tenacity on the other, was the famous Alvaro de Luna, whose career forms the one principal and all overshadowing episode of this reign—the story of his life being indeed the chronicle of Juan II. Alvaro, who had no good right to his proud name of De Luna, was the bastard son of the head of that illustrious Aragonese family, some of whom had settled in Castile. One of his uncles was Pedro de Luna, elected Pope by the schismatics at Avignon in 1394; another was Archbishop of Toledo, the Primate of Castile and most powerful ecclesiastic in Spain. A lady of this race had been a queen of Sicily in the generation before, while many of its members had intermarried with the Mendozas, the Ponces de Leon, and the highest families of Castile and of Aragon. Alvaro began his career at Court as a page in the service of Queen Catherine, where he was chosen as a playmate for the young King Juan, who became so fond of him that he could not bear to be out of his sight, day or night. The young Alvaro, who was of the same age as his master, was distinguished from his earliest years not only for the beauty and grace of his person, but his many accomplishments, his lively disposition, and his excellence in all manly and courtly games and exercises, whether wrestling, dancing, singing, fencing, or other youthful pastime. He was the best also at hunting the wild boar or the bear, for he was very daring and active, a great horseman, and strong in the arm. So well trained had been his body from a tender age that, as his fond biographer avers, there was none to equal him in agility or strength, though he was not big or lofty of stature. "But though his limbs were graceful and delicate, he was very well made, all sinew and bone, so that he did everything well, and became every garb he wore, and endowed with a very good air both the clothes he wore and the beasts he bestrode, as well as everything to which he put his hands. And because he was so graceful and well-mannered, and of a beautiful and gentle disposition, and of a very sweet discourse, the duennas and the damsels of the queen, and all the other great ladies, bestowed on him great favour for what he did and said, more than on any one of all the others." And therefore great envy grew among the young nobles and courtiers at young Alvaro's sudden advancement, and they did not rest till they had parted the king from his favourite playfellow—first sending him to Aragon in the suite of Doña Maria, the king's sister, who went to wed the Prince Alfonso, heir to that kingdom, and afterwards on various pretexts keeping them separate, until they both arrived at manhood, when Alvaro secured his place firmly by the side of the king in spite of his enemies.

The struggle between him and the nobles continued during all this reign, and make up the whole record of Juan II. The first to disturb the peace of the realm, under pretence of ousting the favourite from Court, was the Infante Enrique of Aragon, the king's cousin —a turbulent and ambitious prince, who for several years was a thorn in the side of Don Alvaro. With the connivance of Lopez de Avalos, the Constable of Castile, who like all the other grandees was jealous of Don Alvaro's sudden elevation and extraordinary influence, Don Enrique seized upon the person of the young king at Tordesillas, and carried him away a prisoner to Avila. It was only by the prudence and coolness of Don Alvaro, who temporised with Enrique, that the king was preserved from a worse fate, perhaps from a violent death. The audacious rebel so far prevailed over the king's weakness as to procure his consent to the summoning of the Cortes at Avila, before whom Juan was induced to declare that he approved of Enrique's strong measures, whose zeal in the royal cause had freed him from his enemies. Taking advantage of the festivities held in celebration of Enrique's marriage with Juan's sister Catalina, the king, under the pretext of hunting, escaped from his captors, accompanied by Don Alvaro and some of his adherents. The triumph of the favourite was now complete. The Archbishop of Toledo and the greater part of the nobles, who dreaded the influence of the Infante Enrique more than they disliked their lesser rival, rallied to the king's side. Juan showed his gratitude to his deliverer by loading him with the dignities and estates of the disgraced nobles. Don Alvaro was advanced to the high rank of Constable of Castile, which office was made one of greater power and emolument so that its holder became the second person in the kingdom, the commander of the king's army, the head of the executive, and the dispenser of the royal bounties and honours. The new

Constable, who knew his master's taste for shows and festivities, celebrated his appointment by a series of entertainments more splendid and gorgeous than had ever been witnessed in Castile, so as to cause great wonder and admiration among the people. Banquets, jousts, and plays, were held in public, in which the king and all his Court took much joy and pleasure. There were exhibited before the amazed eyes of the sober Castilians all the knights and squires of the Constable's household, among whom, we are told, were many sons of counts and other great people, most sumptuously dressed and harnessed—all with coats of silk, bordered with excellent new devices, rich girdles, collars, and chains, set with jewels of great price, and sumptuous trappings for the horses and hackneys, so that the whole Court shone and glowed with splendour. And if the chronicler is to be believed, who writes with a tenderness of the great Constable which reaches to the pathetic, there were other and more substantial causes for the popular rejoicing, for the cities and towns of the realm were governed with much justice, and all the people rested in peace and contentment; the roads were safe, malefactors restrained, and the king's commandments observed with great reverence.

So passed several years, during which the Constable was at the height of the king's favour and at the top of his power—years which were probably as happy for the king as for his people, who found themselves both vigorously ruled without the trouble of asserting their freedom. There is reason to believe that never had the kingdom enjoyed so long a period of rest or the people so good a time, for it is clear that Don Alvaro took pains to win their favour as his best support against the malice of the envious nobles. The Cortes, however, began to murmur at the costliness of the king's affection for his minion. They complained that the exchequer suffered from the sovereign's excessive prodigality, and he was restrained from granting any new pensions or land for twenty-five years. Taking advantage of the discontent aroused by the favours extended to Don Alvaro and resenting the munificence with which these were dispensed by the latter among his own kinsmen and followers, the enemies of the favourite began to rear their heads again. A league against Don Alvaro was formed, at the head of which were the kings of Aragon and Navarre, whose pretence for joining it was to obtain the release of their brother, the Infante Enrique, who had been kept in duress since the day had gone against him some years before. In 1427 the enemies of Don Alvaro were powerful enough to procure his removal from Court for eighteen months. The king was weak and, in spite of himself, was forced to yield to the demand. The Constable was prudent, and bowed to the storm —retiring to his castle of Ayllon. In a few months he so managed, through his influence over the king, which was sedulously kept alive during his absence by the courtiers who were mostly his own creatures, that he was recalled, to take his place once more at the head of affairs with greater power than ever. The re-entry of the Constable into the Court is described in the chronicle with a minuteness which bespeaks the eye-witness and an amplitude of effusion which betrays the too partial retainer. With an imposing train of cavaliers, all accoutred in their bravest apparel, on which the artificers, not only of the country but of foreign parts, had been employed for many days—for the Constable was one who took delight in the preparation of pageants as well as of all things pertaining to chivalry—Don Alvaro himself simply though richly accoutred, with a chosen band of pages mounted on horses of rare quality, such as their master knew how to select—some of them carrying lances and riding jennet-wise, others on warhorses all covered with embroidered trappings, with trumpets blowing before them—the Constable went forth to the Court—the king meeting him half-way, at the head of the most distinguished nobles and prelates, among whom were all the principal dignitaries of the kingdom, accompanied, for the greater triumph of Don Alvaro, by his chief enemy—the Infante Enrique and the King of Navarre. Who shall describe, says the enthusiastic chronicler, the great pleasure which all the ladies and damsels of the Queen took in seeing the Constable again, to do honour to whom so many illustrious persons had condescended?

With some of those who were then reconciled to him the truce was but a short one, for presently the kings of Aragon and Navarre were in the field again in great force, whom the Constable marched forth to oppose with all the array of Castile. But the Pope's legate intervened just when they were on the point of battle, and afterwards Queen Maria of Aragon attempted to intercede between her husband and her brother. They not being able to agree on the terms of peace, the war continued, and the Constable gained much honour by taking some frontier places from the Aragonese and doing them much damage. On the other side, in Estremadura, the restless Don Enrique was once more in arms, giving trouble by seizing on the outlying towns and ravaging the country. Against him the Constable, who seems to have been everywhere and occupied in everything, was sent from the borders of Aragon, speedily reducing the rebels and driving them before him to take refuge in Portugal.

Ever indefatigable in the service of his king the Constable, during a brief intermission of rebellion, sought for honour in a more legitimate field. The truce with Granada being ended, he led a great host into the Moorish territory, sending a cartel, according to the fashion of the then prevailing chivalry, to Mahommed-ibn-Azar, the Moorish king, to announce his coming and call him forth to the field. The Moor showing some reluctance to despatch the requisite number of his cavaliers to meet the Christian challenge, the Constable consoled himself by burning several towns and villages within the Moorish frontier, advancing into the *vega* close up to the walls of Granada, and compelling the Moors to come out and fight him—which they did at last, to their great detriment. But just in as great a measure as Don Alvaro's glory increased did the envy of the great lords grow more and more intense, and their hatred of the general favourite become more bitter. Even in the royal camp before Granada was a conspiracy hatched against the Constable's life, which led to the break-up of the expedition, and prepared the way for the still greater enhancement of Don Alvaro's power. He now touched the highest point of all his greatness, and was in the full meridian of his glory. No subject in Spain, noble or commoner, layman or ecclesiastic, had ever reached to so high a dignity. He was not only Constable of the kingdom but Master of Santiago, the richest and most powerful of the military orders. His brother was advanced to the Archbishopric of Toledo. He himself had the Dukedom of Truxillo, besides various countships. He was lord of seventy towns and castles, not including those pertaining to the Order of Santiago. He maintained a retinue of three thousand lances, with a great household full of the youth of good families. By his two marriages he was allied with the noblest blood of Castile. His revenues were on a scale corresponding to the greatness of his rank and the number of his offices. He was as liberal of largess as greedy of emolument; and got and gave with equal magnificence. And though he served himself generously, he was not less profuse to his numerous dependants. In the midst of it all, he was without reproach as a loyal servant of the king and no less steady in his attachment to those principles of honour embodied in that institution of chivalry which had in that age reached its highest development. It is no wonder that a man of this character, who seems to have been as sedulous in the performance of his public duties as eager in the pursuit of pleasure or of fame, should have raised up both devoted friends and bitter enemies. The first were never tired of reciting his acts of goodness, as the second were unweary of ill-doing to his prejudice.

An episode which occurred about this time, in 1439, known in history as *El Seguro de Tordesillas* (The Pledge, or Pact, of Tordesillas), serves to illustrate, in a striking manner, the spirit of the age, with its mingled faithlessness, mutual mistrust, unveracity, and exaggerated sense of honour. The nobles had combined with the King of Navarre and the Prince Enrique, heir of Castile, in one of their numerous attempts to shake the power of the favourite, Alvaro de Luna. After much negotiation, and many passages of arms, and interchange of demands and promises, lightly made and gaily broken, it was agreed between the two parties that a discussion should be held, in some neutral place, of all the matters in dispute. But not being able to trust each other to observe any kind of honourable truce, or to fix upon any town which would be equally safe for the partisans of the king and of the nobles, it was decided to appoint an umpire, who should have absolute power to control the discussion, to arrange the place of meeting, and to fix on the number of those who should attend on each side; and should be invested with the responsibility of keeping the peace between the partisans, ensuring their safety while engaged in the deliberations and becoming security for the observance of such compact as might be made. The man chosen by common consent for this high and most onerous office was Don Pedro Fernandez de Velasco, Conde de Haro, of an ancient Castilian family—of moderate wealth and power, esteemed among all men for his honesty, loyalty, and patriotism, which had won him the name of *The Good Count*. The town selected for the meeting, which the Count of Haro undertook to garrison with a chosen body of his own retainers, was Tordesillas. Thither, under his safe conduct, came the King Juan, with his Constable, and a select band of retainers, on one side; and the King of Navarre, Prince Enrique, and the discontented chiefs, on the other, their numbers being equal; and deliberated under the protection of the Good Count, agreeing, after much discussion, to certain articles of accommodation, which they were bound over by the umpire faithfully to observe; which pact they did religiously keep for the unwonted space of two years—as long as the authority of the Count of Haro lasted. Afterwards they fell to quarrel and war again as before.

The country, under the firm and vigorous rule of Don Alvaro de Luna, enjoyed a long period of peace and prosperity; and if we are to judge of the Constable's character by the success of his policy, we must allow him to be a man gifted in a very extraordinary degree with all the qualities, moral and intellectual, essential to greatness. At last the day came for him to experience the universal lot decreed to those who trust in princes. A new combination of his enemies was formed, headed as usual by his implacable foe, the Infante Enrique—whose life the Constable had more than once spared—sufficiently powerful to drive him from the Court. The king, who was now beginning to waver in his attachment to his old favourite, and perhaps had cause for jealousy, on his own account, in Don Alvaro's ever-increasing popularity, agreed to summon a Cortes at Valladolid to consider the demands of the confederates, who were joined by the king's only son, Prince Enrique. All measures for a peaceful accommodation between the malcontents and the Constable having proved ineffectual, both parties prepared for war. To the honour of Don Alvaro it should be said that, rather than plunge the country in a civil war, he offered to resign his places and retire into Portugal. King Juan, however, who could not bring himself to dispense with his old councillor, dissuaded him from this purpose. Finding the confederates—whose ranks were now reinforced by his queen as well as his son—too strong to be openly resisted, King Juan attempted to temporise, undertaking to banish the Constable from Court for six years. Again the weak and vacillating monarch returned to his favourite, after many changes of fortune winning a decisive battle over the confederate nobles at Olmedo, in which the archdisturber of the public peace, the Infante Enrique, came by his death. But his victory only seemed to re-kindle the king's own jealousy of his favourite, who had offended his master by forcing on him a second marriage with a princess of Portugal. King Juan now sought for an opportunity to rid himself of Don Alvaro, going about the design with a mixture of timidity and treacherousness which serves to show not only his meanness of character but the extraordinary power still wielded by the favourite. Don Alvaro, who was probably not unaware of his master's intentions, took no measures for his own security. Being at Burgos, apart from the great body of his followers, he found his house suddenly surrounded by two hundred men-at-arms, to whom, after a show of resistance, he surrendered himself, on a pledge that his life and liberty should be respected. By the king's command he was brought before a court, hurriedly summoned, who, after a show of trial, condemned him to death. Don Alvaro was removed to Valladolid, where the sentence was carried out. King Juan's fear and remorse were extreme, and to the last he hesitated in his purpose—even sending messages to those who guarded the Constable's person ordering a respite, which are said to have been intercepted by the queen, who, chosen by Don Alvaro himself for that dignity, was now his bitterest enemy. In the last scene of his life the Constable behaved with a manly grace and decency such as moved even his persecutors to pity. A great scaffold was set up in the public square of Valladolid, of proportions and a splendour such as had never been seen in Castile, so as to give due emphasis to so extraordinary an act as the execution of this powerful and famous lord. The Constable was set upon a mule and led through the streets, strongly guarded—the king's herald going before him and declaring his crime and punishment. Mounting to the scaffold, Don Alvaro spoke to the bystanders, declaring that he deserved his death for all his sins but that he had ever been true to his king, and then laid his head on the block—the executioner plunging his knife into his throat, according to the barbarous custom of the time, before cutting off his head. A great wail, we are told, arose from the multitude who had assembled to witness

EFFIGY OF DON ALVARO DE LUNA.

this strange and solemn tragedy, when they saw the deed done, men and women weeping as they who had lost a father or some one whom they much loved.

Whatever might have been Don Alvaro's errors or his crimes—and they had need to be great to equal his noble qualities and his services to his ungrateful king—he bears a name which deserves to be ranked among those of statesmen of the very highest class who have held power in any country of Europe. There can be little doubt that his rule, extending over a period of nearly thirty-five years, was beneficial to his country. The people at least had reason to regret an administrator who, whatever might have been his personal vices, was just, vigorous, and enlightened — who maintained order and peace in Castile as (if we may judge from the unanimous testimony of the native historians) they had never been maintained before. Some of the features of the great Constable's character, as well as the manner of his death, seem to recall a conspicuous personage in English history, whose fate and fortune were such as to liken him to the Castilian. Sir Walter Raleigh never rose so high, and was, perhaps, of harder fibre and broader nature; but the same superabundant vitality, the same soaring spirit and unquenchable appetite for greatness, the same superb infirmities and noble defects, the same splendid contempt for the smaller moralities, distinguished the English and the Castilian adventurers. As to the king, who deserted and betrayed an old servant, who never failed in his duty to his sovereign, who was the chief and indeed the only distinction of his reign—he lived

MONUMENT OF JUAN II. AND HIS QUEEN.

but a year after Don Alvaro's execution, leaving a name which has become a by-word in history for imbecility and faithlessness. By posterity he is chiefly remembered as the father of the good queen Isabel. On his death-bed he is said to have lamented his ill-spent life, regretting that "he had not been born the son of a mechanic instead of King of Castile."

Among the characteristics of the age of Juan II. was a singular growth of the spirit of chivalry—of chivalry as embodied in the order and institution of that name, having honour and a fantastic reverence for womanhood for its bases. Imported from abroad, this was an exotic which took root and flourished with extraordinary luxuriance in the congenial soil of Spain, a hundred years after it had waned in other parts of Western Europe. The first great impetus which was given to chivalry, as an accomplishment worthy of cultivation by men aspiring to the honourable profession of arms, was in the wars of Pedro the Cruel against his brother Enrique of Trastamara. Then for the first time were seen on Spanish ground the two great rival bodies of knights, the choicest in the world, the English and the French, each under a leader of the highest renown for proficiency in the art and practice of romantic and cultured fighting. The Black Prince on one side and Bertrand du Guesclin on the other were patterns of knighthood, obeying a law of conduct while pursuing their warlike game which must have greatly impressed the Spanish mind, hitherto intent on the more practical aim of battle, which was to kill your enemy for the sake of his land. In the collision between the highly trained and

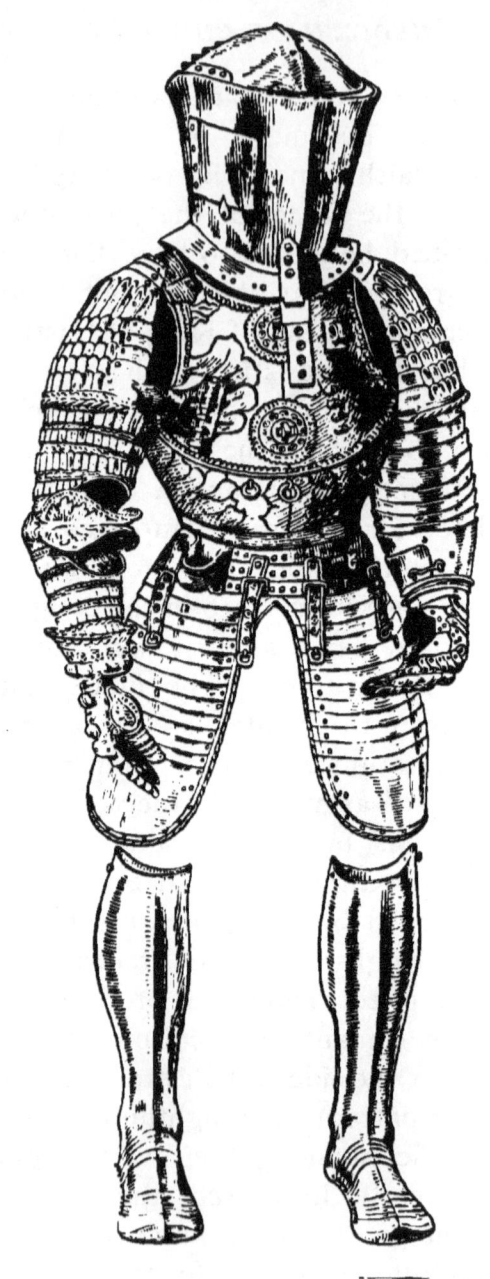

ARMOUR OF FIFTEENTH CENTURY.

splendidly accoutred foreign cavaliers, who came to fight out their own quarrels in Spain, who were less concerned with the comparative merits of Pedro and Enrique than with their own reputations as gallant knights, the Spaniards had a spectacle such as never before had been afforded them on so grand a scale. It is no wonder that a taste grew up for an institution so fascinating in itself and so agreeable to the national humour—that its fantastic and romantic side had a special attraction for the noble souls thirsting for distinction and not finding employment enough, through the decline of the religious sentiment, in fighting their legitimate enemy, the Moor.

The reign of Juan II. was particularly favourable to the development of chivalry. The king himself was much given to take his pleasure in the innocent game of jousting, and his favourite, Don Alvaro, often appeared in the lists as an *aventurero* or a *mantenedor*,[1] earning much distinction for skill and dexterity with lance and shield. But the most striking illustration of the extent to which the practice of chivalry, as a system of honour regulated by fixed laws and ordinances, was carried in the Fifteenth century is afforded by the strange story of the *Paso Honroso*, or Honourable Passage of Arms, held in the year 1434, before the king and of his whole Court, at the bridge of Orbigo, near the city of Leon. One Suero de Quiñones, a knight of illustrious birth, who had borne round his neck for a considerable time a collar

---

[1] The *mantenedor* was the defender who undertook to meet all comers on any occasion. The *aventurero* was the challenger, his opponent.

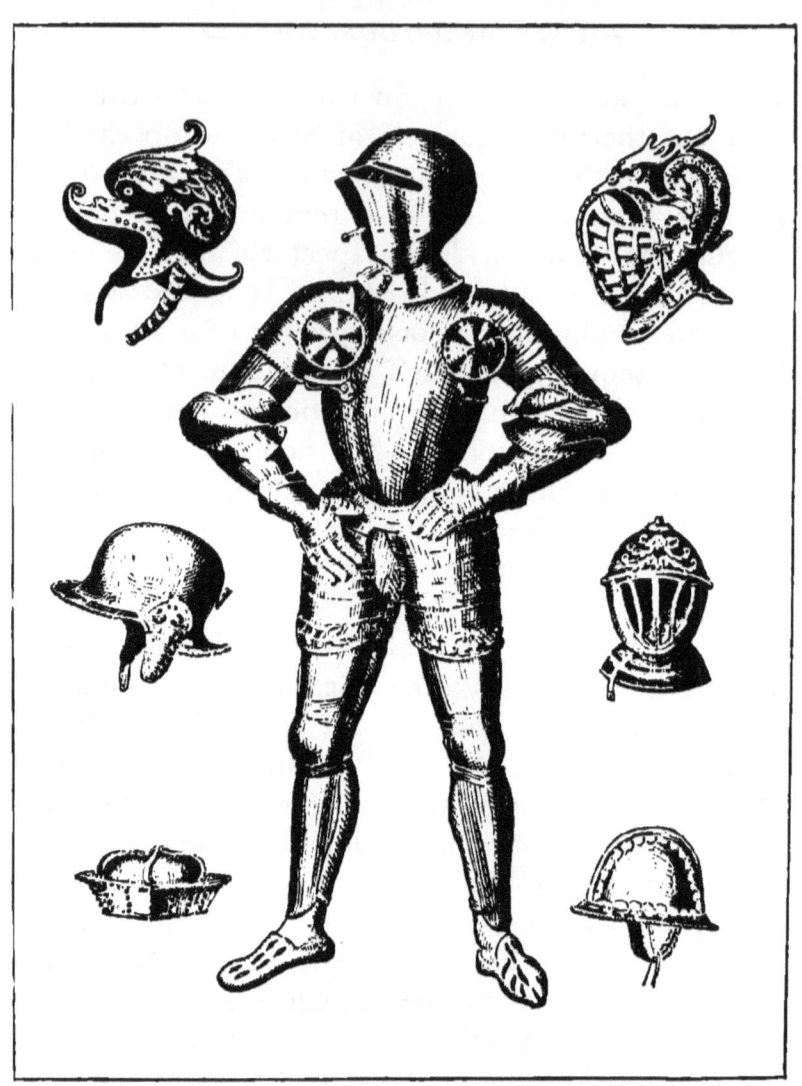

ARMOUR AND HELMETS, FIFTEENTH CENTURY.

of iron, in token of being vassal to his lady love—pleading that it was just and reasonable that they who were in captivity should seek deliverance—formally petitioned the king that he might be allowed, with nine of his friends, to joust with any who came against them, for a period of thirty days—pledging himself and them to break three hundred lances, having achieved which feat he was to be freed from his self-imposed penance. The king having given his license, and the conditions of the tournament which were twenty-two in number and most minute and precise, being settled, the Cortes formally voted the money required to defray the cost of the ceremony—advice of which was sent round to all the courts of Christendom, with an invitation to all knights of spirit to compete. No fewer than sixty-eight knights responded to the appeal, coming some of them from Germany, Italy, Brittany, and Portugal. These were the *aventureros*, or challengers, against whom Suero de Quiñones and his nine companions had to keep the field. After a series of tiltings, in which seven hundred and twenty-seven courses in all were run, one knight from Aragon being killed and many severely wounded, among the latter Suero de Quiñones himself, it was solemnly decided by the judges that he had fulfilled his vow, and the King of Arms was ordered to remove the iron collar from his neck—all which great and shining deeds, which raised the character of Spanish chivalry to the highest pitch and moved the envy of surrounding nations, are set forth minutely and in becoming order in a chronicle expressly devoted to the *Honourable Passage of Arms*.

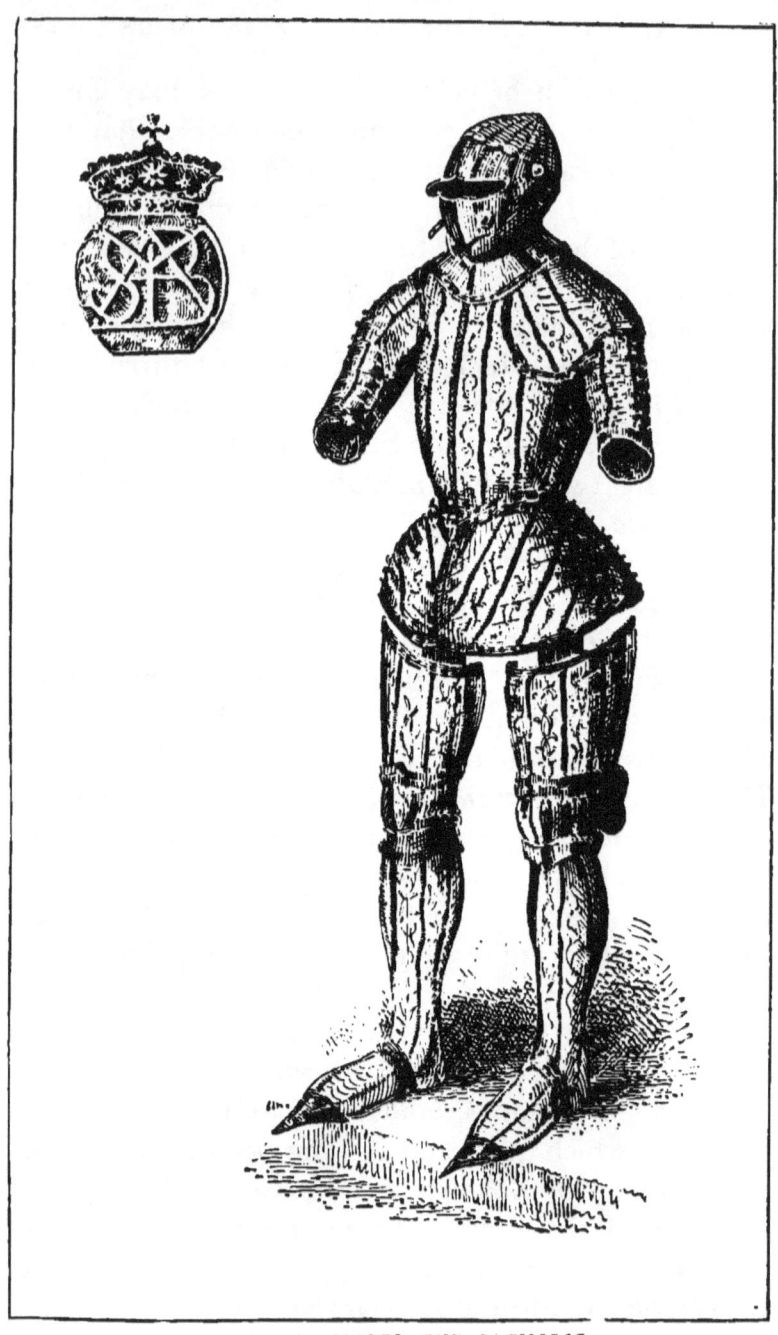

ARMOUR OF ISABEL THE CATHOLIC.

XI.

REIGN OF ENRIQUE IV.—CIVIL WAR AND DISORDER —MARRIAGE OF FERNANDO AND ISABEL— UNION OF CASTILE AND ARAGON.

(1454–1474.)

JUAN II. on his death in 1454 left three children— one son, Enrique, by his first wife Maria of Aragon, and a son and a daughter much younger, Alfonso and Isabel, by Isabel of Portugal, the grand-daughter of King Joam and his Queen Philippa. Enrique IV., who from his early prodigalities earned the name of *The Liberal*, to be exchanged soon afterwards for the title unflattering to his manhood by which he is better known in history, ascended the throne of Castile under favourable auspices. The old king had kept himself aloof from his people. The new sovereign had, in his physical endowments, all the semblance of one who promised to be popular. He was of large stature and stout of limb, with an aspect, says the chronicler, ferocious and like unto a lion, whose gaze struck terror in those at whom he looked. He had red hair and a long beard, seldom trimmed, large blue eyes, wide apart, and a very fair skin. The possessor of these graces, however, quickly proved himself to be, with all his brave shows, but an indifferent valiant. With all the weakness of his father he had few of his more amiable qualities, and did more during his reign to degrade the office of king than any monarch of his house. His first acts were gracious and princely. He confirmed all his father's servants in their offices, and pardoned and released his enemies. He made peace with his Christian neighbours. But to prove that he was not deficient in that taste for war which was looked for in every King of Castile he summoned his Cortes at Cuellar, to whom he made a speech—dwelling on the evils to which a nation was exposed which preferred idleness and luxury to the wholesome exercise of battle, and pointing out that war with the Moors was the necessary and legitimate employment of a Christian people, for the Moors were not only usurpers of their soil but enemies of their faith, whom it was right and proper to destroy, and that there were three reasons why they should presently engage in a crusade—the first, seeing they had a just cause; the second, for they had a clear right; and the third, because such a design was holy and approved by God. The Cortes lending a favourable ear to the king's proposition which, in default of any other internal occupation such as civil war or an attack upon a neighbouring state, was always popular, and in fact a work which had never been wholly lost sight of, though greatly neglected, during the last hundred years, Enrique gathered a large army together, and with great pomp and warlike apparatus proceeded to take the field against the Moors of Granada. Entering the *vega* at the head of a large army, the king rather disappointed the expectations raised of his martial prowess—especially by an order given to his cavaliers that they were not to engage in single skirmishes with the enemy, for the Moors, he said, in this kind of war, were more dexterous than the Christians, so that the number of Christians who died was greater than that of Moors. Therefore he commanded that they were only to make a succession of forays, so as to cause the enemy great hunger and failure of victuals, and then he could have them in a ring and take them. And so counselling, the king bade them remove the royal camp to a safe place. Such an issue of the great crusading enterprise, the object of which was finally to sweep the Moors out of Spain and recover the land for the true Faith, was naturally most distasteful to the great lords and the knights who had been summoned to the expedition, and no less so to the people on the border, who complained of the sacrifices to which they had been exposed in feeding and lodging so large an army—averring that the war had been made against them and not against the infidels. The murmuring rose to the height of a conspiracy against the king's person, with the object of preventing him from disbanding the army. This was the beginning of the Castilians' discontentment with their new king, him of the large stature and the lion's aspect. For three or four years in succession did Enrique lead an army into the plains of Granada, but only to plunder and burn, retiring when the Moors appeared in force, or when some great Christian leader had been slain, in one of the numerous petty skirmishes in which the agility, lighter equipment, and good horsemanship of the enemy gave them an advantage.

In his domestic affairs the king was no happier than in war. He had married a princess of Portugal, but his conduct towards her and her manner of resenting it, led to much scandal and to a long series of troubles, during which the worst days of Castilian civil war were revived. In the matter of favourites Enrique was even weaker than his father had been, with a worse taste. They were chosen for qualities less than respectable, and changed as shamelessly. His first favourite was Juan de Pacheco, whom he advanced to the Marquisate of Villena, and endowed with immense estates. He was wantonly displaced in favour of Beltran de La Cueva, whose relations with the queen made his influence over her husband still more odious to the people. The public contempt and disgust for the royal pair was carried to the height when, at a great tournament held near Madrid in the presence of the Court and of the English ambassador, Beltran de La Cueva appeared as one of the defenders in a passage of arms, maintaining the supreme beauty of his mistress, the queen—a feat which made the king so glad that he erected a monastery in its celebration.

Incensed by Enrique's follies and by the conduct of his upstart minions, the nobles—on this occasion representing the people—who had been equally disgusted and irritated by the king's disregard of their rights, by his arbitrary invasions of their ancient privileges, by his petty exactions, and the numerous disorders which were caused by the relaxation of authority—set about once more to conspire for their monarch's dethronement. The crowning act of the national disgrace, in their eyes, was Enrique's requiring the Cortes to swear allegiance to a daughter born of the queen, who from her reputed paternity was nicknamed *La Beltraneja*, as heir to the throne. The confederate nobles, assembling at Burgos, protested against this act, declaring the child to be illegitimate; maintaining the right of Prince Alfonso, the king's half-brother, to be his successor; drawing up a catalogue of the public abuses which they required to be amended; insisting upon the dismissal of Beltran de La Cueva, the favourite; and entering into a solemn compact not to lay down their arms until their wrongs had been redressed. The king made submission so far as to promise compliance with these demands. He delivered his brother Alfonso into the hands of the confederates, agreeing to recognise him as heir to the crown on condition of his marrying his daughter, Juana—*La Beltraneja*. He promised to appoint a commission to inquire into the state of the kingdom and provide a redress for the popular grievances, and he undertook to dismiss Don Beltran from his employments. But these concessions, and especially the facility with which they were made, only served to augment the public distrust of King Enrique. The confederates openly defied his power, and declared their intention of setting up his brother Alfonso as king in his stead.

Alfonso was even proclaimed King of Castile and Leon at Valladolid.

How low the authority of Enrique had fallen, and how strong was the feeling against him, is proved by an extraordinary scene which was now (1465) enacted near Avila. In the open plain near the city there was erected on an eminence so that all might see, a scaffold on which was placed a chair of state, and on this an effigy of King Enrique, clothed in black and adorned with all the emblems of sovereignty— a crown on his head, a sceptre in his hand, and a sword by his side. Then from the midst of the distinguished assemblage, composed of the highest dignitaries of the kingdom, a herald stood up, and reciting the chief matters of complaint against the king, declared him to be deprived of his four principal functions: the first, of his royal dignity, when the Archbishop of Toledo rose and took the crown off the effigy; the second, of the administration of justice, when the Count of Plasencia removed the sword; the third, of the government of the realm, at which the Count of Benavente snatched the sceptre away; the fourth, of the throne and title of king, whereupon Don Lopez de Zuñiga, uttering foul and furious words, flung the effigy from its throne, which was kicked about the plain amidst the mingled curses and acclamations of the bystanders. Then Prince Alfonso, a youth of tender age, was raised to the royal seat, and all the prelates and nobles, taking it on their shoulders, cried aloud—"*Castilla! Castilla! por el Rey Don Alfonso!*" amidst the blare of trumpets and the beating of drums. Considering the almost superstitious reverence in which the person of the king was held in Castile, even by those who rebelled against him, this was a monstrous and unparalleled outrage, of which the terrified chronicler, though half-approving, cannot speak but in interjections of pity and horror.

By some historians Alfonso is recognised as actually King of Castile, during his short life-time. There were thus two kings at least in the land, the great cities of Toledo, Seville, Cordova, and Burgos, together with nearly all the districts of the south, joining with the enemies of Enrique. The country was in the greatest confusion. Both sides flew to arms, the cause of Enrique being the stronger in Asturias, and his party being recruited, in spite of his unworthiness and timidity in the field, by those who still adhered to the ancient Castilian standards of loyalty, and those who were jealous or fearful of the growing power of the confederate nobles. The Marquess of Villena, the chief of the insurgents, entered into a traitorous correspondence with Enrique with the object, apparently, not so much of bringing the dispute to an end as of keeping it alive, by preserving an equilibrium between the rival forces for his own ambitious ends. An indecisive battle ensued between the two parties at Olmedo, in which the turbulent Archbishop of Toledo (there is always an Archbishop of Toledo on these occasions) was in the forefront of the fight, receiving a lance thrust in the arm. A papal legate who came on the field to intervene was dismissed with jeers and threats of personal violence. He was told, in contumelious words, that "the Pope had no business to interfere in the temporal concerns of Castile—that the Castilians had a perfect right to depose their king, having grounds sufficient, and would exercise that right without hindrance." Then the king himself, who had a constitutional aversion to bloodshed, consented to meet

ALEAZAR OF SEGOVIA.

the insurgent leaders at Segovia, to arrange an accommodation. A period of chaos and confusion ensued, without precedent even in the history of Castile. City fought against city; street against street. The churches were fortified and used for places of war. The powerful nobles who had their own particular feuds to settle took that opportunity for waging war with each other. The great houses of Guzman and of Ponce de Leon, each claiming to be supreme in Andalusia, fought desperately, with armies rivalling those of kings, while the Moors looked on with wonder and hope, expecting a consummation as bissful for them as when the vices of the Goths led to the subversion of Spain.

From his own personal perplexities Enrique was for a time relieved by the sudden death of his brother and rival, Alfonso, in July, 1468, under circumstances, as usual, suggestive of poison—one very suspicious circumstance being that three days before the prince expired his death was announced throughout the kingdom—" a thing of great marvel," says the chronicler, in innocence or in irony. Alfonso was the Marcellus of his age and country, the worthy brother of the Princess Isabel, who, had he survived—he was only fifteen when he died—would have changed the whole current of Spanish history. His death brought his sister Isabel to the front as the legitimate successor to the crown. The confederate nobles turned towards her as their only hope. Isabel, however, though only sixteen years of age, behaved with a prudence and magnanimity which gave auspicious presage of her future career. Up to the date of the battle of Olmedo she had sided with the king—at least, had continued to dwell in his family—a trial she had endured not so much out of love for her half-brother as for the sake of his protection and as a refuge from the numerous suitors whom her personal charms and brilliant expectations had brought to her feet. She then found an opportunity of seeking shelter with Alfonso and his adherents. Upon his death she betook herself to a monastery at Avila. There she was visited by the Archbishop of Toledo who, in the name of the confederates, offered her the crown. Isabel, however, with equal sagacity and nobility of heart, refused to accept that perilous and onerous dignity, desiring to intercede between the king and the nobles. There being no other member of the royal family in whose name the confederates could hope to gain the people, they gave a reluctant consent to come to terms with Enrique. The conditions of the peace were, that a general amnesty should be proclaimed; that the Queen Juana, whose conduct had given rise to so much scandal, should be divorced from her husband and sent back to Portugal; that Isabel should be recognised as heir to the crowns of Castile and Leon, with the principality of Asturias for her present estate; that the Cortes should be summoned to give a legal sanction to her title, and for the amendment of the flagrant abuses of the government; lastly, that Isabel should be free to marry whom she pleased, provided her choice was confirmed by her brother. A meeting took place between Enrique and his sister near the spot marked by the mystic sculptured monsters, supposed to be of præ-Roman origin, called the *Toros de Guisando*, on the 9th of September, 1468, which was made the occasion of a solemn function—the nobles present tendering their homage to Enrique as king, and kissing the hand of Isabel as their future queen.

Thus happily, for a time at least, was concluded the long and most disastrous quarrel between Enrique and his subjects, in a manner more fortunate for the king than he had any right or claim to expect.

The next trouble was how to dispose of Isabel's hand, which was solved by that princess in a manner very characteristic of her good sense and firmness of character. Among her wooers were scions of most of the royal houses of Europe, including the Duke of Clarence, brother to King Edward IV. of England, and the Duke of Guienne who held the same relation to King Louis XI. of France. A Prince of Aragon also, as to the fabled casquets of Belmont, " came to his election presently "—in the person of Fernando, son of Juan II. of that country. Isabel had shrewdly sent a trusty agent to inspect the French and the Aragonese pretenders, who came back with a report that the Duke of Guienne was an effeminate man, with limbs so emaciated as to be almost deformed, and rheumy eyes which unfitted him for the exercises of chivalry. Prince Fernando, on the other hand, was declared to be a very proper man, of a comely visage and figure, and a spirit equal to anything. Isabel fixed her choice upon her kinsman of Aragon ; and never in the annals of courtly marriage was a match so happy and so entirely blessed. Fernando, now in his eighteenth year, had every qualification to fit him to be Isabel's husband, while being heir to Aragon their marriage would bring peace and unity to the two countries which between them made up Spain. Such a union had been longed for by the wisest and coolest heads in both countries, but hitherto it had been defeated, more than once, when to all seeming it had been ripe for accomplishment, by old jealousies and national prejudices, kept alive by interested courtiers on either side.

Nor was it without some delays and after much negotiation and disputing that the well-assorted couple were made one. The chief of the late insurgent nobles, the Marquess of Villena, saw in this alliance the ruin of all his hopes of future distinction. Isabel, by this marriage, would have in her service a strong arm, able to keep down all the enemies of the Crown. Moreover, Aragon had claims over the greater part of the estate of Villena, which were likely to be vigorously enforced when the countries were united. The great family of the Mendozas, for other reasons equally selfish, were averse to the marriage. An intrigue was entered into with Portugal by the malcontent nobles, into which the worthless King Enrique was drawn—the bait to him being a marriage between *La Beltraneja*, whom Enrique had never ceased to claim for his own daughter, with the son and heir of King Alfonso of Portugal. This match, which would unite the two kingdoms in the next reign, was proposed by the faction of Villena as an alternative to the union with Aragon. The King of Portugal himself, who was a widower, paid his addresses to the Princess Isabella, but his suit was pressed so roughly by the king, who endeavoured to force his sister into the marriage, in violation of the compact by which he promised to respect her wishes, that the people rose in revolt. Songs insulting to Portugal and friendly to Aragon were sung in the streets. Supported by a powerful section of the nobles, by the Archbishop of Toledo, who represented not only the higher clergy but a very formidable military force, and by the entire people, Isabel felt herself justified in taking steps to conclude her marriage with Prince Fernando, without further regard to her brother's wishes. The marriage articles were signed on the 7th of January, 1469. By these Fernando, on whom had now been bestowed by his father the title of King of Sicily, was bound strictly to respect the laws and customs of Castile; to reside within that kingdom, never leaving it without his queen's permission; to recognise her as the sole fountain of honours and benefices in Castile; and indeed to accept his consort as an equal partner with himself in all the right of sovereignty in respect of the two kingdoms. Even after this contract was signed, the terms of which illustrate in a striking manner the jealousy which still existed between Aragon and Castile, the match was on the point of being broken of by violence. The Marquess of Villena, in concert with the king, made an attempt to capture Isabel's person, which was only defeated by the vigilance of a few faithful adherents and the activity of the Archbishop of Toledo, who collected a body of horse and carried the princess off in safety to Valladolid, before the enemy could reach her. The adventures of Prince Fernando in quest of his bride were scarcely less strange and stirring. He had to run the gauntlet of King Enrique's guards and the partisans of Mendoza and Villena, before he could pass the frontier, and was compelled to disguise himself, incurring much peril and discomfort, including shortness of money, before he could arrive at any place in the power of Isabel's adherents. However, his courage and address, which were worthy of a knight of romance, were at last crowned with all the success due to so gallant an enterprise. After finding shelter for a while in a faithful town of Leon, Fernando was brought to Valladolid and introduced to his mistress. The rest of the business, which for its romantic interest as well as for all the important issues which hung thereby has occupied so large a space in history, may be here passed over briefly. The marriage of Fernando and Isabel, that union so auspicious for Castile and Aragon, was solemnised on the 19th of October, 1469, amidst a scene of popular enthusiasm which made amends for the lack of more courtly ceremonies. The King Enrique was dutifully informed by his sister of the step she had taken, and returned a churlish answer that he would "take counsel with his ministers."

The counsel he followed was such as might be expected from a man of his worthless character, smarting under a rebuff so public and humiliating. His first step was to convoke the Cortes in order to get his supposed daughter, Juana (the hapless Beltraneja), once more recognised as his heir, to the exclusion of Isabel—his compact with whom at Toros de Guisando he declared had been broken by her disobedience in marrying contrary to his wishes. The Cortes declining to come together for such a purpose, the king, at the instigation of the Marquess of Villena, who now chose to be called by his new dignity of Master of Santiago, offered Juana to the

Duke of Guienne, with a view to cement his alliance with France. At a meeting between the representatives of the two countries, Juana was formally affianced to the Duke in October, 1470. But once more Enrique's plans for the assertion of his much doubted paternity were doomed to be disappointed. The Duke of Guienne died suddenly, "of herbs," administered, it is suggested, by his brother Louis XI., to which astute monarch the prospect of his relative's aggrandisement by the Spanish marriage was probably less attractive than it was to Enrique. The prospects of Isabel and Fernando were still somewhat gloomy, owing to the frightful state of anarchy in which the country was plunged, which seemed to promise a total dissolution of the social order. A picture of the universal demoralisation is given in some satirical verses which were now in the mouths of the people, called *Coplas de Mingo Revulgo*, in which, with mystic phrases made purposely obscure, but probably clearer to those of that time than they are to us, the vices of the Court, the clergy, and the higher orders are lashed with a fierce and bitter sarcasm. A prophet, under the guise of a shepherd named *Gil Arribato*, addresses *Mingo Revulgo* (a personification of "the people"), asking him why he is so gloomy and depressed. *Mingo Revulgo* answers that it is by reason of his misfortunes ; that he has a shepherd who deserts his flock, who goes after his own pleasures and lusts. Meanwhile the four dogs which should guard the flock, Justice, Fortitude, Prudence, and Temperance, are destroyed, so that the wolves are come in to the sheep and are devouring them. Then the prophet retorts that the evil is not wholly the shepherd's fault, but proceeds from the vices of the people, suggesting that if Faith, Hope, and Charity were to reign, they would not suffer the ills they have. Such is the general purport of these celebrated couplets, which seem to have had a vogue far in excess of their poetical merit, though they abound in picturesque and forcible passages, because they expressed, as without doubt they may be taken to do, the popular opinion respecting the evils and disorders of this miserable period. There is little doubt that some of the stanzas, purposely veiled in obscurity, are intended to presage the coming of a better time, when, under the new kings, Isabel and Fernando, justice and truth will prevail, and the people have a purer and stronger government.

Meanwhile the last years of Enrique were spent in a continuous series of intrigues to keep out his sister from her inheritance, which he was doing his best to spoil by his mingled rapacity, profligacy, and feebleness. In an age of general depravity, Castile had sunk to the lowest point of wretchedness; and when Enrique terminated his inglorious life, in 1474, the relief to the nation was hailed with universal joy. With him ended the line of Trastamara, which had reigned in Castile for a hundred years.

Before we take up the story of Isabel it is necessary, to the due understanding of her husband's position, that we should return to the affairs of Aragon.

Fernando I., the Castilian prince, who had been elected as King of Aragon in 1411, had but a brief reign, which was disturbed by the efforts of the Count of Urgel to regain possession of the kingdom. Under his successor, Alfonso V., a prince of great capacity and boundless ambition, Aragon greatly increased her importance in Europe by foreign annexations. Throughout the greater part of his reign Alfonso was engaged in wars and intrigues for the extension of his dominion in Italy and in the islands of the Mediterranean, the details of which, scarcely belonging to our history, may be briefly given. In Sardinia and Corsica, the Aragonese had been for some time in possession of the supreme authority, which was perpetually disturbed by risings among the native population, and by the enterprises of the Genoese Republic, now nearing the height of its greatness. Under Alfonso V., vigorous attempts were made to re-establish the Aragonese authority, which was for a season diverted into a more promising quarter. Joanna, Queen of Naples, weary of her husband and his nation, had expelled the French from her dominions. Fearing the vengeance of France, she placed herself under the protection of Aragon, offering to adopt Alfonso as her heir, on condition of his supporting her on the throne. In spite of the advice of his council, who then, as always, were averse to foreign conquest, which called away their sovereign from his native affairs and laid heavy burdens on the exchequer, Alfonso accepted this proposal, and thus became involved in a war with both France and Genoa, during which he had sufficient opportunity to judge of the fickleness of the Neapolitans. Received as a conqueror on his arrival with a powerful fleet at

Naples, it was not long before the capricious queen made an attempt to take his life, first by poison, next by the dagger. He was then assailed by the combined forces of the Neapolitans and the French, and found himself besieged in a narrow quarter of the city. Reinforced by troops from Spain, Alfonso was enabled to recover Naples and drive the French from the walls. Called back to attend to his own affairs in Aragon, once more the tide of fortune turned against Alfonso at Naples—the French, with their allies, regaining possession of the kingdom. A few years afterwards, Queen Joanna once more justified the character of her sex, by quarrelling with the French, turning out the Duke of Anjou, and seeking the aid of Alfonso. Pope Martin also, who had a few years before excommunicated the King of Aragon, turned round and espoused his cause, upon some quarrel with the French. In 1432, Alfonso set sail with a powerful armament, with which he landed in Sicily. Two years afterwards, Queen Joanna being dead, Alfonso landed at Gaeta, to claim his promised kingdom of Naples. But a new combination of states, more powerful than the old, was formed against Aragon, France having secured the alliance not only of the Genoese, but of their rivals, the Venetians and the Florentines, together with the new Pope and the Duke of Milan. A great naval battle was fought off the Neapolitan coast, which proved most disastrous to Aragon—her ships being destroyed or captured, and the king himself, with his two brothers, Juan and Enrique, being taken prisoners. This was the severest blow ever inflicted on the maritime power of Aragon, which transferred the command of the inland sea from them to their jealous commercial rivals, the Genoese and the Venetians.

Alfonso himself, through the chivalrous generosity of his captor, the Duke of Milan, was almost immediately released, without ransom, only to renew, on his return to Aragon, his designs upon Naples. In 1438 he was once more before Naples, in opposition to his old competitor, the Duke of Anjou, gaining victories by sea and land, and in the end obtaining possession of the city, after a great battle in which the French, Genoese, and Papal troops were defeated. Finally Alfonso succeeded in winning over Pope Eugenius, and on condition of holding the kingdom of the Two Sicilies as a fief of the Holy See was confirmed in his Italian dominion. Dying soon afterwards, in 1458, the King of Aragon, who did little for his own country, left his Spanish dominions, together with Sicily, Sardinia, and the Balearic Islands, to his brother Juan, who was then King of Navarre, and Naples to his bastard son, Fernando, whom he had induced the Pope to declare legitimate.

With Juan II., who is chiefly known in history as the father of the prince under whom Aragon was made one with Castile, this history has little to do. He was, like all his house, a restless and turbulent monarch, ever busy with designs of conquest, who, while King of Navarre, was engaged in an unnatural contest with his own son Carlos. As King of Aragon, he was involved in a dangerous quarrel with a portion of his own subjects, the Catalans, who, instigated by Louis XI. of France, broke out into rebellion, at one time setting up a republic, at another offering themselves as vassals to the King of Castile, and finally giving themselves to the Infante of Portugal, who had some claim, on the maternal side, to the crown of Aragon. In the tangled series of wars and intestinal troubles which followed, in which Louis XI. followed his usual tortuous policy, first playing with one side and then with the other as it suited his interest, which was to gain possession of Roussillon and some coveted frontier forts as Perpignan, King Juan was greatly assisted by his second wife, the daughter of the Admiral of Castile, and by her son, Fernando. Dying in 1479, Juan II. was succeeded in Aragon, Sicily, and Sardinia, by Fernando, who was already consort of Isabel, the Queen of Castile and Leon.

XII.

REIGN OF ISABEL AND FERNANDO—UNION OF CAS-
TILE AND ARAGON—PEACE AND ORDER IN
SPAIN—THE INQUISITION—WAR WITH THE
MOORS AND CAPTURE OF GRANADA—THE
END.

(1474-1492.)

WITH the accession of Isabel to the throne of Castile there began a new era for Spain. She was proclaimed at Segovia by an assembly of the great nobles, the clergy, and the principal dignitaries of state, amidst the acclamations of all classes of the people, on the 15th of December, 1474—being the second of her line to whom the designation of *reina propietaria* belongs. The jealous Castilians from the first took care to separate her title from that of her husband, for though the union was popular in both countries it was not until many years afterwards that Aragon and Castile were made one. Fernando, who was still only prince of Aragon—his father the king, being alive—was not present when his consort received the homage of her subjects. He seems to have made, through his relatives and personal adherents, a somewhat ungracious attempt to claim the exclusive sovereignty as its lawful inheritor, being the male representative of the house of Trastamara. But the question being submitted to the arbitration of the two archbishops of Toledo and Seville they decided that, according to the law of Castile which, unlike that of Aragon, did not exclude females from the throne, Isabel was the sole rightful heir of the kingdom, and

CROWN OF ISABEL THE CATHOLIC.

that Fernando's authority was only such as he derived from his wife. This decision being given, a contract in the terms of the marriage settlement was made, which Fernando, to his honour, ever afterwards loyally observed, the subsequent happiness which ensued to the two countries through this marriage being greatly due to the judicious and politic fidelity with which that prince interpreted the duties of his double position.

The young couple, on whom devolved the arduous task of lifting the much distracted country out of the misery and disorder into which it had been plunged by years of misrule, were not unworthy of each other, in graces of person as in gifts of mind. Isabel was now in her twenty-fourth year ; in form and aspect fitted to command universal love and homage—tall of stature, with the fair skin, ruddy hair, and blue eyes, which marked her northern descent,[1] with regular features, and a serene and open countenance. Her charm of manner and benignity of disposition were equal to her beauty of person, making up a queen such as to her delighted people seemed expressly bestowed by Heaven for the relief of an afflicted realm. The chroniclers are too much enamoured of her to speak with due composure of her merits. By her contemporaries and by posterity she has had the rare good fortune to be equally praised. She was Shakespeare's "queen of earthly queens" —by Francis Bacon pronounced "an honour to her sex and the corner-stone of the greatness of Spain." She was the embodiment of all that poets and painters have feigned or imagined of grace and majesty—the flower of womanhood—in virtue as excelling as in wisdom, and truly a creature of rare mould, in form, heart, and mind, who came as near to be the type of the perfect sovereign as any king or queen who ever reigned. Fernando, whatever he may have become afterwards when he lost his partner and his good genius, was in early manhood not unworthy to

---

[1] Isabel was descended from the Plantagenets on both sides, her father being the grandson, and her mother the great-grand-daughter, of John of Gaunt.

FERNANDO THE CATHOLIC.

be the mate of Isabel. He was a year younger than his wife and somewhat less in stature—a prince of excellent endowments, physical and mental, such as made him not unequal to his good fortune and his dignity—of "a blood and judgment well commingled,"—sober, astute, active, and cool-headed. The first days of their joint government were not without the usual troubles of a new reign in Castile. Although the great body of the nobles and the clergy, with probably the mass of the people, who longed for nothing so much as repose and security, had accepted Isabel as their queen with warmth and gladness, there were still some malcontents who could not brook the new order which seemed unpropitious to their designs and unfavourable to their interests. At their head was the young Marquess of Villena, son of the arch-rebel of the late reign, whose vast estates made him the most powerful subject in Castile. He and his faction were joined by the old Archbishop of Toledo, once a zealous adherent of Isabel, but now—through jealousy of his brother of Seville, the Cardinal Mendoza, who had quickly risen into the place of the queen's chief adviser—turned into a bitter enemy. These traitors proposed to Alfonso V., King of Portugal, a scheme for marrying his niece Juana (*La Beltraneja*), and thus securing to himself her title to the inheritance of Castile. Alfonso, a man of ardent and warlike character, better fitted for a knight-errant than a king, who had acquired the name of "the African" by his sterile victories over the Moors of Barbary, permitted himself to be drawn into this wild adventure. Crossing the frontier with a powerful army, Alfonso met his destined bride, now thirteen years of age, at Plasencia. After being solemnly affianced to her the pair were proclaimed, in all form, King and Queen of Castile. Isabel and Fernando seem to have been taken by surprise by the Portuguese invasion, and had some difficulty in finding the necessary supplies with which to raise an army. Aided, however, by the patriotic devotion of the people, and especially by the clergy, who did not hesitate (to the disgust of the zealous churchmen of a subsequent age), to sacrifice one half of their plate for the national cause, the royal pair, mainly through Isabel's personal exertions, were able to collect a sufficient force with which to encounter the King of Portugal. The two armies met on a plain near the city of Toro, and after a battle, in which the international hatreds fed by three centuries of incessant hostility had full vent, the Portuguese were utterly defeated. The disgrace of Aljubarrota was amply avenged. The King of Portugal narrowly escaped being taken prisoner, and was forced to retire into Portugal, leaving Isabel and Fernando undisturbed in their dominion. The unlucky *Beltraneja*, the innocent cause of so many evils, was parted from her would-be husband by a bull from the Pope, and remitted to a convent; while the Marquess of Villena and the Archbishop of Toledo were forced to seek for pardon at a heavy sacrifice of money and estate.

In the measures subsequently taken for the pacification of the kingdom Isabel took an active personal share. While her husband was engaged in securing the frontier of Aragon on the side of Navarre and in winning over the wily Louis XI.—" ever strong upon the stronger side"—to his cause, Isabel led an army into Estremadura, reducing the strongholds of the insurgent nobles and confirming her authority. At length, in 1479, a treaty of peace was made with Portugal, by which Alfonso relinquished his claim on Juana, gave up her pretensions to the throne, and agreed to take the infant daughter of Isabel and Fernando, then in her cradle, for a wife to his son and heir, Don Juan. The poor *Beltraneja*, tossed about from husband to husband, who had witnessed her hopes of being settled in life so often frustrated, finally disposed of herself and ended her troubles by becoming a nun.

The death of the old King of Aragon in 1479 raised Fernando to the throne of that kingdom, and thus were the two countries united at last, after a separation of nearly eight hundred years. There was still a corner of Spain, extending over the border, which for a few years longer retained a nominal independence, chiefly through its geographical position which made it neither all Spanish nor wholly French. But Navarre also fell to the mingled force and address of Fernando; and thus was laid the last stone to the fabric which, in the next century, towered to such a height in Europe.

The first care of Isabel and Fernando, after they were fairly established in their sovereignty, was to redress that social order which by the crimes and weaknesses of their predecessors had been so seriously damaged. The strong hand and the cool head required to deal with the enormous evils which had sprung from the almost total decay of the executive authority, during the last two feeble reigns, were fortunately found in Isabel and her consort. Aided by her wise and sagacious counsellor, the Cardinal Mendoza, the queen—on whom devolved the principal share of the work of internal administration—went about her reforms with a vigour, promptitude, and courage, such as must have amazed that careless and profligate age, when the people had almost ceased to believe in kings and judges. The greatest and most sweeping of Isabel's reforms was the establishment, or rather the re-institution, of that tremendous engine of law, the *Santa Hermandad* or Holy Brotherhood. By an adroit stroke of policy the Holy Brotherhood, hitherto an instrument in the hands of the enemies of order, which was practically never used except against the crown, was turned into a very potent weapon in support of the executive. Originally a kind of vigilance committee, of irregular and uncertain action, which overrode and set aside the formal operation of justice, the Holy Brotherhood, to which every householder had to contribute, whose affairs were regulated by a central body chosen from the principal citizens throughout the kingdom, was erected into a most formidable tribunal, which had its own officers, and executed its own sentences, by the most simple and summary of processes. In a few years, in spite of the great nobles, who viewed with alarm this dangerous encroachment on their prerogatives, the Holy Brotherhood succeeded in restoring an unwonted degree of order and security throughout the country. The personal influence of Isabel was no less conspicuous in the measures taken to curb the insolence and rapacity of the grandees, who had possessed themselves by force or trickery of fortresses belonging to the crown, under pretence of their being included in their estates, from which they had been accustomed to wage war on each other or against the king. In the province of Galicia alone, we are told, more than fifty castles—the abodes of petty brigand knights, who lived by spoiling their neighbours—were razed to the ground. Highway robbers, taken in the red hand, were executed on the spot, being shot to death by arrows, their bodies exposed on the road tied to stakes.[1] For the first time, perhaps, in the annals of Spain, the roads were made safe to unarmed travellers. The people, freed from their old oppressors, blessed God, we are told, for "a deliverance from an evil worse than captivity." Nor were Isabel's labours confined to the improvement of the process of justice. The higher tribunals were re-organised, their proceedings simplified, the judges made more independent. New laws were passed for securing the liberty of the subject, for the punishment of corrupt or unjust magistrates, and for securing a cheap and speedy trial for offenders. For the better maintenance of the law in its dignity and popularity the sovereigns themselves were accustomed to preside on the judgment bench,

---

[1] The readers of "Don Quixote" will remember Sancho Panza's terror of the Holy Brotherhood when engaged with his master in his knight-errantries. The severity of the law, however, had been much relaxed before the time of Cervantes—the Emperor Charles V., out of his great clemency, decreeing that the malefactor should be strangled before being pierced by arrows.

after the ancient custom of the Castilian kings. At the great Cortes held at Toledo, 1480, which confirmed these and many other salutary measures, it was ruled that the king should take his seat in the Council one day in every week. Freed from civil war, rapine, and bloodshed, the people might well believe that the Golden Age had returned. The change in the condition of the country was nothing short of a revolution, perhaps the most thorough and wholesome which had ever been made in the life of a nation. Not without warrant does Fernando de Pulgar, an eye-witness of these reforms and secretary to the "Catholic Kings," write that "whereas the kingdom had been filled with robbers and malefactors of every kind, who committed the most devilish outrages, in open contempt of the law, there was now such terror impressed on the hearts of all that none dared lift his hand against another, or even assail him with reproachful or discourteous language. The knight and the squire, who had formerly oppressed the labouring man, were intimidated by the fear of that justice which was certain to be executed on all; the roads were swept of robbers; the castles, the strongholds of violence, were thrown down; and the whole nation, restored to tranquillity and order, looked for no other redress than that afforded by the operation of the law." The reform of the judicature was accompanied by a new codification of the laws, which, taking for their basis the *Siete Partidas* of Alfonso X., were brought into conformity with the spirit of the age and the demands of the nation. The civil revenue and expenditure were ordered and controlled;

the various branches of the executive duly defined and their duties prescribed ; the Cortes remodelled and the rights and privileges of the deputies placed on a surer footing. The power of the sovereign which had necessarily increased as the feudal system (which had never taken very firm root in Spain) fell into decay—perhaps rather as the grandees exhausted themselves in their petty civil wars—was itself regulated and restrained, and if it reached, as doubtless it did, during the reign of Isabel and Fernando to a higher point than ever, leading the way to the autocracy of Charles V. and of Philip II., it was as much through the prestige acquired from the personal character of Isabel and of her consort as by any direct assertion of a higher royal prerogative.

Unfortunately for the reputation of Isabel with posterity, the queen was not content to be the protector of the bodies of her subjects. Inspired by a zeal which, in the eyes of the native historian, constitutes her chief glory, as being the basis of her claim to the appellation of "the Catholic," Isabel, who in such matters was entirely under the power of her spiritual advisers, undertook to purge the souls of her people. Cardinal Mendoza, whose influence over the sovereigns had gained him the title of " Tertius Rex," does not appear, indeed, to have been the principal agent in turning Isabel's mind to the re-establishment of the Holy Inquisition, with a view to the uprooting of heresy. That honour is due to the famous Torquemada, the queen's confessor in her early days, who is said to have extorted a pledge from her that when she came to the throne she would devote herself to the extirpation of heresy "for the glory of God and the exaltation of the Catholic faith." Isabel, we are told, on coming to the throne, resisted for a long time the importunities of her ecclesiastical advisers, who urged her to the fulfilment of her vow ; and it was not until 1478 that, at the instance of her husband (the Inquisition was already of long standing in Aragon), she was prevailed upon to ask for a bull from the Pope, to introduce the Holy Office into Castile.

There can be no greater injustice than to condemn one century by the standard to which a later has arrived, through long ages of trial and a slow process of development; nor does it become us, in times which have witnessed the deportation of a whole people from their country and homes, by the arbitrary decree of a monarch who ranks among the greatest of European princes, to be too severe on Isabel because, true to the creed in which she had been suckled, she resolved upon the forcible conversion of the Jews. To bring that ancient race within the bosom of the Church was the chief object of the Inquisition. For greater aggravation of their sin of heresy the Jews, then as now, got riches—while good Christians, "old and rank," such as Sancho Panza took his chief glory in being, remained poor "The accursed race," to the scandal and confusion of true nobility, even dared to ally themselves by marriage with the great Christian families, and so to pollute the pure stream of blue Gothic blood. First introduced into Aragon in the early part of the Thirteenth century for the special benefit of the Albigenses, the Inquisition, contrary to what its apologists have maintained, was never to the taste of the Spanish people. It required all the authority of the Church, then rapidly growing into its monopoly of power and absorbing all the wealth and intellect of the kingdom, to force it upon a reluctant nation. It was not until after many delays and much opposition from all the secular bodies in the state that the Holy Office was instituted. Isabel herself, who has borne with posterity an undue share of the odium of this baleful measure, gave her consent to it with reluctance, doing her best to mitigate its severities. It is significant that the Cortes, who, as Prescott notes, were sitting at the time, engaged in passing severe laws against the Jews, abstained from making any reference to the new tribunal, whose powers, as novel as they were terrible to the people, were doubtless jealously regarded by the proud Castilians. However, the priests prevailed, having on their side King Fernando, who, less from piety than from policy, was not disinclined to a measure which promised to divert a large portion of the wealth of the unbelievers into the ill-furnished national exchequer. The Inquisition was formally proclaimed on the 2nd of January, 1481, by a decree which required all persons guilty of heresy—that is, of not accepting the Catholic faith—to make public confession of their fault, on pain of being burnt at the stake. Some late defenders of the Holy Office. using an argument which would have scandalised its founders, have set up the plea that the delinquents were not burnt for defect of belief, but for sedition, or at least incivism—that they were punished, in fact, not because they were heretics but because they were traitors—that the Inquisition really took no man's life, seeing that it handed over every one it condemned to the "secular arm." By a parity of argument one might acquit Judge Jefferies of his butcheries, for it is certain that the judge did not hang the west-country rebels with his own hands. The fact remains that, within the period dating from the promulgation of the decree to their final expulsion, in 1492, shortly after the fall of Granada, two thousand Jews were burnt alive in Andalusia, while seventeen thousand were permitted to make "reconciliation," that is to say, to save their lives by giving up all their property and submitting to lesser penalties, such as civil incapacity, or imprisonment, or banishment. The Jews, at whom the stroke was levelled, by a piece of cold-blooded barbarism from which even the persecuting Muscovite has recoiled, were not even permitted to get away—to carry their heresies and their lives elsewhere. They would like to have taken refuge with the Mahommedans of Granada, but then both their souls and their properties would have been lost to the Christian state; and confiscation of the Jewish treasure was one of the means through which Isabel and Fernando hoped to raise the fund for the still greater work of faith which was now thrust upon them—that final enterprise which was to crown and consummate their work of empire — namely, the destruction of the one remaining Moorish kingdom, and the total extirpation of the infidels from Spanish soil.

The war with Granada, now the only Moslem state in the Peninsula, where was concentrated all that was left of the once proud heritage of the

Omeyyad Khalifs, broke out not by the choice of the Catholic sovereigns but through an act of hare-brained audacity on the part of the Moorish king, Abu-l-Hassan. Fernando was slow in responding to the challenge. The Catholic kings were still occupied in the settlement of their domestic affairs—in the arrangements for the cure of heresy. It may be doubted whether Isabel, though not wanting in the martial spirit of her race, engaged in the war with any view to conquest or increase of dominion. When finally prevailed upon to consent to the expedition against Granada, it was probably less through motives of policy than of piety. As in her subsequent compact with the Genoese adventurer, one Christopher Colon, the queen was moved not so much by a desire to extend her empire as to add to the number of souls to be saved. The thought of recovering the lost soil of Spain, of revenging the disaster of Guadalete, of rounding off and completing the Christian kingdom, had as yet not entered into Isabel's mind. The Moors, though their dominions were much shrunk, had dwelt for so many years side by side with the Christians on terms not always unfriendly, that their existence seemed not incompatible with the security and integrity of the Spanish kingdom. There had been an interchange of good offices quite recently between the two powers. The kings of Granada had mostly paid tribute, and such desultory attempts as had been made to disturb their reign had not always been attended with advantage to the Christians. Though now comparatively few in number, the Moors were concentrated in a strong position. Their capital city, now at the height of its splendour, larger and richer than any town in Spain, could itself send out, on short notice, an army of fifty thousand men, better equipped and furnished than any force which could be raised in Spain—skilled in war, and highly trained by constant exercise therein, of whom the light horsemen and archers were reckoned among the best in Europe.

The Moors themselves, though enervated by luxurious living and torn by family feuds, still retained their old capacity for war, nor had lost their martial temper. With an infatuation, engendered perhaps by his successes in the field against the feeble Enrique IV., the Moorish king, when required to pay his annual tribute in 1476, sent back a message that "the mints of Granada no longer coined gold but steel." In 1481 Abu-l-Hassan, without warning or direct provocation, marched across the frontier and took by storm the frontier fort of Zahara. This led to a reprisal, in an enterprise singularly characteristic of the Castilian temper, as showing that whether the sovereign was prepared or not, there were those within the kingdom who were ready to force his hand. A body of men, the personal retainers of the famous Marquess of Cadiz, Rodrigo Ponce de Leon, marched into the heart of the territory of Granada, and took by assault the city and fortress of Alhama. Alhama, within eight leagues of the capital, was believed to be impregnable. It was the pearl of the Moorish realm—the favourite seat of the king, renowned for wealth and luxury—the centre of a world-famous silk industry—whose loss spread grief and terror throughout all Moordom, in proportion as the exploit, to be counted among the most brilliant feats of Spanish chivalry, filled the Christians with mingled joy and wonder. So deep was the sensation created by this disaster, that no one in Granada was permitted to speak of it on pain of death. The news of this daring stroke helped to spur on the Catholic sovereigns to that task which, at first, they seem to have entered upon with reluctance. Preparations were made in all haste for the reinforcement of the heroic captors of Alhama, who were now in turn besieged by a formidable army of Moors. The defence of the place was no less glorious to the Castilian arms than its capture had been. In vain did the besiegers bring all their overwhelming resources, in men and in engines of war, to bear upon the town. Ponce de Leon held out until— to make the romantic story complete—he was relieved by his deadly hereditary foe, the Duke of Medina Sidonia, the head of the Guzmans, who, without waiting for King Fernando to join him, hastened at the head of all the power of his great house, which comprised half the manhood of Andalusia, to the aid of the beleaguered garrison. The King of Granada retired on the approach of the Christians. The Duke of Medina Sidonia, after sacking and despoiling the city, withdrew his army, leaving a small garrison to defend the fortress. Once more the Moors invested the place, bringing with them a large train of artillery, which they had been in too great a hurry to provide in the first siege.

Vigorous measures were now taken to prosecute the war on the Christian side. Isabel, who at first had been lukewarm in the enterprise, now urged it with equal ardour and wisdom—insisting that Alhama, as the key of the enemy's frontier, must be retained at all cost, and infusing her own spirit into her people and her passionless consort. Preparations for the campaign were now made on a scale which betokened that this was to be no mere military promenade as those in the last reign, or a foray for plunder, or even a campaign for the enlargement of the border; but a war for the faith, having for its object the final extinction of the Moorish dominion.

The main army under the command of Fernando in person entered the *Vega* of Granada in July, 1482, its first aim being Loja—a city set upon the hills, which offered a vigorous resistance to the Christians. Fernando, who was no great general, handled his men so badly, getting them into a difficult position, that the Moors were enabled, with a comparatively small force, to repulse the king's army, and even to inflict upon him a defeat which might have ended in a total rout but for his personal coolness. The Castilians were forced to retire from before Loja with heavy loss, including their artillery and baggage—Fernando betaking himself for refuge to Cordova, while the Moors recovered nearly all their lost ground.

At this crisis, when the hopes of Christian Spain were at the lowest, and even the indomitable soul of Isabel was in despair, one of those chamber revolutions broke out in Granada, so common in Oriental history, and changed the whole aspect of affairs. The King Abu-l-Hassan was expelled from Granada by a rising of the people, led by his son Abu Abdallah, or rather by the Queen Zoraya, of Castilian descent. Indignant at her husband's preference for a younger wife, Zoraya, with her clansmen of the Zegries, between whom and the Abencerrajes there raged a deadly blood feud, stirred up that revolt which led to the downfall of her race and kingdom. The romantic story of these troublous times in Granada has been elsewhere told so fully that it need not occupy us longer here. The civil war between Abu-l-Hassan and his son materially contributed to the triumph of the Christians, and precipitated the fall of Granada. The war languished for a time, through the exhaustion of both parties. The Moors, divided as they were between the partisans of the old king whose seat was at Malaga, and Abu Abdallah (better known by his Spanish nickname of *El Rey Chico*—the Little King) at Granada, even won some battles in the field. At last Abu Abdallah was defeated and made prisoner at Lucena, upon which the fickle citizens of Granada, inspired by the Abencerrajes, took back Abu-l-Hassan, his father. But Abu Abdallah being liberated, by the shrewd policy of Fernando, upon a pledge of paying up all arrears of tribute and becoming a faithful vassal of the Christian kingdom, went back to Granada, to weaken his kingdom once more by civil dissension. Weary of the calamitous civil war which was being waged in the face of the enemy, the Moorish chiefs resolved to get rid of both father and son—setting up another Abdallah, a younger brother of Abu-l-Hassan, called from his lustihood *Es-Zagal* (the Valiant One). Ez-Zagal well justified his name and the confidence of his countrymen, making a stout fight of it and inflicting a severe defeat on the Christians in the defiles of the Axarquia. Stirred to action by this reverse, Fernando—who would rather have turned his arms against France in prosecution of his claims on Roussillon—consented to join his queen in a great armament which was now prepared for the invasion of Granada and the final subjugation of the Moors, which included ten thousand horsemen and forty thousand foot, with the largest supply of artillery and munitions of war ever seen in Spain. Volunteers from all parts of Europe joined the army, including a contingent of Swiss—a people who had lately earned great military renown by their victories over the Duke of Burgundy—and some English knights, among whom were the Earl of Rivers and Lord Scales. Queen Isabel herself accompanied the army, with her daughter and a train of damsels, splendidly mounted on mules, by the side of whom rode the Cardinal Mendoza—lately advanced, by the death of his old rival Alfonso de Carrillo, to the Archbishopric of Toledo. The Spaniards, taught by their recent reverses, advanced leisurely into the field, taking town after town in their march, in spite of all the attempts of the gallant Ez-Zagal to arrest their progress by cutting off their detached foraging parties and laying waste the country in their rear. The iron chain round the devoted city was gradually drawn tighter on the north and west. The people of Granada still continuing to receive supplies from the coast, it was resolved to send an expedition against Malaga—then an important seaport town the chief *entrepôt* of the Moorish foreign trade. Malaga was taken, after a brave resistance, in 1487. The war was then, for a time, suspended, to enable the sovereigns to visit Aragon, to suppress certain disorders in that kingdom, and to raise reinforcements for the army in Granada. The resources of Fernando and Isabel were at this time exposed to a double strain through their alliance with the Duke of Brittany against France. On the other hand the Christians were greatly helped by the split among the Moors, whose shrunken kingdom was now divided in two—Abu Abdallah reigning in Granada, while Ez-Zagal was supreme in Baeza. An expedition against the latter from the eastward was defeated by the vigilance and activity of the Moors; nor was it until the spring of 1489 that the main army, now swelled to nearly a hundred thousand men of all arms, resumed active operations in the field under the personal command of Fernando. The siege of Baeza, now the second city in importance of those left to Granada, which Ez-Zagal had made his capital, was pressed with vigour but for many months without success. Fernando's troops were more than once repulsed, and had the Moors been aided by their brethren from the capital, it is probable that the doom of Baeza, in which was necessarily involved that of Granada, might have been averted or at least postponed. But the *Rey Chico* made no sign, even when the Christians, foiled in all their attacks upon Ez-Zagal's stronghold, proposed to withdraw from the siege. But for Isabel's stout heart, who would not listen to those who counselled the abandonment of the war, or at least its postponement to a more fortunate season, all the work of the campaign would now have been undone. The queen was indefatigable in her exertions, by voice and letter, to keep up the spirits of her husband and her followers, and in her efforts to arouse the national enthusiasm in favour of her enterprise, which she was now convinced was one for God's service. The operations before Baeza having begun to flag, and a pestilence breaking out in the besieger's camp, Isabel came herself to the army, attended by her ladies ; "and her presence," says Peter Martyr, her faithful secretary, " seemed at once to gladden and reanimate our spirits, drooping under long-protracted vigils, dangers, and fatigue." [1] At last the Moorish garrison, worn out by the toils of war, reduced by sickness, and seeing no hope of relief, agreed to surrender. With Baeza was given up the whole of the dominion of Ez-Zagal, including the larger portion of what remained of the territory of Granada. The King Ez-Zagal himself made submission, being treated with all knightly courtesy by Fernando and his queen, and permitted to retain his title with a small estate and revenue, under vassalage to Castile.

King Abu Abdallah, having pledged himself by the treaty of Loja that he would surrender Granada whenever Baeza and the adjacent domains had capitulated, was now called upon by the Catholic king to carry out his foolish promise. But Abu Abdallah made excuses, urging that his people would not

---

[1] Peter Martyr (Pietro Martire) was a cultured Italian of good family who was in the train of Isabel throughout the war. His letters are the best and most authentic source of the history of these times.

let him give up the city, and were resolved upon its defence. Another campaign was necessary before the war could be brought to the end which was now in all men's minds. It is a proof of the martial quality still remaining in the Moors, that, though reduced to a mere handful of warriors, with one city and its dependencies only remaining to them of all their wide dominion, with the wound still green of all their sufferings and an open sore of civil dissension in their midst, they should have offered so formidable a front to the Christians that it required two years more of preparation—and a new army of at least fifty thousand men, before Granada was finally reduced. Fernando, whose camp was graced, as usual, by the presence of Isabel—without whom it appeared that the chivalry of Spain could not be put in motion—sat down before Granada for the last time, in April, 1491. For six months a series of perpetual skirmishes took place between the advanced posts on either side, in the course of which individual acts of prowess were performed which shed much glory on both Christian and Moorish knighthood. At last the king, Abu Abdallah, despairing of succour from any quarter, and probably fearing for his own life amidst the hostile factions in the city, made overtures for surrender. The conditions were liberal, and, if intended to be observed (which is grave matter of doubt), such as reflected credit on the generosity of the conquerors. The inhabitants of Granada, who were reckoned—with the remnants of the population which had crowded into the city from the other captured towns—at not less than a quarter of a million, were confirmed in the possession of their places of worship, with free exercise of their religion, and guaranteed the full enjoyment of their property, with liberty to go where they pleased; those who chose Africa for residence to be furnished with the means of transport thither, with their families and household goods; those preferring to remain in Granada, to be subject to their own laws, administered by their own judges and magistrates, under the general control of the Spanish governor.

These conditions having been agreed to, Abu Abdallah rode forth from his stately palace-fortress of the Alhambra, on the 2nd of January, 1492, to meet the triumphal calvacade of the conquerors, headed by Fernando with a brilliant train of knights and courtiers. Meanwhile the Cardinal Mendoza had been sent, with a chosen body of troops, to make a circuit of the hill on which the Alhambra stands, and enter the palace by a side gate. Soon the great silver cross, which had been carried in front of the king throughout the war, was seen to gleam from a high tower, and the banners of Castile and Aragon to wave from the *Torre de la Vela*, the loftiest pinnacle of the fortress. Then all the Christian host fell on their knees, and gave thanks to God for His great mercy vouchsafed to the armies of the Catholic kings, who had recovered the soil of Spain from the Moslem conquerors—hailing Isabel and Fernando, when they appeared in the midst of the enraptured soldiers, in terms which no Spanish sovereign had ever heard, as saviours of their country, sent from heaven for the glory of the nation and the salvation of the faith.

Thus was brought to a close the long duel between Spaniard and Moor, which had lasted for seven hundred and eighty-one years. By the fall of Granada, the defeat of the Goths was avenged. The whole land of Spain, for the first time since the death of Roderick, was restored to the native dominion. The victory, largely due to the courage and constancy of Isabel and the wisdom and prudence of her husband, made of Spain one whole and entire kingdom, redressed the balance between the Cross and Crescent in Europe, and almost consoled Christendom for the loss of Constantinople.

APPENDIX.

CALENDAR OF LEADING EVENTS IN THE HISTORY OF SPAIN FROM THE MOORISH CONQUEST TO THE FALL OF GRANADA.

A.D.
711. Tarik, Lieutenant of Musa, Mahommedan Governor of Western Africa, lands at Algeciras, April 30th.
—— Battle of Guadalete, end of July. After three days' (seven days?) fighting the Gothic army defeated by the Moors under Tarik, the Gothic king slain and his kingdom overturned.
712. Musa lands in Spain and completes the subjugation of the country.
713. Theodomir, the Goth, by treaty with the Moors, established in a semi-independent sovereignty in Murcia.
718. Pelayo, or Pelagius, rallies the Christians in Asturias.
720. (?) Battle of Covadonga. Defeat of the Moors by Pelayo.
737. Death of Pelayo.
739. Alfonso I. reigns as King of Asturias.
756. Cordova made capital of Moorish kingdom by Abderahman, founder of the Omeyyad Dynasty.
776. Charlemagne leads an army into Spain.
777. Rout of the rear-guard of the Frankish army under Roland, at Roncesvalles.
801. Barcelona recovered from the Moors.

A.D.
850. Leon founded by Ordoño I., and made capital of the kingdom.
885. Garcia reigns, first King of Navarre.
921. Battle of Val de Junquera. The Christians under Ordoño II. defeated by the Moors under Abderahman III.
929. Abderahman III. assumes the title of Khalif.
934. Battle of Simancas. Victory of Ramiro I. over the Moors.
982. Burgos founded and made capital of Castile.
996. Leon taken and sacked by Almanzor, the Moorish general.
1002. Death of Almanzor the Conqueror.
1009. Fall of the Omeyyad Dynasty in Spain.
1025. (?) Birth of the Cid, Rodrigo Diez de Bivar.
1065. Death of Fernando, first King of united Castile and Leon.
1071. Defeat of the Leonese by the Castilians at the battle of Carrion.
1080. Ecclesiastical Council of Burgos establishes the Roman Ritual in place of the Gothic.
1085. Toledo captured by Alfonso VI.
1094. Dynasty of the Almoravides begins.
1095. Valencia captured by the Cid.
1096. Battle of Alcoraz. Defeat of Moors and Castilians by Pedro I. of Aragon.
1099. Death of the Cid.
1102. Valencia retaken by the Almoravides under Yussuf.
1108. Battle of Uclés. Defeat of the Christians and death of Sancho, only son of Alfonso VI.
1118. Saragossa taken by Alfonso *El Batallador.*
1135. Alfonso VII. crowned Emperor of all Spain.
1137. Petronilla, daughter and heiress of Ramiro of Aragon, married to Raymond Berenger IV., Count of Barcelona.
1148. The Almohades from Africa replace the Almoravides.
1161. Military Order of Santiago founded.

A.D.
- 1170. Alfonso VIII. marries Eleanor, daughter of Henry II. of England.
- 1189. First Cortes met at Burgos, where deputies from the towns were present, with nobles and clergy.
- 1195. Battle of Alarcon. Christians under Alfonso VIII. defeated by the Moors.
- 1212. Great victory of Las Navas de Tolosa by the Christians under Alfonso VIII. over the Moors.
- 1228. Majorca conquered by Jayme I. of Aragon.
- 1230. Castile and Leon finally united under Fernando III.
- 1235. Cordova taken by Fernando III.
- 1239. Valencia recaptured by Jayme *El Conquistador*.
- 1240. Murcia taken by Fernando III.
- 1248. Seville taken by Fernando III.
- 1252. Death of Fernando III. (San Fernando) at Seville.
- 1258. The *Siete Partidas* promulgated by Alfonso XI.
- 1290. Tarifa taken.
- 1309. Gibraltar taken by Alonso *El Bueno*.
- 1334. Algeciras taken by Alfonso XI., after twenty months' siege.
- 1340. Battle of the Salado. Defeat of the Moors under Emperor of Morocco by Alfonso XI.
- 1367. Battle of Najera. Defeat of Enrique of Trastamara and French allies by the Black Prince.
- 1369. Death of Pedro the Cruel at Montiel.
- 1385. Battle of Aljubarrota. Victory of the Portuguese and English allies over the Castilians and French companies under Juan I.
- 1386. John of Gaunt crowned King of Castile and Leon at Santiago.
- 1387. Marriage of Catherine, daughter of John of Gaunt, with the Infante Enrique of Castile.
- 1411. Fernando, Prince of Castile, elected King of Aragon.
- 1439. El Seguro de Tordesillas.
- 1453. Execution of Don Alvaro de Luna at Valladolid.
- 1465. Mock dethronement of Enrique IV. at Avila.

A.D.
1469. Marriage of Isabel and Fernando, October 25th.
1474. Accession of Isabel to the throne of Castile and union with Aragon.
1476. Battle of Toro. Defeat of the Portuguese and Castilian insurgents under Alfonso V. of Portugal by King Fernando.
1481. The Holy Inquisition established in Castile, January 2nd.
1482. Capture of Alhama by Ponce de Leon.
1487. Malaga taken by King Fernando.
1491. Siege of Granada commenced, in April.
1492. Surrender of Granada, January 2nd.

APPENDIX.

GENEALOGICAL TABLE SHOWING THE CONNECTION BETWEEN THE ROYAL HOUSES OF CASTILE AND ENGLAND.

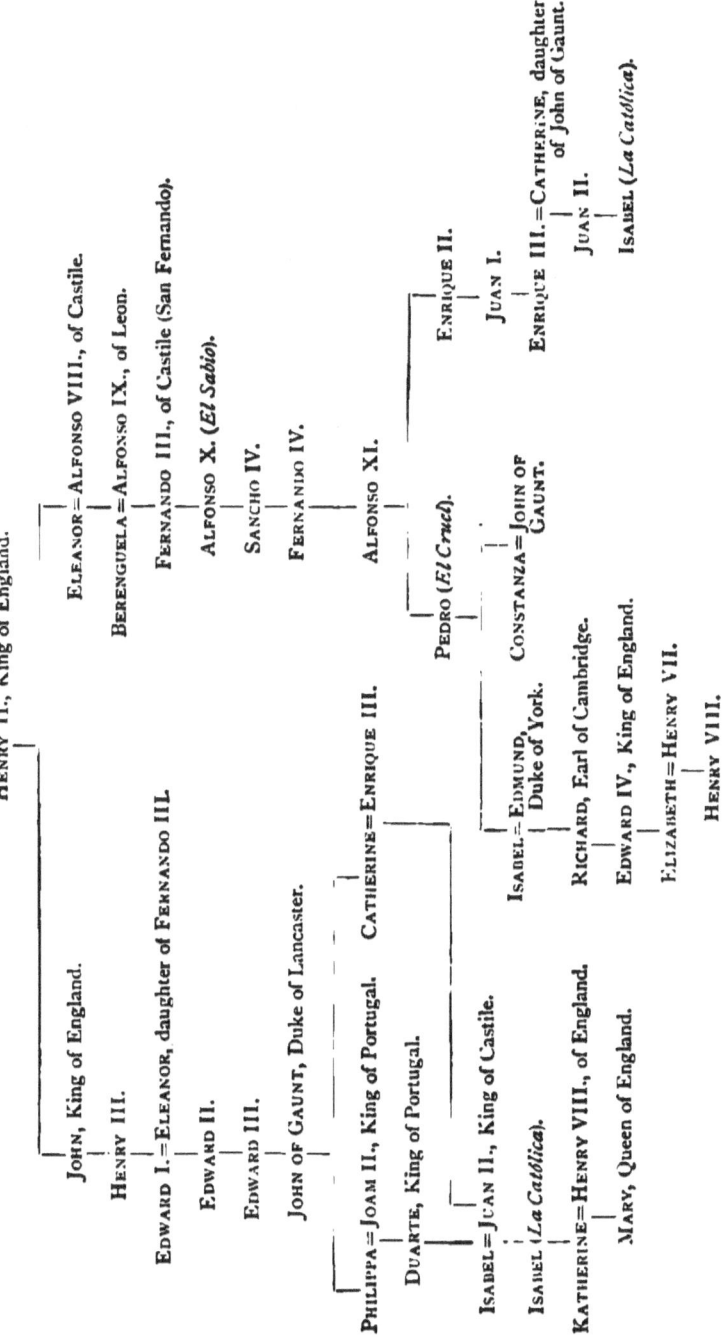

TABLE OF THE KINGS OF SPAIN FROM PELAYO TO ISABEL AND FERNANDO.

Dates of Accession.	Asturias and Leon.	Castile.	Navarre.	Barcelona.
A.D.				
718	Pelayo.		Occupied by Frankish adventurers till the first independent Count, Sancho Iñigo.	Occupied by Moors till—
737	Favila.			
739	Alfonso I.			
757	Fruela I.			
768	Aurelio.			
774	Mauregato.			
788	Bermudo I.			
791	Alfonso II.			
842	Ramiro I.			
850	Ordoño I.	Counts dependent on kings of Asturias till—		
856	Alfonso III.		A.D.	A.D.
910	Garcia.		873 Sancho Iñigo.	858 Wifredo I.
914	Ordoño II.		885 Garcia I.	872 Salomon.
923	Fruela II.		905 Sancho I.	884 Wifredo II.
925	Alfonso IV.	A.D.	924 Garcia II.	912 Miro.
930	Ramiro II.	932 Fernan Gonsalez.	970 Sancho II.	928 Seniofredo.
950	Ordoño III.	970 Garcia Fernandez.	(*El Mayor*).	967 Borello.
				993 Raymundo I.

APPENDIX. 309

LEON.	CASTILE.	NAVARRE.	BARCELONA.	ARAGON.
A.D. 955 Sancho I. 967 Ramiro III. 982 Bermudo II. 999 Alfonso V. 1027 Bermudo III. 1037 Fernando I. 1065 Alfonso VI. 1109 Urraca. 1126 Alfonso VII. 1157 Fernando II. 1188 Alfonso IX. 1230 Fernando III. (also King of Castile).	A.D. 995 Sancho Garces. 1021 Garcia Sanchez. 1027 Sancho *el Mayor* (also King of Navarre). 1035 Fernando I. (also King of Leon). 1065 Sancho II. 1072 Alfonso I. (also King of Leon as Alfonso VI). 1109 Urraca (also Queen of Leon). 1126 Alfonso II. (Alfonso VII. of Leon). 1157 Sancho III. 1158 Alfonso III. (better known as Alfonso VIII.). 1214 Enrique I. 1230 Fernando (also King of Leon).	A.D. 1035 Garcia III. 1054 Sancho III. 1076 Sancho IV. (also King of Aragon as Sancho I.). 1092 Pedro I. (also King of Aragon). 1104 Alfonso I. (also King of Aragon). 1134 Garcia IV. 1150 Sancho V. 1194 Sancho VI. The succession passed to French princes till 1425, when Blanche of Navarre married Juan, son of Fernando I., King of Aragon.	A.D. 1017 Berengario Raymundo 1035 Raymundo II. 1076 Raymundo III. 1082 Raymundo IV. 1131 Raymundo V., married Petronilla, daughter and heiress of Ramiro, King of Aragon. Barcelona merged into Aragon.	The greater part of Aragon was held by the Moors till the Eleventh century, the districts in the west, possessed by the Christians, being a dependency of Navarre. Sancho *el Mayor* left Aragon to his son A.D. 1035 Ramiro I. 1063 Sancho I. 1094 Pedro I. 1104 Alfonso I. (sometimes called Alfonso VII. of Castile).

TABLE OF THE KINGS OF SPAIN FROM PELAYO TO ISABEL AND FERNANDO (*continued*).

CASTILE AND LEON.

A.D.
1252 Alfonso X. (*El Sabio*).
1284 Sancho IV.
1295 Fernando IV.
1312 Alfonso XI.
1350 Pedro I. (*El Cruel*).
1369 Enrique II.
1379 Juan I.
1390 Enrique III.
1407 Juan II.
1454 Enrique IV.
1474 Isabel I.
(Castile united with Aragon.)

ARAGON.

A.D.
1134 Ramiro II.
1137 Petronilla.
1163 Alfonso II.
1196 Pedro II.
1213 Jayme I. (*El Conquistador*).
1276 Pedro III.
1285 Alfonso III.
1291 Jayme II.
1327 Alfonso IV.
1336 Pedro IV.
1387 Juan I.
1395 Martin.
1412 Fernando I.
1416 Alfonso V.
1458 Juan II.
(Also King of Navarre.)
1479 Fernando II.
(Aragon united with Castile.)

INDEX.

A

Abdelaziz, 3, 21
Abd-el-Melic, 32, 33
Abdelmumen, 109
Abderahman I., 30, 32
Abderahman II., 41
Abderahman III., 47, 50
Abelda, 40
Aben Hud, 123
Abu Abdallah, 295, 297, 299
Abu Said, 203
Abu-l-Hassan, 182, 183, 187, 292
Africa, 8, 68, 109, 114
Alarabi, 32, 33
Alarcon, battle of, 113
Albigenses, 125
Albuquerque, 196, 197
Alcalá de Henares, 224
Alcalá de los Gazules, 181
Alcántara, 225
Alcañiz, 230
Alcoraz, battle of, 97
Alfonso I., of Leon, 28
Alfonso II., of Leon, 36, 38
Alfonso III., of Leon, 42
Alfonso IV., of Leon, 47
Alfonso V., of Leon, 53
Alfonso VI., of Castile and Leon, 59, 61, 64, 68, 69, 70, 158, 169
Alfonso VII., Emperor, 107, 108
Alfonso VIII., of Castile, 111, 112, 119
Alfonso IX., of Leon, 113, 119
Alfonso X., *El Sabio*, 129, 139
Alfonso XI., 178, 180

Alfonso I., of Aragon, *El Batallador*, 70, 101, 105, 106
Alfonso II., of Aragon, 115
Alfonso III., of Aragon, 190
Alfonso IV., of Aragon, 192
Alfonso V., of Aragon, 273
Alfonso, Prince of Castile, 261, 262, 265
Alfonso V., of Portugal, 281
Alfonsos, the, 139
Alphonsine Tables, 143
Algarve, 137, 141
Algeciras, 16, 67, 181, 184, 187, 217
Aljubarrota, 220
Alhama, 292
Alhamar, 129, 136
Alhambra, 300
Almanzor, 11, 51, 52, 54, 99
Almohades, the, 8, 109, 112
Almoravides, the, 8, 66, 69, 105
Alvar Fañez, 82, 89
Alvaro de Luna, 236-248
Andalusia, 7, 20, 29, 58, 105, 114, 117, 123.
Aquitaine, 98, 106
Arts and crafts, 166, 167
Aragon, 32, 56, 70, 96, 107, 155, 157, 189, 228, 272, 274
Architecture, 169, 171
Asnar, Don, 93
Asturias, 22, 23, 30
Aurelio, king, 30
Avignon, 210
Avila, 202

Avis, Master of, 219, 220
Axarquia, 296
Ayala, Pedro de, 201

B

Baeza, 123, 297, 298
Balearic Islands, 126
Barcelona, 98, 99, 124
Basques, the, 33, 95, 96
Bellido Dolfus, 61, 77
Beltran de la Cueva, 260
Beltraneja, la, 261, 268, 270, 281, 283
Benedict, pope, 229
Beni Hud, 81
Berbers, the, 4, 17
Berengaria, queen, 113, 119
Bermudo I., 31
Bermudo II., 11, 52
Bermudo III., 56, 58
Bernard, Archbishop, 158, 169
Bernardo del Carpio, 34, 37
Bertrand du Guesclin, 205, 207, 209, 211, 213, 214
Biscay, 202, 207
Blanche of Bourbon, 196, 204
Borello, Count, 99
Burgos, 152, 211

C

Calatañazor, 33
Calderon, 201
Calverley, Sir Hugh de, 207, 209
Campeador, 76
Canga de Onis, 23, 27
Captal de Buch, 209
Cardeña, S. Pedro de, 91
Castile, 42, 44, 47, 54, 77, 121
Catalonia, 98, 131
Catherine, Queen, 223, 228, 235
Ceuta, 184
Chandos Herald, 208
Chandos, Sir John, 209
Chanson de Roland, 34
Charles Martel, 3
Charles V., of France, 205
Charles VI., of France, 220
Charles of Anjou, 191
Charlemagne, 31
Chindaswind, 23
Christian renegades, 11

Crónica, General, 143
Cid, the, 12, 59, 62, 63, 71-91
Clarence, Duke of, 231, 267
Clavijo, victory of, 39
Compostella, 39, 51, 52
Comunidad, the, 150
Cordova, 32, 50, 52, 54, 69, 124
Cortes, 43, 136, 142, 152, 258, 286, 287
Coruña, 39, 222
Costanza, of Castile, 216, 219
Courts of Love, 228
Covadonga, 25, 27

D

Daroca, battle of, 105
Derby, Earl of, 185
Douro, the, 42, 45, 58
Dozy, Professor, 53, 74
Dunham, Dr., 73

E

Ebro, the, 97
Edmund, Duke of York, 216, 219
Edward I., of England, 140, 191
Edward, the Black Prince, 206, 208, 209, 211, 218
Eleanor of Castile, 140
Eleanor of England, 111, 112
Empecinado, El, 73
English in Spain, 111, 185, 208, 219
Enrique I., 119
Enrique II., 196, 203, 209, 212, 214, 216, 218
Enrique III., 223, 225
Enrique IV., 257-272
Enrique, Infante of Aragon, 237, 242, 245
Euric, king, 144
Ez-Zagal, king, 295

F

Fadrique of Trastamara, 198, 199
Farfanes, the, 223
Favila, king, 27
Fernan Gonsalez, 47, 49
Fernando I., 58, 59
Fernando II., 111
Fernando III., 119, 120, 124, 134, 136, 139, 146

INDEX.

Fernando IV., 176, 177
Fernando of Aragon, 231
Fernando the Catholic, 267, 269, 276, 277–301
Florinda, 17
Foix, Comte de, 185
Fraga, 106
French in Spain, 216, 221
Froissart, 206, 209, 214
Fruela I., 30
Fruela II., 47
Fuero Juzgo, 144, 146, 147
Fueros, the, 150, 153

G

Galicia, 28, 285
Galician dialect, the, 143
Ganelon, 34, 61
Garcia, king, 45
Garcia of Navarre, 95
Garci Ordoñez, 79
Gascons, the, 207
Gascony, 140, 217
Genoese, the, 194, 274, 275
George, St., of Aragon, 97
Germany, Emperor of, 140
Gibraltar, 17, 180, 187
Golpejara, battle of, 59, 62, 77
Goths, the, 56, 158
Granada, 15, 129, 226, 242, 259, 290
Guadalete, battle of, 1, 16, 19
Guadalquivir, the, 137
Guadiana, the, 42, 67
Guienne, Duke of, 267, 271
Guzman, Alonso de, 175
Guzmans, the, 265

H

Haro, Conde de, 244
Haroun-er-Rashid, 32
Hisham III., 92
Holmes, Sir Ralph, 214
Holy Brotherhood, the, 284
Holy Inquisition, 288, 289
Huelgas, Las, 140

I

Iñez de Castro, 219
Iñigo of Navarre, 11
Innocent III., pope, 114

Isabel, princess, of Castile, 216
Isabel, queen, the Catholic, 265, 269, 277–301
Isabel, Queen of Portugal, 258
Isidro, San, 116
Ismail, King of Granada, 179
Italian wars, 157

J

Jaen, 134
Jayme I., *El Conquistador*, 125–134
Jayme II., 191
Jews, the, 4, 225
Joam II. of Portugal, 220
Joanna, Queen of Naples, 273
John of Gaunt, 209, 216, 217, 219, 222, 223
Juan I., 218, 224
Juan II., 232, 234, 251
Juan I. of Aragon, 228
Juan II. of Aragon, 275
Juan, Infante, 173, 174
Juan, Don, *el Tuerto*, 179
Juan Manuel, Don, 180, 185
Justicia, the, 155
Justiciero, the, 201

K

Khalif, the, 19, 92

L

La Cerdas, the, 141, 173, 174, 175, 179
Laras, the, 111, 119, 141, 176
Latin language, the, 162
Learning and letters, 162, 163, 165
Leon, city of, 45, 50, 52, 58, 233
Leon, cathedral of, 171
Leonora, Doña, of Aragon, 202
Leonora de Guzman, 196
Lisbon, 219
Loja, 299
Louis XI. of France, 276, 283
Lucanor, Conde de, 180

M

Madrid, 113
Mahommedans, the, 4, 19, 52, 68, 166

Malaga, 296
Maria de Padilla, 196, 200, 204
Mariana, 28, 39
Marsilio, king, 33
Martin, pope, 279
Martin, King of Aragon, 229
Masdeu, 73
Mauregato, king, 30
Medina Sidonia, Duke of, 293
Mena, Juan de, 235
Mendoza, Cardinal, 281, 284, 287
Mendozas, 268
Mingo Revulgo, 271
Miramolin, 115
Moctadir, 81
Montfort, Simon de, 125, 140
Montiel, 213
Moors, the, 8, 10, 12, 51, 171, 232, 291, 299
Morocco, 8, 67, 69, 116
Morocco, Emperor of, 142
Motamid, 79
Moutamin, 82
Mozarabes, the, 105, 158
Mudejars, the, 167
Murcia, 20, 129, 131, 173
Muret, siege of, 125
Musa, 3, 7

N

Najera, battle of, 208
Naples, 274, 275
Navarre, 43, 56, 93. 167, 183
Navas de Tolosa, battle of, 14. 114, 117
Normans, the, 38, 51
Nuño Fernandez, 94

O

Olmedo, battle of, 246
Omeyyad Khalifs, the, 51, 54, 92
Oppas, Bishop, 16, 25
Ordoño I., 40
Ordoño II., 45
Ourique, battle of, 108
Oviedo, 38

P

Pampeluna, 32
Paso, Honroso, el, 253
Pedro the Cruel, 187, 195, 214

Pedro I. of Aragon, 97
Pedro II. of Aragon, 124
Pedro III. of Aragon 187, 193
Pelayo, 21, 23, 25
Peter Martyr, 298
Petronilla, 100
Philip II., 74, 201
Philip IV. of France, 142
Philippa, princess, 222
Poem of the Cid, 80
Ponce de Leon, 265
Pope, the, 103
Portugal, 58, 59, 69, 108, 206, 217, 219
Pulgar, Fernando de, 286

Q

Quixote, Don, 27

R

Ramiro I., 38
Ramiro II., 47
Ramiro III., 51
Ramiro I. of Aragon, 96
Raymond Berenger, 84
Raymond, Count of Burgundy, 108
Raymundos, the, 100
Recared, king, 158
Recceswinth, king, 6
Ricos Hombres, 157
Rivers; Lord, 296
Roderick, king, 3, 18
Rodrigo, Archbishop of Toledo, 27, 39, 114, 115
Rodrigo Ponce de Leon, 292, 293
Roger de Lauria, 190
Roland, 33, 35, 37
Rome, 158, 160
Roncesvalles, 33, 35, 208
Rowlands, James, 214

S

Salado, battle of the, 183
Salamanca, 40
Salisbury, Earl of, 185
Sancho I., 49, 59
Sancho II., *El Mayor*, 56, 58, 95
Sancho III., 111
Sancho IV., *El Bravo*, 173, 175

INDEX. 315

Sancho Iñigo, 43
Sancho Panza, 166
Santiago, 39, 73, 171, 222
Santiago, Archbishop of, 286
Santiago de Peñalva, 167
Santillana, Marquis of, 234
Saragossa, 32, 67, 105, 193
Sardinia, 192, 194, 229
Scales, Lord, 296
Sebastian, bishop, 26
Segovia, 142, 264, 277
Sepulveda, battle of, 103
Seville, 130, 199
Sicily, 189, 191, 229, 274
Sierra Morena, 114
Siete Partidas, 143, 148, 256
Silo, king, 38
Simancas, battle of, 47
Sobrarbe, Fueros de, 95, 154
Spanish nationality, 38
Suero de Quiñones, 253

T

Tadmir, land of, 21
Tagus, the, 58
Tarifa, 175, 182, 187
Tarik, 3, 4, 16, 17, 20
Tarragona, 105
Tello, Don, 201
Tenorio, Archbishop, 225
Thames, the, 219
Theodomir, Duke, 18, 20
Theroulde, 34
Toledo, 20, 61, 66, 83, 152, 198
Tordesillas, 238, 244, 245
Torquemada, 287
Toro, 61, 199, 282
Trastamara, line of, 272
Trial by battle, 159

U

Ubeda, 123
Uclés, battle of, 101
Urge, Count of, 230
Urraca I., queen, 47
Urraca II., queen, 59, 61
Urraca III., queen, 70, 101

V

Val de Junquera, 47, 95
Valencia, 58, 66, 69, 88, 124, 127, 128, 230
Valladolid, 247
Vandals, the, 17
Villanueva, 27
Villena, Marquess of, 260, 263, 268
Villena, Enrique de, 234
Violante, queen, 228
Visigoths, the, 28
Visigothic laws, 142–144
Voltaire, 21

W

Wifredo, Count, 99
Wight, Isle of, 217
Witiza, king, 3, 6, 16

X

Xeres, 181
Ximena, 77, 89

Y

Yahia, 66
Yussuf, Almoravide, 67, 68

Z

Zallaca, battle of, 67
Zamora, 52, 59, 61, 77
Zegries and Abencerrajes, 295
Zoraya, queen, 295
Zumalacarreguy, 73

The Story of the Nations.

Messrs. G. P. PUTNAM'S SONS take pleasure in announcing that they have in course of publication, in co-operation with Mr. T. Fisher Unwin, of London, a series of historical studies, intended to present in a graphic manner the stories of the different nations that have attained prominence in history.

In the story form the current of each national life is distinctly indicated, and its picturesque and noteworthy periods and episodes are presented for the reader in their philosophical relation to each other as well as to universal history.

It is the plan of the writers of the different volumes to enter into the real life of the peoples, and to bring them before the reader as they actually lived, labored, and struggled—as they studied and wrote, and as they amused themselves. In carrying out this plan, the myths, with which the history of all lands begins, will not be overlooked, though these will be carefully distinguished from the actual history, so far as the labors of the accepted historical authorities have resulted in definite conclusions.

The subjects of the different volumes have been planned to cover connecting and, as far as possible, consecutive epochs or periods, so that the set when completed will present in a comprehensive narrative the chief events in the great STORY OF THE NATIONS; but it is, of course not always practicable to issue the several volumes in their chronological order.

The "Stories" are printed in good readable type, and in handsome 12mo form. They are adequately illustrated and furnished with maps and indexes. Price, per vol., cloth, $1.50. Half morocco, gilt top, $1.75.

The following volumes are now ready (May, 1893):

THE STORY OF GREECE. Prof. JAS. A. HARRISON.
" " " ROME. ARTHUR GILMAN.
" " " THE JEWS. Prof. JAMES K. HOSMER.
" " " CHALDEA. Z. A. RAGOZIN.
" " " GERMANY. S. BARING-GOULD.
" " " NORWAY. HJALMAR H. BOYESEN.
" " " SPAIN. Rev. E. E. and SUSAN HALE.
" " " HUNGARY. Prof A. VÁMBÉRY.
" " " CARTHAGE. Prof. ALFRED J. CHURCH.
" " " THE SARACENS. ARTHUR GILMAN.
" " " THE MOORS IN SPAIN. STANLEY LANE-POOLE.
" " " THE NORMANS. SARAH ORNE JEWETT.
" " " PERSIA. S. G. W. BENJAMIN.
" " " ANCIENT EGYPT. Prof. GEO. RAWLINSON.
" " " ALEXANDER'S EMPIRE. Prof. J. P. MAHAFFY.
" " " ASSYRIA. Z. A. RAGOZIN.
" " " THE GOTHS. HENRY BRADLEY.
" " " IRELAND. Hon. EMILY LAWLESS.
" " " TURKEY. STANLEY LANE-POOLE.
" " " MEDIA, BABYLON, AND PERSIA. Z. A. RAGOZIN.
" " " MEDIÆVAL FRANCE. Prof. GUSTAVE MASSON.
" " " HOLLAND. Prof. J. THOROLD ROGERS.
" " " MEXICO. SUSAN HALE.
" " " PHŒNICIA. Prof. GEO. RAWLINSON.
" " " THE HANSA TOWNS. HELEN ZIMMERN.
" " " EARLY BRITAIN. Prof. ALFRED J. CHURCH.
" " " THE BARBARY CORSAIRS. STANLEY LANE-POOLE
" " " RUSSIA. W. R. MORFILL.
" " " THE JEWS UNDER ROME. W. D. MORRISON.
" " " SCOTLAND. JOHN MACKINTOSH.
" " " SWITZERLAND. R. STEAD and Mrs. A. HUG.
" " " PORTUGAL. H. MORSE STEPHENS.
" " " THE BYZANTINE EMPIRE. C. W. C. OMAN.
" " " SICILY. E. A. FREEMAN.
" " " THE TUSCAN REPUBLICS. BELLA DUFFY.
" " " POLAND. W. R. MORFILL.

Heroes of the Nations.

EDITED BY

EVELYN ABBOTT, M.A., FELLOW OF BALLIOL COLLEGE, OXFORD.

A SERIES of biographical studies of the lives and work of a number of representative historical characters about whom have gathered the great traditions of the Nations to which they belonged, and who have been accepted, in many instances, as types of the several National ideals With the life of each typical character will be presented a picture of the National conditions surrounding him during his career.

The narratives are the work of writers who are recognized authorities on their several subjects, and, while thoroughly trustworthy as history, will present picturesque and dramatic "stories" of the Men and of the events connected with them.

To the Life of each "Hero" will be given one duodecimo volume, handsomely printed in large type, provided with maps and adequately illustrated according to the special requirements of the several subjects. The volumes will be sold separately as follows:

Cloth extra $1 50
Half morocco, uncut edges, gilt top . . . 1 75
Large paper, limited to 250 numbered copies for subscribers to the series. These may be obtained in sheets folded, or in cloth, uncut edges 3 50

The first group of the Series will comprise twelve volumes, as follows:

Nelson, and the Naval Supremacy of England. By W. CLARK RUSSELL, author of "The Wreck of the Grosvenor," etc.

Gustavus Adolphus, and the Struggle of Protestantism for Existence. By C. R. L. FLETCHER, M.A., late Fellow of All Souls College, Oxford.

Pericles, and the Golden Age of Athens. By EVELYN ABBOTT, M.A., Fellow of Balliol College, Oxford.

Theodoric the Goth, the Barbarian Champion of Civilization. By THOMAS HODGKIN, author of "Italy and Her Invaders," etc.

Sir Philip Sidney, and the Chivalry of England. By H. R. FOX-BOURNE, author of "The Life of John Locke," etc.

Julius Cæsar, and the Organization of the Roman Empire. By W. WARDE FOWLER, M.A., Fellow of Lincoln College, Oxford.

John Wyclif, Last of the Schoolmen and First of the English Reformers. By LEWIS SARGEANT, author of "New Greece," etc.

Napoleon, Warrior and Ruler, and the Military Supremacy of Revolutionary France. By W. O'CONNOR MORRIS, sometime Scholar of Oriel College, Oxford.

Henry of Navarre, and the Huguenots in France. By P. F. WILLERT, M.A., Fellow of Exeter College, Oxford.

Alexander the Great, and the Extension of Greek Rule and of Greek Ideas. By Prof. BENJAMIN I. WHEELER, Cornell University.

Charlemagne, the Reorganizer of Europe. By Prof. GEORGE L. BURR, Cornell University.

Louis XIV., and the Zenith of the French Monarchy. By ARTHUR HASSALL, M.A., Senior Student of Christ Church College, Oxford.

To be followed by:

Cicero, and the Fall of the Roman Republic. By J. L. STRACHAN DAVIDSON, M.A., Fellow of Balliol College, Oxford.

Sir Walter Raleigh, and the Adventurers of England. By A. L. SMITH, M.A., Fellow of Balliol College, Oxford.

Bismarck. The New German Empire: How It Arose; What It Replaced; and What It Stands For. By JAMES SIME, author of "A Life of Lessing," etc.

William of Orange, the Founder of the Dutch Republic. By RUTH PUTNAM.

Hannibal, and the Struggle between Carthage and Rome. By E. A. FREEMAN, D.C.L., LL.D., Regius Prof. of History in the University of Oxford.

Alfred the Great, and the First Kingdom in England. By F. YORK POWELL, M.A., Senior Student of Christ Church College, Oxford.

Charles the Bold, and the Attempt to Found a Middle Kingdom. By R. LODGE, M.A., Fellow of Brasenose College, Oxford.

John Calvin, the Hero of the French Protestants. By OWEN M. EDWARDS, Fellow of Lincoln College, Oxford.

Oliver Cromwell, and the Rule of the Puritans in England. By CHARLES FIRTH, Balliol College, Oxford.

Marlborough, and England as a Military Power. By C. W. C. OMAN, A.M., Fellow of All Souls College, Oxford.

G. P. PUTNAM'S SONS

NEW YORK
27 WEST TWENTY-THIRD ST.

LONDON
24 BEDFORD ST., STRAND

www.ingramcontent.com/pod-product-compliance
Lightning Source LLC
Chambersburg PA
CBHW030000240426
43672CB00007B/770